# A Field Guide in Colour to
# INSECTS

# A Field Guide in Colour to

# INSECTS

### By Dr. Jiří Zahradník

### Illustrated by František Severa

Translated by Olga Kuthanová
Graphic design Aleš Krejča

English version first published 1977 by
Octopus Books Limited
59 Grosvenor Street, London W1

Reprinted 1978

ISBN 0 7064 0582 X

Printed in Czechoslovakia
3/07/06/51-02

# Contents

# Foreword

Insects have inhabited our planet for some 350 million years, which is far longer than man, who first walked the earth little more than one million years ago. When man first appeared on earth insects already had behind them a long and varied evolution, and this evolution continues to this day. Some insect orders are only now beginning their development, so that the present era may be said to be not only the age of man but also the age of insect evolution.

Long before the primitive beginnings of human civilization, before the discovery of primitive tools, insects knew how to do many of the things man succeeded in doing only in the recent past. Long before man began his first experiments to produce 'paper', wasps already knew how to make quite durable paper from wood, and they used it as building material for their nests. Long before man developed the first drilling tools, various beetles and other insects had mastered the technique of drilling tunnels, even in wood that was quite hard. Insects are so good at narcotizing and paralysing their prey that it remains fresh for many days or even weeks. But these are not the least of their abilities. Since time untold insects have produced sweet syrups, wax for the protection of their bodies and as construction material for their nests, thick encrustations of shellac, kilometres of fine silk fibre and extremely fast carmine dyes. Insects are also able to glow, transforming chemical energy into cold light within their bodies by a very complex process which man is only just beginning to understand.

Insects are also excellent construction builders, producing and using a remarkable range of building materials. Many species of insects make small nests for their offspring by cementing various materials together. Termites make strong 'concrete' with soil and their own saliva and droppings and use it to build tall and sturdy structures whose practical design and positioning evoke the greatest admiration. Insects are also skilled at cutting, sewing, weaving and even burying the dead. Another characteristic that must not be overlooked is the collective phenomenon, for insects were the creators of the first organized society, a sort of state, sharply divided into various castes. All members 'obey' the queen, who is not only the founder of the state but as a rule also the mother of all the members of the community, be they ants, bees, wasps or termites.

Insects are resourceful also in caring for their eggs, often making beautiful silken containers in which to put them or else 'sewing' leaves together for this purpose. Sometimes such care is even carried a step further in that the adult insect keeps watch over the eggs, licking them and keeping them clean. It may even care for the young larvae, providing them with food and on occasion even living to see the next adult generation.

Many animals, including insects, were man's companions from the very beginning of his existence, a fact recorded even by ancient civilizations. In the days of the Egyptian pharoahs the bee often appeared in pictures, and the scarab, regarded as a symbol of creation and creative power, was held sacred. All these relics strike us as being very old, but in the context of the evolution of all living things several millenia are as nothing.

The gradual development of human civilization and farming, however, brought with it a clash of interests. In ancient times as well as in more recent centuries man was defenceless against insects, waging war against them with bare hands or a stick, or by exorcism. Insects

6

caused diseases and also hunger. The swarms of locusts that invaded the countryside and devoured everything down to the last blade were regarded as God's punishment.

Cultivation of the land brought with it marked changes in the landscape. Forest stands gave way to cultivated steppes and later to forest monocultures. The composition of the insect population likewise changed. In most cases the insects that had inhabited the original stands disappeared and their places were taken by new and different ones which, finding ample food here, soon became established in their new home and in time became pests of field and forest. In the end man was forced to seek various ways and means of controlling these uninvited guests which he himself had been instrumental in bringing to his neighbourhood.

It would be neither right nor just, however, to take note of only the negative aspect of the relation between insects and man. Since time immemorial insects have also been extremely beneficent, a fact that has been duly appreciated primarily by our own day and age. Insects are important pollinators, thus ensuring not only the propagation of various useful plants but the very existence of the plant world itself. Predatory insects feed on species that are often very unpleasant and undesirable from man's point of view, thus regulating the numbers of various pests. In their role as scavengers, small armies of insects remove quantities of decaying organic matter, both plant and animal. Last but not least, insects delight man by their very presence. Next time you come upon a forest clearing stop and take a good look at the shimmering beauty of butterfly wings, the graceful flight of the dragonfly, the remarkable shapes of the many small insects and their lovely colouring and ornamentation. Learn something about their life habits and you will marvel at the extraordinary efficiency of all the various phenomena. Insects as such definitely merit our attention, for they are an important part of the life around us.

# What are Insects?

Laymen wrongly apply the term 'insect' to all kinds of creatures that are not true insects — creatures such as spiders, mites, book scorpions, centipedes, millipedes, and even woodlice or sowbugs. These creatures are, nevertheless, all related to the insects. They are all members of a vast group of animals known as arthropods. This is by far the largest group in the animal kingdom and it is made up of many classes, of which the insects are but one. The class of insects is itself extremely large and varied and it includes more than thirty orders, which makes finding characteristics common to all of the insects no easy task.

Most insects, like many other arthropods, have a body made up of three distinct parts: the **head, thorax,** and **abdomen.** The head of an insect consists basically of six segments, the thorax is made up of three, and the abdomen contains eleven segments, but it is not easy to make out all of the segments, especially on the head, because they are closely united. The head bears the mouthparts, the antennae, the compound eyes, and sometimes also some simple eyes called ocelli. The thorax bears three pairs of legs in adult insects and, in the majority of adult insects, it also carries the wings. This is where the insects really differ from the other arthropods, for none of the other arthropod groups ever has wings. Most adult

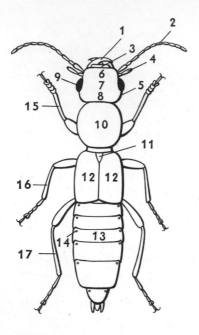

**1 Diagram of an insect body (a rove beetle):**
1 — mandible 2 — antenna 3 — labrum
4 — maxillary palp 5 — head 6 — clypeus
7 — frons 8 — vertex 9 — compound eye
10 — scutum 11 — scutellum 12 — first pair
of wings (in this case elytra) 13 — abdomen
14 — spiracle 15-16-17 — front, middle and
hind pair of legs

insects have two pairs of wings, but some groups have only one pair, and some species and even whole orders have vestigial wings or no wings at all. The legs, eyes, antennae and mouthparts may also be reduced in various ways or entirely wanting. The abdomen never has any legs in the adult insect, but it often carries various outgrowths at the hind end. These are very often concerned with mating and egg-laying.

The body of an insect is covered with an outer protective layer of varying thickness. This layer is known as the cuticle and it consists mostly of a horny material called chitin. The cuticle may be very thin, but it is usually quite rigid and in many species it is very hard. It forms the so-called exoskeleton. The separate pieces that make up the external skeleton are called sclerites. They are rigid, but they are joined to each other by flexible membranes, and the body as a whole is thus flexible. The sclerites often overlap. Thanks to this hard chitinous skeleton, many insects, such as beetles, bugs, moths, grasshoppers and so on, can be kept in collections as dry specimens.

The smallest of the body parts is the **head**. It varies in shape and may project straight forward (the prognathous head), be bent downward (orthognathous) or be below the body and pointing towards the hind end (opisthognathous). The head bears the mouthparts, the antennae and the eyes (both compound eyes and ocelli). The head itself is divided by sutures into several portions. Right at the front, overlying the mouth, is the upper lip or labrum. Behind and above the labrum is the transverse portion called the clypeus, then comes the frons, the vertex, and last of all the occiput at the back. Located behind the eyes and running down to meet the mouthparts are the lateral portions of the head called the genae or cheeks. The various portions, however, cannot always be clearly distinguished.

The *antennae*, which serve primarily as organs of smell, are a pair of jointed appendages bearing numerous sensory hairs. They may vary greatly in form as well as number of segments. Antennae may be filiform or threadlike (long and made up of thin, uniform segments), moniliform or necklace-like (the segments more or less bead-like), serrate or saw-like (segments triangular, projecting like the teeth of a saw), pectinate or comb-like (segments having long processes on one or both sides like the teeth of a comb), clavate or club-shaped, geniculate (bent abruptly at right angles near the centre), flabellate or fan-

**2 Head of an insect:**
1 — antenna 2 — compound eye
3 — ocellus 4 — frons 5 — clypeus
6 — labrum 7 — mandible
8 — maxilla 9 — maxillary palp
10 — labium 11 — labial palp

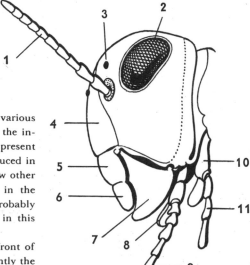

shaped, etc. Many examples of these various forms can be found in practically all the insect orders. Prominent antennae are present in most insects, although they are reduced in the mayflies and dragonflies and a few other groups. They are completely absent in the telson-tails (Protura), their function probably being taken over by the front limbs in this case.

The *mouthparts* are located at the front of the head. The best known and apparently the earliest type are mouthparts formed for chewing, this being most clearly evident in the beetles. They are made up of four parts. Above the mouth opening is the upper lip or labrum which, as we have seen, is really part of the head capsule. Below this are the mandibles, or upper pair of jaws, which are often large, usually strongly sclerotized (hardened), sharp and, in most cases, provided with one or several teeth. These move towards each other from the sides, cutting the food and crushing it into coarse particles. Below the mandibles are the maxillae, or second pair of jaws, to which are attached segmented appendages known as the maxillary palps. Located below the maxillae is the lower lip or labium. It bears a pair of appendages known as the labial palps. The maxillae and labium help to hold the food and push it into the mouth, while the palps are concerned largely with tasting the food and determining its suitability.

Mouthparts of the mandibular type, however, are not the only kind to be found amongst insects. In some they are adapted for piercing and sucking, for licking and sucking, merely for licking, and the like. Among the butterflies and moths the two maxillae are greatly elongated and fastened together side by side to form a sucking-tube known as the proboscis, which is extremely long in some of the hawkmoths. The mandibles and labium are also involved in the piercing 'beaks' of bugs and mosquitoes.

The mouthparts of adult insects often differ from those of the larval stages. The proboscis of the adult butterfly, for example, is very different from the biting jaws of the caterpillar.

Prominent eyes are present in most adult insects. As a rule the insects have a pair of compound eyes and two or three ocelli, but most beetles have only compound eyes and the males of most scale insects have only ocelli. The ocelli of larvae differ in structure from those of adult insects.

The compound or faceted eye may be round, oval or kidney-shaped. It may be flat or convex and is composed of varying numbers of tiny sections, the ommatidia. The ommatidia may be all alike or different. Their numbers vary greatly. The eyes of some insects are composed of only a few ommatidia, whereas in others there may be tens, hundreds and even thousands of them. Eyes with a large number of ommatidia are to be found, for instance, in the dragonflies, burying beetles, etc. Each ommatidium has a separate lens which gathers light from a certain section of space. The images from the various lenses are combined to form a mosaic image of the complete field of view.

In some insects, such as dragonflies and certain true flies (Diptera) and beetles, the eyes are very large, while in other insects they are very small. Their size, however, need not be proportional to the size of the body. Some extremely small beetles have large eyes and vice versa.

The **thorax** is composed of three segments: the prothorax, mesothorax and metathorax. These are usually clearly separate, but they may often be more or less firmly joined together. Each bears a pair of legs, and in winged insects the second and third segments both bear a pair of wings.

The leg of an insect consists basically of five parts, the last of which, the tarsus, is commonly composed of five segments. The coxa is the proximal segment of the leg (the segment nearest to the body) and it is connected to the thorax. The trochanter is the second part of the leg, the femur is the third, the tibia is the fourth and the tarsus, which is terminated by one or two small claws, is the fifth. The basic type of leg is fitted for running and the segments are long and fairly thin as in the ground beetles. Sometimes the last pair of legs is adapted for jumping, having either an enlarged femur, as in the grasshoppers, or a long tibia, as in the leafhoppers. Legs may also be adapted for scraping (mole-crickets, earth-boring dung-beetles and others), seizing prey (praying mantis and mantis fly *[Mantispa]* ), or for swimming (water beetles). It is not uncommon for insects to have one or more pairs of legs reduced (scale insects) or even absent, as in the females of Strepsiptera, certain mealy-bugs, and the like.

As well as being organs of locomotion, the legs also bear various sensory organs. These include organs of smell and taste and various bristles which are sensitive to touch or to air currents. Some insects also carry hearing on their legs as well as stridulating organs whereby

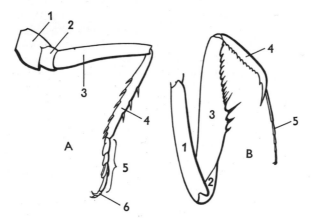

3 **Leg of an insect:**
A — common type:
1 — coxa 2 — trochanter
3 — femur 4 — tibia
5 — tarsus 6 — tarsal claw
B — the large front leg of the praying mantis adapted for seizing prey

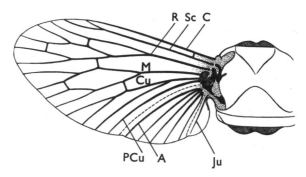

**4 Wing of an insect:**
Principal longitudinal wing
veins: C — costa
Sc — subcosta R — radius
M — media Cu — cubitus
PCu — postcubitus
A — analis Ju — jugum

they produce loud rasping sounds. Grasshoppers, for example, stridulate by rubbing their hind legs against their front wings.

Most adult insects possess well-developed and functional wings, but the members of some insect orders are wingless. The presence or absence of wings was for a long time the principal criterion for the systematic classification of insects into two subclasses: the **Apterygota,** or wingless insects, which contained only a small number, and the **Pterygota,** or winged insects, which included all the remaining insects. However, even amongst the latter group there are many species, genera and even families and orders in which the wings are not developed. Examples include sucking lice, bird lice and fleas, but this is an acquired condition, for all these insects had winged ancestors. Worker ants and termites, certain generations of aphids, female scale insects and some female moths are also wingless, although other forms or sexes of the same species may be winged. Nowadays the division of insects into the Apterygota and Pterygota is fast losing its importance.

Though used for locomotion, *wings* are not true limbs. They are in fact folds of the skin modified in a number of ways. The commonest type is the membranous wing, consisting of two delicate membranes closely applied throughout except along certain hollow lines which are called the veins. The arrangement of these veins forms the venation of the wing. The longitudinal veins are joined by cross-veins. In some wings there are very few veins, but the wing venation is often very intricate, as in dragonflies and lacewings. Each vein has a specific name or designation which is important in determining the various species and genera. The principal wing veins are shown in Fig. 4.

Typical membranous wings include those of bees, wasps and ants (Hymenoptera), flies (Diptera), lacewings (Planipennia), dragonflies and damsel-flies (Odonata), mayflies (Ephemeroptera). They are usually transparent but they are sometimes variously spotted. The membranous wings of butterflies and moths (Lepidoptera) are clothed with overlapping scales of varicoloured hues. The wings of the thrips (Thysanoptera) are tough and narrow with few veins and a wide fringe of hairs, so that they look like minute feathers.

In many groups of insects the front wings show striking modifications. In beetles and earwigs they are thickened throughout, without a trace of venation, and they serve to protect the functional hind wings; wings of this type are termed wing-covers or elytra. In bugs the front wings are thickened at the base and the terminal portion is membranous; such wings are known as hemelytra.

Insects originally had two pairs of wings but here, too, there occur numerous modifica-

11

tions. Thus, for example, in the order Diptera only the front wings are functional, the hind wings being tiny, pin-like organs termed halteres. The males of mealy-bugs or scale insects have similarly modified hind wings. In the Strepsiptera, on the other hand, it is the front wings that are reduced to slender, leathery, club-shaped appendages.

In repose, the wings may be held in various positions. They may be folded parallel with the abdomen, folded roof-like over the abdomen (caddis-flies, certain moths and flies), or held erect above the back (mayflies and butterflies).

For some insects the wings serve only for short flights, but countless other species are masters of the air, notably the hawkmoths and dragonflies. Not only are they rapid, they are also tireless fliers.

The third and terminal part of the insect's body is the **abdomen,** which bears no legs. In the spring-tails (Collembola) the abdomen is equipped with a springing organ that enables the insects to progress by leaps. Some insects have various small appendages at the tail end of the abdomen. Earwigs, for example, bear curved forceps, while cockroaches, mayflies and several other groups carry slender, often thread-like appendages.

In some groups, such as the crickets and certain hymenopterous insects, the females possess a prominent ovipositor with which they lay their eggs.

The internal anatomy of insects also has its interesting aspects but the limits of this book do not allow broader discourse on the subject. If nothing else, however, note should at least be made of the form and function of the respiratory system. Insects breathe by means of a system of air-tubes termed tracheae, which receive air through openings on the body surface known as spiracles (less correctly as stigmata) and deliver it to the various body organs. There is a great difference between breathing by means of gills and lungs and by means of air-tubes. These are brought to the reader's attention purely as an item of particular interest. The number, positioning and shape of the spiracles are important identifying characters in the classification of certain groups of insects.

## How Many Insect Species Occur in the World?

Insects account for about 80 per cent of all the animals on this earth and are thus without doubt the largest class in the animal kingdom. As to species, one can speak only in terms of approximate numbers, for books on the subject differ by as much as tens of thousands. It may be assumed that there are about 800, 000 to 1, 000, 000 described and registered species. However, many more have not yet been determined. The vast territories of tropical Africa, Asia and South America still guard many secrets. Suffice it to point out that thousands of new species are discovered every year in Europe alone, and from the viewpoint of entomology this is a territory that has been investigated quite thoroughly. Authorities estimate that there are about one million more species of insects yet to be discovered, which means that those known to us represent roughly about half the earth's insect population.

The number of existing species is therefore given only approximately. The number of individual insects on the earth cannot possibly be counted or even estimated. The most approximate estimate would be a figure of astronomical proportions.

# Development of Insects

The majority of insects reproduce by laying eggs; such insects are termed *oviparous*. The eggs are usually fertilized before they are deposited. However, in many species the females lay eggs that are not fertilized. This method of reproduction is termed *parthenogenesis*. Examples of such reproduction may be found amongst aphids and certain phasmids (stick insects and leaf insects). A number of insects, including certain aphids and blood-sucking flies, are *viviparous*. This means that the females give birth to live offspring (nymphs or larvae, or very occasionally pupae).

Embryonic development begins from the moment the egg is fertilized and continues until the emergence of the first active stage. This is followed by a very complex development process during which the individual undergoes marked morphological changes. This complex transformation, termed metamorphosis, is not the same in all insects and there are two basic types. The first type is incomplete metamorphosis or hemimetabolous development (insects belonging to this group are known as Hemimetabola) and the second is complete metamorphosis or holometabolous development (insects of this group are called Holometabola).

The duration of the period of development is determined by several factors, first and foremost, however, by the temperature. At higher temperatures development is more rapid. In warm regions a species may appear several weeks earlier than in regions with a lower mean temperature. The more rapid development at higher temperatures may allow a species to produce two or even more generations in a year whereas only one generation may occur in cooler areas.

**Incomplete metamorphosis** is the simplest type consisting of the following three main stages: egg — nymph — adult (imago). The nymphal stages (instars) vary in number and are very similar. The later the instar the more it resembles the adult. With each successive nymphal instar there is an increasing development of the wing rudiments until the last nymphal instar, from which the adult emerges. The adult insect differs from the nymph in size and in having fully developed wings and copulatory organs. In incomplete metamorphosis the changes are gradual and there is no period of inactivity.

Insects which undergo an incomplete metamorphosis include mayflies, dragonflies, locusts, grasshoppers, Homoptera (aphids, etc.), bugs, termites, lice and others.

**Complete metamorphosis** differs from the preceding type by the inclusion of a pupal stage, making four main stages in all: egg — larva — pupa — adult. Whereas a nymph looks like a small, wingless version of the adult, the larva does not look like the adult at all, and it does not become like the adult as it grows. When it reaches full size, the larva turns into a pupa or chrysalis, and it is during this stage that the body is completely rebuilt to form the adult insect.

Insects which undergo a complete metamorphosis include the four orders with the greatest number of species, namely the Coleoptera, Lepidoptera, Hymenoptera and Diptera, as well as several other, numerically smaller, orders such as Siphonaptera (fleas), Trichoptera (caddis flies) and others.

Variations occur in both types of metamorphosis, however, and in some instances there is yet another stage and the development is even more complex. Oil beetles, for example, have

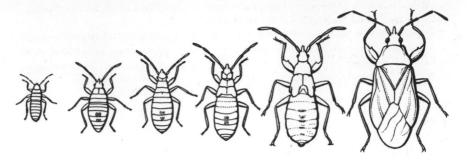

**5 Incomplete metamorphosis of insects:**
5 nymphal stages and the adult (a bug)

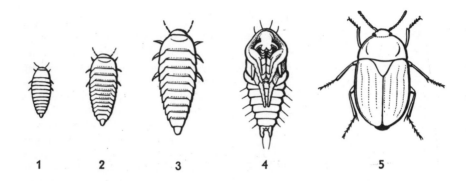

**6 Complete metamorphosis of insects:**
1 to 3 — larval stages 4 — pupa 5 — adult or imago

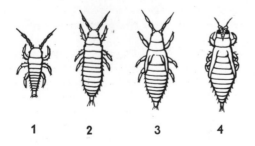

**6a The complex metamorphosis of thrips:**
1 and 2 — larval stages 3 — propupa 4 — pupa 5 — adult

several different kinds of larvae, and thrips also have a complex kind of life history. Further details are given in the descriptions of the various insect orders.

The most primitive insects — the bristletails and other Apterygotes — develop without metamorphosis. The young insect is practically the same as the adult except that it is smaller, often composed of fewer segments, and is unable to reproduce. It undergoes a great many moults — as many as thirty. In this group of insects the adults also moult.

## The Egg

The eggs of insects are generally very small, often even microscopic. In some species, however, they are quite large, the eggs of some large ground-beetles measuring as much as several millimetres. That of *Carabus coriaceus* measures 8 millimetres in length.

The size of the egg depends on the size of the adult, and also on the number laid and on the life-habits of the future larva. Parasitic species lay a great many eggs, often several thousand, for species that undergo a complex development must ensure the existence of the future generation by laying a great number of eggs. However, where the development takes place in sheltered conditions so that the future larvae are protected from enemies as well as from various unfavourable influences, the number of eggs laid is comparatively small. Burying beetles, for example, lay only about ten eggs, for the larvae develop in relative safety underground and are fed by the female. The same is true of the burrowing dung-beetles, which prepare an ample store of food for their young, and the bark-beetles whose larvae are protected by the bark of trees.

Eggs may retain their colour until the time they hatch. They are usually whitish, pale or dark yellow, greenish or dark. In many instances, however, the original colouring changes within a few hours.

The shape of the egg shows marked diversity. It may be spherical, ovate, pointed at one or both ends, or barrel-shaped. The eggs of stick insects and leaf insects have prominent little lids which the emerging nymphs push off. In aquatic species, such as mosquitoes, the eggs are often furnished with floats to keep them on the surface. Some mayfly eggs have tufts of coiled threads which anchor them to water plants. The eggs of the green lacewings are attached to plants by slender stalks.

The external surface of the egg is usually smooth, but in many cases it is richly sculptured. Striking examples are the eggs of butterflies and moths, which are covered with extremely dainty and intricate markings.

Eggs are laid singly, in rows or in clusters. Some insects deposit their eggs on plants, the fur of animals or feathers; others seek a suitable shelter and deposit them in the ground, in cracks in tree trunks or branches, under bark and in wood, or under stones; still others inject them into the bodies of various animals, or lay them in foodstuffs and other stored goods such as grain, spices, flour, fabrics, and so on. The egg-laying females usually seek places where the larvae will find the particular food they need when they emerge. Some moths cover their egg batches with tufts of hairs from their bodies. The eggs of some insects are contained in egg-cases, termed oothecae, or in cases made of leaves. The oothecae produced by cockroaches resemble small ladies' handbags. The eggs of the praying mantis are laid inside a frothy fluid which hardens into a tough covering. Remarkable silken cases are woven by female water scavenger beetles and attached to the water plants before the eggs are laid in them.

The duration of the egg stage differs. Sometimes it may be only a few days, at other times several weeks or even months. Eggs laid in the autumn usually overwinter. They pass through a period of dormancy known as diapause and the larvae emerge the following year.

## The Nymph and the Larva

After a certain period the young insect emerges from the egg. The insect is then said to be in its first instar and, whether it is a nymph or a larva, it begins to feed. As a rule it grows at a rapid rate and its skin soon becomes too small. The skin is then cast off in a process known as moulting or ecdysis. The old skin splits open and the new instar works itself out through the opening. As the second instar nymph or larva feeds and grows, the process is repeated. The majority of insects moult four to five times but many are known to moult even more often than this.

The young insect is usually very active. The conditions under which it passes its life and the food it eats are largely responsible for determining the size of the future imago, for the adult insect itself does not grow. A poorly fed nymph or larva will produce a small adult — perhaps several millimetres shorter than the average adult.

The duration of the larval stage varies greatly. In burying beetles, where the length of the larval stage is determined by the durability of the food, the moults follow rapidly one after the other and the larval life is rather short. In other species the periods between the individual ecdyses may last several days or weeks. Some butterflies and moths and certain beetles hibernate as larvae, and here there may be several months between one ecdysis and the next. The nymphs of one American cicada live for seventeen years before becoming adult.

The form of the young stages of certain orders is characteristic for the given order and makes it easy to recognize them as such. Best known are the caterpillars of Lepidoptera, the caterpillar-like larvae of plant-eating Hymenoptera, the larvae of numerous beetles and flies, and the case-bearing larvae of the caddis-flies. The nymphs of dragonflies and mayflies are also easily recognized.

Nymphs, as we have seen, look very much like small adults, but larvae are very variable. Larvae may be divided according to the form of the body into the following four groups:

(a) Protopod larvae — abdomen unsegmented or with few segments. All are parasites living inside the bodies of other insects. Not common.

(b) Oligopod larvae — a very common type with three pairs of thoracic legs and no abdominal legs. Included in this group are the larvae of caddis flies and lacewings and most beetles. The larvae of this group are of two main types: long-legged campodeiform larvae with prognathous heads and two caudal setae or bristles at the hind end of the abdomen; and C-shaped scarabaeiform grubs belonging to the scarab beetles and their relatives (Lamellicornia).

(c) Polypod larvae — with three pairs of thoracic legs plus varying numbers of paired abdominal legs. Best known of this group are the caterpillars of butterflies and moths and the caterpillar-like larvae of the plant-feeding sawflies (Hymenoptera).

(d) Apodous larvae — without legs. This group includes first and foremost the larvae of flies

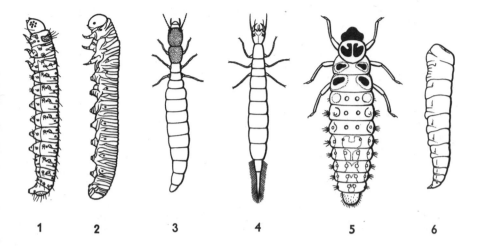

**7 Various types of insect larvae:**
1 — caterpillar of Lepidoptera 2 — caterpillar-like larva of sawfly (Hymenoptera)
3 — larva of a snake-fly (family Rhaphidiidae) 4 and 5 — larvae of beetles 6 — larva of fly
(Diptera)

(Diptera), those of certain beetles (weevils, longhorn-beetles, bark and ambrosia beetles), and the grubs of bees, wasps, and ants (Hymenoptera).

The change at the last moult may be from the nymph to the adult (insects with an incomplete metamorphosis) or from the larva to the pupa. In the latter example the final larval stage often forms a case in which the pupa is enclosed. These cases may be made of silk fibres (the cocoons of many moths) or of bits of earth, sand, stones, faeces and the like cemented together by glandular secretions.

## The Pupa

This is a state of inactivity when the insect does not feed and, apart from a few exceptions, the organs of locomotion are functionless. The pupal state is helpless against such enemies as predacious insects, birds, insectivores and the like, but it is sometimes provided with a protective cover in the form of a cocoon or case. Although inactive in the sense that it does not feed and does not normally move about, the pupa is far from inactive inside, for this is where it undergoes a very complex transformation. Apart from the few exceptions, there occurs a process called histolysis, in which there is a complete dissolution of the tissues. The young pupa is thus filled with a thin liquid. This stage is followed by the growth of new tissue and the formation of the internal organs of the future adult insect.

17

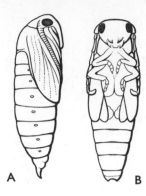

**8 Pupa of a butterfly (A) and of a beetle (B)**

The pupae of certain insect orders have a distinctive and characteristic form. In general two types are commonly recognized:
(a) Obtect pupae — pupae which have the legs and wings concealed within a mummy-like casing, although their outlines are usually visible. The pupae of butterflies and moths are generally of this type.

(b) Exarate pupae — pupae which have the legs, antennae and wings free and clearly visible, as in most beetles and Hymenoptera.

The duration of the pupal state varies. In species where the pupa is dependent on certain specific conditions, or where it has no protective covering and is attached freely to plants (e. g. ladybirds), it is very brief. In many cases, however, this quiescent period lasts several weeks or even months. The pupal state may also be the one in which the insect overwinters, and some moths even spend two winters in the pupal stage.

## The Adult

The adult, or imago, is generally soft, moist, and either a light colour or white when it first emerges from the pupa, and the wings are crumpled. After several minutes or several hours the wings expand and the skin hardens and acquires its permanent coloration.

Many beetles and some other insects emerge from the pupal stage in the autumn but, though the days are still warm and sunny, they remain underground until the next spring.

The lifespan of the adult insects varies from species to species, ranging from just a few hours to as long as several years. Adult mayflies and the males of Strepsiptera and scale insects live no more than a few hours. The average lifespan of butterflies and moths is about three to five weeks, although some live for several months. Long-lived insects include certain beetles and the queens of some of the social insects. Queen ants live for up to fifteen years, while termite queens are believed to survive for as much as 50 years. Primitive wingless insects also have long lives. The little silverfish *(Lepisma saccharina)*, for example, lives for two to three years.

In many insects the adult stage is very short but their development may take several years. The adult cockchafer, for instance, lives only four weeks but its development may take as long as three to four years. Wood-feeding beetles may also take a long time to grow up, but few are as long-lived as the seventeen-year cicada already mentioned.

# Distribution of Insects

Practically all parts of the world are inhabited by insects. They are to be found in the tropics, subtropics and the temperate zone and even beyond the Arctic and Antarctic Circles. Insects are most abundant in the tropics, however, and it is here that one will also find the largest and most brightly coloured species.

The world is divided into the following nine zoogeographical areas: Palearctic, Nearctic, Neotropical, Australasian, Oriental, African, Madagascar, Arctic and Antarctic. Though certain groups of insects may be found in more than one of these regions, those of each given region have certain specific characteristics.

The Palearctic is the largest of the nine regions. Roughly it includes North Africa, nearly all of Europe (as far as the Arctic Circle), a large part of the U.S.S.R. and China, Japan, Asia Minor, the Middle East and the northern part of the Arabian peninsula. It is a region of widely differing habitats and climatically it is located in the temperate and subtropical zones. It has few giant-sized insects but is the home of many economically important species.

The Nearctic includes North America and part of Central America. The Grande del Norte River valley in Mexico marks the boundary between this and the Neotropical region. The entomofauna of the Nearctic region is very similar to that of the Palearctic and therefore the two regions are often referred to jointly as the Holarctic region.

The Neotropical region extends from the Grande del Norte River to the southernmost promontory of South America. It has a great wealth of large insect species. Found here are the world's largest beetles, *Titanus giganteus, Macrodontia cervicornis, Dynastes hercules* (the Hercules beetle) and others, and also the moth *Thysania agrippina* — the largest of all lepidopterous insects. There are also the beautiful members of the genus *Morpho,* and other striking butterflies. Many other striking insects are undoubtedly to be found here, for the entomofauna of the region has still not been adequately investigated.

The Australasian region includes first and foremost Australia, together with Tasmania, New Zealand, New Guinea, the Celebes, Moluccas and neighbouring smaller islands. It is a remarkable territory with an unusual fauna, for which reason it is often divided into several independent regions.

The Oriental region, also designated as the Indo-Malayan region, borders on the Palearctic and includes India and Pakistan, South-East Asia, Ceylon, southern China, Taiwan and the Philippines. It is noted for its magnificent stag beetles and chafers, as well as large and brilliant butterflies and moths and curious stick and leaf insects.

The African region includes Africa south of the Tropic of Cancer and the southern promontory of the Arabian peninsula. The insect fauna of this region is extraordinarily striking and varied and some of the insects here attain huge dimensions. Examples include Goliath beetles, giant swallowtails, and a fascinating array of large grasshoppers.

Madagascar is generally included in the African region, although authorities are increasingly inclined to consider it an independent region of its own, separate from the African land mass. Madagascar certainly supports a wealth of strange insects that are not found elsewhere.

Located near the north and south poles are the Arctic and Antarctic regions, respectively, both of which boast very little in the way of animal life. Only the very hardy and adaptable species are to be found here. Certain Lepidoptera and large bumblebees occur on the arctic plains, where they get food from the bright flowers in summer, but wingless springtails and other small species are the only insects to be found in the Antarctic.

# System of Insect Classification

Insects *(Insecta)* are a group of animals that belong to the phylum **Arthropoda,** which, for purposes of easier orientation, is divided into several smaller groups according to several different criteria — firstly the form and arrangement of the mouthparts and, secondly, the method of respiration.

The following outline will best show where the arthropods rank in the zoological system and where the insects fit in amongst the arthropods.

Kingdom:      *Animalia* — all living species of animals.
Subkingdom: *Metazoa* — all animals having the body composed of cells differentiated into tissues and organs (as opposed to the subkingdom Protozoa, composed of unicellular animals).
Phylum:       *Arthropoda* — animals with segmented legs and a segmented body consisting of three basic parts: head, thorax and abdomen. The phylum is further divided into two sections according to the form of the mouthparts, namely:
(a) **Amandibulata:** mouthparts without biting jaws: made up in living species of chelicerae and pedipalpi. The Amandibulata include two subphyla: **Trilobitomorpha** (extinct) and **Chelicerata,** which includes the class **Arachnida** (scorpions, spiders, and others).
(b) **Mandibulata:** mouthparts with one pair of mandibles and two pairs of maxillae (the second pair is termed the labium in insects). The Mandibulata include two subphyla: the **Branchiata,** with aquatic respiration (by means of gills) — the class **Crustacea** belongs to this group; and the **Tracheata,** with aerial respiration (by means of air-tubes or tracheae). The Tracheata includes four classes, namely **Symphyla, Diplopoda** (millipedes), **Chilopoda** (centipedes) and **Insecta** (insects).

Insects are further divided into a great number of lesser categories. A commonly used division is into two very unequal groups — the **Apterygota** and the **Pterygota.** The former contains a relatively small number of primitive, wingless insects, such as silverfish and the firebrat, which have never passed through a winged stage during their evolution. The Pterygota is a much larger group, containing all the winged insects as well as a large number which have become wingless through evolutionary changes. Wingless insects of the first group (the Apterygota) are little known to man despite the fact that they are very plentiful. Because of their small size, concealed habits and inconspicuous appearance they are not collected by amateurs and are usually studied only by professional scientists. Opinions have been voiced that this group does not belong to the class of insects. The springtails (Collembola) for example, possess an odd springing organ not found elsewhere, and the telson-tails (Protura) have what might be termed rudimentary legs on the first three abdominal seg-

ments — a character absent in insects. The Diplura, too, are often considered as not belonging to the insects. According to these views, then, primitively wingless insects would include
only the Thysanura (Archaeognatha and Zygentoma).

In view of the established traditions and lack of agreement between the many different
opinions, all the orders of wingless insects have been retained in the class Insecta. There are
also practical reasons for this, inasmuch as those who take at least the slightest interest in
life about them will regularly come across many representatives of this group on their
nature trips.

## Classification of Insects

CLASS: **INSECTA** (insects)

        **Apterygota** (wingless insects)

        Sub-class:    **Entotropha**

        Orders:      *Diplura* (two-pronged bristle-tails)

                    *Protura* (telson-tails)

                    *Collembola* (springtails)

        Sub-class:    **Ectotropha**

        Orders:    * *Archaeognatha*

               * *Zygentoma*

        **Pterygota** (winged insects)

        Hemimetabolous insects

| Orders: | | |
|---|---|---|
| *Ephemeroptera* | — | mayflies |
| *Odonata* | — | dragonflies and damselflies |
| *Plecoptera* | — | stoneflies |
| *Embioptera* | — | web-spinners |
| *Dermaptera* | — | earwigs |
| † *Mantodea* | — | praying mantids |
| † *Blattodea* | — | cockroaches |
| *Grylloblattodea* | — | (no common name) |
| *Isoptera* | — | termites or white ants |
| *Zoraptera* | — | (no common name) |
| *Phasmida* | — | stick- and leaf-insects |
| O *Ensifera* | — | crickets and bush crickets (long-horned grasshoppers) |
| O *Caelifera* | — | locusts or short-horned grasshoppers |
| *Psocoptera (Corrodentia)* | — | psocids or book lice |
| *Mallophaga* | — | bird lice or biting lice |

---

\*    These two orders are more often grouped together to form the order *Thysanura*
†    These two groups are generally considered to be sub-orders of the order *Dictyoptera*
O   These two groups are generally considered to be sub-orders of the order *Orthoptera*

| | |
|---|---|
| *Anoplura* | — sucking lice |
| *Thysanoptera* | — thrips |
| ◇ *Homoptera* | — cicadas, leaf-hoppers, aphids, scale-bugs, white flies |
| ◇ *Heteroptera* | — true bugs |
| Holometabolous insects | |
| △ *Megaloptera* | — alder flies |
| △ *Raphidioptera* | — snake flies |
| △ *Planipennia* | — lacewing flies |
| *Coleoptera* | — beetles |
| *Hymenoptera* | — bees, wasps and ants |
| *Trichoptera* | — caddis flies |
| *Lepidoptera* | — butterflies and moths |
| *Mecoptera (Panorpata)* | — scorpion flies |
| *Diptera* | — true flies (two-winged flies) |
| *Siphonaptera* | — fleas |
| *Strepsiptera* | — twisted winged insects or stylopids |

## Development of the System and Nomenclature

The system of classification of insects has been in use for more than two hundred years and is as yet still far from definite. The foundation for the system was laid down by the Swedish naturalist *Carolus Linnaeus* (Carl von Linné) in the tenth edition of his famous work *Systema Naturae* (1758).

The basic unit of classification is the species. Ever since Linnaeus's day it has been designated by two names, the first designating the genus to which it belongs and the second the actual name of the species. Modern systematics has added further categories, the chief one being the sub-species — geographical race, which is designated by three names — the generic, the specific, and thirdly the subspecific of the race. Often even lower categories are used, e. g. morpha, natio or simply form.

The generic, specific and subspecific names are furthermore followed by the name of the scientist who first described the species or other category (i. e. the biologist who first named it). As a rule the naturalist's name is written out in its entirety; only in the case of Linné and Fabricius is it permitted to use the initials L. or F.

The only name universally recognized is the scientific name of a category, derived either from the Latin or Greek. Besides its scientific name a given species also has a common name by which it is known in the different languages. Such names, however, are not universally recognized. In some languages the system of common names is worked out in detail but in others it is not definite nor uniform and one and the same species may have several

---

◇ These two orders are sometimes considered to be sub-orders of the order *Hemiptera*

△ These three orders are sometimes considered to be sub-orders of the order *Neuroptera*

common names. For this reason both popular and scientific literature use not only the common but also the scientific names.

# A Survey of Insect Orders

**Apterygota** (wingless insects)

Sub-class **Endotropha**

1. Order **Diplura** — two-pronged bristle-tails

These wingless arthropods look more like larvae than adult insects. They are sightless, pale-coloured and measure 3—50 millimetres in length. The head bears long filiform antennae and the mouthparts are withdrawn into the head, a fact which gives rise to the name of the subclass (Endotropha means internal mouthparts). The abdomen bears a pair of appendages (cerci) that may be long, bristle-like and many-jointed, or forceps-like. The ventral side of the abdomen bears small appendages (styli) which are believed to be vestigial legs.

The Diplura are basically herbivores, though they may sometimes also be predacious. They are fond of damp and dark situations and may be found under moss, under stones, in the ground, in decaying wood of tree stumps and in caves.

More than 700 species exist, and they are most abundant in tropical regions. Although thermophilous (warmth-loving), some species occur far to the north. The genus *Campodea,* for example, is well represented in Europe and North America. The largest diplurans are species of *Heterojapyx,* found in Australia.

2. Order **Protura** — telson-tails or proturans

Members of this order look the least like insects. The narrow, elongate body, measuring about 2 millimetres in length, is coloured yellowish or yellowish-white. The creatures are sightless and lack antennae, the function of the latter apparently being taken over by the forelegs which are held forward and provided with a number of sensory bristles. The abdomen is twelve-segmented in the adults. In the young it is eight-segmented, one new segment being added with each moult. The first three abdominal segments bear vestigial legs on the ventral side.

The telson-tails are small predators that also eat plant food. They are found in damp situations, in the humus-rich soil of deciduous woods, in moss, under stones, under rotting bark, and the like. They easily escape notice in the wild because of their small size, unobtrusive colouring and concealed habits and consequently very little is known about their life-habits and development.

There are more than 500 known species in the world, of which about 100 occur in Europe. About 30 species are known in Australia and about 70 in North America.

Like most wingless insects, the telson-tails can be identified with certainty only with the aid of a microscope.

### 3. Order **Collembola** — springtails

Members of this order are fairly small insects usually measuring 3 millimetres and only very occasionally 7 — 9 millimetres in length. The body, covered with a very fine skin, is sometimes elongate, at other times stout to globose and composed of the head, three thoracic segments and at most six abdominal segments.

They are often brightly coloured, though many species are a sombre grey, blue-grey, yellowish or whitish. The head bears a pair of antennae, a number of simple eyes and mouthparts concealed and apparently retracted into the cavity of the head.

A characteristic feature of most springtails is the springing organ consisting of a spring (furcula) and catch (retinaculum). At rest, the spring is folded under the abdomen where it is held by the catch. This springing organ is typical of the springtails and found in no other group of insects. The springing movement made possible by the furcula, however, is not the usual form of locomotion. As a rule springtails crawl forward with the aid of the three pairs of slender legs, employing the springing apparatus probably only when danger threatens. Another organ possessed only by the springtails is the ventral tube situated on the ventral side of the first abdominal segment.

Springtails feed on various kinds of decaying organic substances as well as living plant matter. They occur abundantly in the upper layers of humus, their numbers decreasing rapidly at greater depths, though some species may be found even at depths of several decimetres. Numerically they are among the most plentiful of insects. It is estimated that in Europe there are as many as 50,000 to 400,000 individuals to a square metre (depth 30 centimetres). They may be encountered high up in the mountains and their range extends even into the Antarctic.

Propagation is by means of eggs which are laid in small groups. Springtails moult many

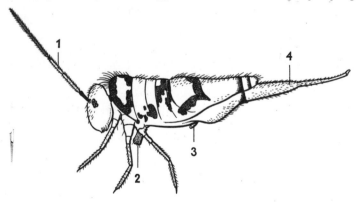

9 **Diagram of a Springtail** (Collembola)
1 — antenna 2 — ventral tube (collophore) 3 — retinaculum (hamula) 4 — furcula or spring extended

times both during development and in the adult state. The regeneration of lost limbs and antennae occurs quite frequently.

Springtails inhabit widely varied situations. They may be found in the ground, on plants (many species on mosses and fungi), in the neighbourhood of water as well as on water, on decaying vegetable and animal matter, in ants' nests, caves and the like. As a rule they occur throughout the year, even in winter. Springtails play an important role in the balance of nature for they participate in the disintegration of organic matter and thus in the formation of humus.

From the viewpoint of evolution the springtails are a very old group, for they existed in the Devonian more than 300 million years ago.

There are more than 8,000 known species, of which about 2,200 are found in Europe and several hundred in North America. About 215 species are known in Australia. More new species, however, are being discovered every year. Reliable identification and determination is possible only with the aid of a microscope.

Sub-class **Ectotropha**

## 4. Order **Archaeognatha**

Apart from a few large diplurans, the members of this order are the largest of the wingless insects, measuring up to 20 millimetres in length. The body is covered with fine scales, which are greyish or may form striking patterns, and it tapers towards the hind end. It bears the cerci, plus a single, long, median caudal filament which resembles the cerci in form. The antennae are long and filiform, and the mouthparts are adapted for chewing. The head is furnished with ocelli. As in the Diplura and Protura, several of the abdominal segments bear styli. The long, slender legs are easily broken off but new limbs grow to replace the lost ones. Archaeognatha run very fast.

Archaeognatha are found in stone debris, quarries, under piles of stones in fields and under the bark of tree stumps. They emerge in the evening and run very fast when disturbed. They feed on small plants — algae, lichens and fungus threads; they also eat small animals.

Development is comparatively slow. The females lay only a few eggs which are very small, almost microscopic. The young moult many times.

There are about 250 known species in the world. Identification is difficult because the insects lose their scales and colouring after preparation. Accurate identification generally requires the use of a microscope. Specimens are kept in 70—80 per cent alcohol; they may be cemented to labels but they usually dry up. The arrangement of the scales is best recorded by macrophotography.

## 5. Order **Zygentoma**

Members of this order are wingless insects with elongate bodies measuring 5—12 millimetres in length and often covered with fine scales. The antennae are long and jointed. There are no ocelli. The abdomen bears a pair of long cerci plus a median caudal filament.

These insects feed on plant and animal matter. They are most often found in ants' nests and in human habitations, where the best-known species are the silverfish and the firebrat. Development is slow; adults often have a lifespan of several years and moult many times.

About 300 species are known and the group is found all over the world, although most of the species live in the warmer regions. There are few in Europe and North America, but about 25 species in Australia. The insects are preserved in 75—80 per cent alcohol.

Members of this and the preceding orders are usually grouped together in the single order *Thysanura* — the bristle-tails. The difference between the two lies in the presence or absence of ocelli and in the form and attachment of the mandibles.


## Pterygota — the winged insects

This group includes all the remaining orders of insects, most of which have membranous or variously modified wings. Some forms, however, are without wings — female scale insects, worker ants, fleas, lice and the like — but the wingless condition in such a case is an acquired one.

### 6. Order **Ephemeroptera** — mayflies

Members of this order are insects with a very delicate skin measuring from 3 to 40 millimetres in length without the cerci. The antennae are small and composed of two short, stout segments succeeded by a slender bristle. The mouthparts are vestigial. A characteristic feature of mayflies are the long, many-jointed, outspreading cerci, often with a third long caudal filament in the middle. There are usually two pairs of wings, though sometimes the hind wings are absent. When at rest, the wings are held upright above the body, and are thus easily distinguished from most other aquatic insects. The wings have a great many longitudinal veins connected by numerous cross veins. They may be transparent, yellowish, whitish or brownish, sometimes even glossy. The legs are usually not alike; in the males the first pair is extremely long.

Adult mayflies do not feed and they live only a few hours. They are found in the vicinity of water where they are most abundant in the later afternoon and after sundown. Formerly they occurred in large swarms but nowadays they are becoming less common as a result of the growing pollution of lakes, ponds and streams.

The metamorphosis of mayflies is incomplete. The females deposit their eggs in water, and the nymphs (sometimes called naiads) live in the water for between one and three years, depending on the species. There exists a transitional stage between the naiad and the adult called the subimago, which greatly resembles the adult. The duration of the subimago stage is only a few hours or days.

The nymphs of mayflies prefer clear, well-aerated waters. They climb over stones and green water plants, or else they burrow in the mud at the bottom. They breathe through tracheal gills located on the sides of the abdomen. Both nymphs and adults are important items in the diet of fish and other animals, including birds and bats.

Mayflies are a very ancient group of insects that existed as long ago as the Carboniferous period. Many fossils of both adults and nymphs have survived from that time.

At present there are about 2,000 known species of mayflies in the world, and about a quarter of these are found in North America. 200 species or so live in Europe. About 125 species are known in Australia. Specimens are preserved and kept in glass tubes in alcohol. Only for exhibition purposes are they mounted with outspread wings in the manner of dragonflies or butterflies.

7. Order **Odonata** — dragonflies and damsel-flies

Members of this order are large insects measuring 20—80 millimetres in length and with a wing expanse of up to 110 millimetres. The body may be slender and elongate or short and stout. It is usually brightly coloured, often variously striped or spotted. The head is attached to the thorax by a slender peduncle. The antennae are short and the compound eyes are very large; they play an important role in procuring food and contain thousands of ommatidia. The mouthparts are fitted for chewing. All four wings are membranous, both pairs nearly of the same size. They are narrow and elongate and either clear or ornamented with darker patches and spots. When at rest the wings are either held close together above the body (damsel-flies) or extended horizontally (dragonflies). Some Odonata are slow and vascillating in flight (the damsel-flies), whereas others are noted for their rapid and sustained flight. The long legs are terminated by three-jointed tarsi. The abdomen bears short unjointed cerci at the caudal end.

The Odonata are predacious insects that capture their victims in flight. They feed primarily on insects that live near water, for example, mosquitoes, flies and the like, as well as many other species. A few dragonflies fly by night, but most fly on sunny days in spring and summer, generally in the vicinity of water and especially above the surface of still or slow-flowing water courses, but they travel far from their birth sites and may be encountered in forest clearings, roads, in fields and even in city streets. Young individuals regularly leave the vicinity of water, flying away for a time but always returning again after a certain period.

**10 Diagram of a Dragonfly**
(Odonata)
1 — antenna 2 — compound eye
3 — cerci 4 — pterostigma
5 — spiracle 6 — copulatory organ
of male

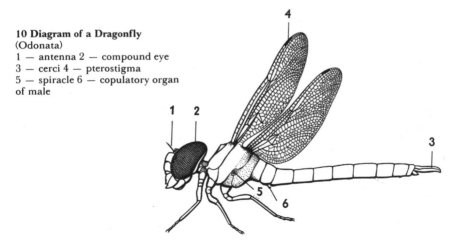

The metamorphosis is incomplete. The females deposit their spherical, fairly small (0.5 — 2-mm) eggs either directly in water, in mud or in sand, or else in the stems of aquatic plants which they puncture with their ovipositors. Sometimes this is done with the assistance of the male who holds on tightly to the female's neck with his anal claspers. First to emerge from the egg is the maggot-like pronymph, which within the space of a few minutes, or even seconds, becomes a nymph. The nymphs are predacious, feeding on various animals such as small crustaceans, small worms and the like. For capturing their food they are furnished with a formidable weapon called the mask, which is the greatly enlarged and specially formed lower lip. The nymphs live in pools, ponds, lakes and streams, and the like. The duration of their development may be one to four years, depending on the species. When fully grown the nymph stops feeding, climbs up on a plant until it is either partly or entirely out of the water and after a few hours transforms into the adult. Adult dragonflies in temperate regions normally die at the onset of winter, leaving just eggs or nymphs to pass the winter, but certain species in Europe, North America, and Australia will sometimes hibernate in the adult state.

The Odonata are very useful for they often feed on troublesome blood-sucking insects. They are also a lovely sight as they skim over the surface of lakes and streams. It is an exaggeration to say that the nymphs are pests of fish-hatching ponds.

The Odonata are a very old and primitive group of insects existing as early as in the Paleozoic period, mainly in the Permian. Some species had a wing expanse of as much as 700 millimetres.

Today there are more than 4,500 known species distributed all over the world. There are about 400 species in North America, 120 in Europe, and 250 in Australia. The Odonata are divided into two main sub-orders; *Zygoptera* (damsel-flies), smaller as regards the number of species, and the larger *Anisoptera* (dragonflies). A third sub-order contains just two living species from India and Japan.

Specimens are dried for mounting in collections.

### 8. Order **Plecoptera** — stoneflies

Members of this order include both large and small insects (wing expanse 50 millimetres at the most) with soft, elongate bodies. The caudal end of the abdomen bears two jointed cerci which may be long or short. The antennae are long and many-jointed. A characteristic feature is the form of the wings and position in which they are held when at rest. The forewings are simple and oval, the hind wings are broader. When at rest the wings are folded flat upon the abdomen. The legs are similar in form and terminated by a three-jointed tarsus.

Adults feed on algae, small lichens or pollen, or else eat nothing at all. Their lifespan is fairly short. Males live one to two weeks, females about a week longer.

Most stoneflies do not fly much, and when they do they go only short distances. They are usually found on plants, on logs near water, under stones and on bridge supports. They avoid direct light. They are known to communicate by means of a drumming sound registered by sensory organs on the legs.

The metamorphosis is incomplete. The females lay their eggs cemented together in a mass which they immerse in water. The nymphs then develop in the water. The development lasts

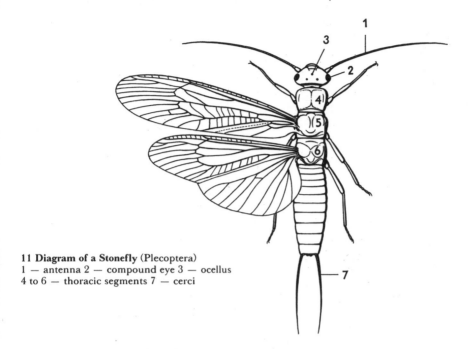

**11 Diagram of a Stonefly** (Plecoptera)
1 — antenna 2 — compound eye 3 — ocellus
4 to 6 — thoracic segments 7 — cerci

one or more years, during which time they moult 20 to 30 times. They require well-aerated water and therefore are most abundant in mountain brooks and streams. They live on the bottom of the stream and under stones. They may be predacious, herbivorous or omnivorous. Respiration is by means of gills. When fully grown the nymph leaves the water, climbing up on a stone or aquatic plant where it transforms within a short time into the adult.

The nymphs of stoneflies, as well as the adults, are food for fish and other animals, and the nymphs, like those of mayflies, serve as indicators of the purity of water courses. Stoneflies, too, are a very old group of insects existing as long ago as the early Carboniferous.

Of the 2,000 known species, there are about 100 in central and western Europe and a further 400 in North America. Nearly 100 live in Australia. They are divided into three sub-orders.

In collections they are generally kept in glass tubes filled with alcohol, because the copulatory organs are the only sure means of identification and these become deformed in dry specimens.

9. Order **Embioptera** — web-spinners

Members of this order are small insects with elongate bodies measuring only a few millimetres in length. The mouthparts are adapted for chewing. The head bears compound eyes with no ocelli. The male usually has two pairs of wings similar in form, with very few veins.

The females are wingless. Web-spinners are easily recognized by the tarsi of the forelegs, the first segment of which is ovate and contains numerous silk glands.

These insects feed on bits of plants and debris. They are often gregarious and live together in silken nests or galleries which they spin in turf and debris under stones, or else under loose bark. The female deposits the eggs in the galleries, guards and cleans them, and sometimes even brings food which the larvae eat on emerging.

There are more than 200 known species, found mainly in the tropical regions. Several species live in southern Europe, especially in coastal regions, and there are about nine species in North America. About 70 species inhabit the warmer parts of Australia and New Zealand.

## 10. Order **Dermaptera** — earwigs

Members of this order are very much alike. They have an elongate, flattened body measuring up to about 25 millimetres in length, with a pair of forceps-like appendages at the tail end. These are either smooth on the inner side or furnished with one or more teeth. The coloration of earwigs is generally yellowish or brownish.

The head is prognathous (projecting straight forward) and is clearly demarcated from the thorax. The mouthparts are fitted for chewing; the antennae, which are not strikingly long as a rule, may be made up of thirty or more segments. Ocelli and compound eyes are present. The prothorax is covered by a tergal plate — the pronotum. Most earwigs have two pairs of wings. The fore wings (elytra) are very short, smooth and leathery and without veins, while the hind wings are large and membranous and elaborately folded under the fore wings. Sometimes the hind wings are absent. The legs are adapted for running and terminated by three-jointed tarsi. The legs are all similar in form. The males are distinguished from the females by the shapes of the forceps, those of the males being more strongly curved than those of the females. Usually only the male cerci bear teeth.

Earwigs are dark-loving insects and thus seek out sheltered spots by day. They may be found under stones, under old wood, under the bark of tree stumps, and often also in rural dwellings in cellars, pantries and the like. Some live in sandy banks. They feed on both plant and animal matter. Two strange groups of earwigs are parasitic on bats and rats in Indonesia and tropical Africa.

The metamorphosis is incomplete. The females lay their eggs in underground chambers, arrange them in small piles and brood over them, protecting them from fungal attack by licking them. They take similar care of the newly hatched nymphs.

As a group, the earwigs are primarily tropical insects. Of the 1,300 described species only about 20 are to be found in Europe, with about the same number in North America. About 60 species live in Australia. The oldest preserved fossil remnants date from the Jurassic.

Specimens are dried for mounting in collections.

## 11. Order **Mantodea** — mantids

The mantids, measuring 4—8 centimetres in length (up to 16 centimetres in the tropics), are distinguished by the unusual form of the front legs which are adapted for seizing prey. The femora and tibiae are armed with sharp spines and the tibia of each can be folded back against the femur to keep a secure hold on the seized victim. The remaining pairs of legs are long and slender.

The head, which is bent downward, bears moderately long antennae, compound eyes, ocelli and large mandibles. The prothorax is very long and freely movable. The wings are folded flat on the body. The fore wings are narrower and tougher than the hind wings. The mantids, however, are not particularly good fliers.

Both adults and nymphs are predacious, feeding primarily on various other insects. They may stalk after their prey, or else they lie in wait until an insect comes within range of the front legs.

The metamorphosis is incomplete. The females lay their eggs in fairly large oothecae, constructing several of these during their lifespan; they are usually fastened to the stems or twigs of plants. The oothecae protect the eggs not only from enemies but also from drying out or overheating. The nymphs shed their skin several times during their development.

All species of this order are warmth-loving insects and are chiefly inhabitants of the tropics and subtropics. Of the more than 1,800 known species, several occur in southern Europe, but only one reaches as far north as Paris. Several species occur in North America, particularly in the southern states, and about 120 live in Australia.

Specimens are dried for mounting in collections.

12. Order **Blattodea** — cockroaches

Most cockroaches are moderately large insects, even though some species measure only 5 millimetres in length. The body is strongly depressed and the abdomen bears two caudal appendages. Besides these, males have two further appendages. The colour is mostly brown-

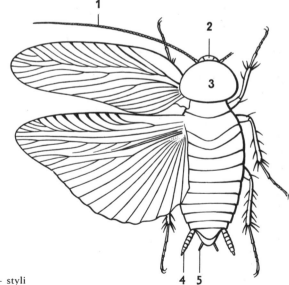

12 **Diagram of a Cockroach**
(Blattodea):
1 — antenna 2 — head
3 — pronotum 4 — cerci 5 — styli

ish-black or ochre. The head is bent downward and covered by a shield-like pronotum. The mouthparts are formed for chewing. The antennae are long and many-jointed. There are usually four wings, though some species may be wingless. They are more fully developed in the males; in the females they may be reduced or absent. The two pairs of wings differ in size and structure. The fore wings are generally stronger, tough and elytra-like, the hind wings broad and membranous. They are not used much for flight, however, for cockroaches fly only short distances, the chief organs of locomotion being the legs which have greatly developed coxae and five-jointed tarsi. Cockroaches are very good, fast runners.

Species living in the wild are mostly plant-feeders, whereas 'domestic' cockroaches are omnivorous. Unlike the former, the 'domestic' species feed at night and are furthermore troublesome pests.

The metamorphosis is incomplete. The eggs are enclosed in characteristic purse-like oothecae which the females carry at the end of the abdomen — often for several days — until they find a place to conceal the capsule.

From the geological aspect cockroaches are a very old order, many genera and species having existed as early as the Carboniferous and Permian. Cockroaches are closely related to the mantids, and the two groups are often combined to form the order Dictyoptera. Blattodea and Mantodea then become sub-orders and not full orders.

It is estimated that there are about 3,000 species of cockroaches altogether, most of them inhabitants of the tropics. Australia has about 450 species, but only about 30 species are found in Europe, with rather more in North America. Most of the 'domestic' species are aliens which have arrived from warmer regions.

Specimens are dried for mounting in collections.

## 13. Order **Grylloblattodea** — grylloblattids

This tiny order, with less than a dozen known species, is not likely to be seen by many amateur naturalists, for the insects live under stones high in the mountains — at altitudes up to 2,000 metres or more. The grylloblattids range from 15 to 30 millimetres in length and, being wingless, they look rather like large springtails from above, although they have no springing organ. The antennae are long and slender, and there is a pair of long cerci at the tail end. The insects feed on plant and animal matter by night. Most of the known species come from the Rocky Mountains, with some in Japan and Russia.

## 14. Order **Isoptera** — termites

The termites are considered close relatives of the cockroaches. Their body, however, is only slightly depressed; it is elongate with delicate cuticle. The length may be from several millimetres to 2.2 centimetres, but mature egg-laying females of some species may be 10 centimetres long. The mouthparts are fitted for chewing and the antennae are short. The eyes are usually absent. The legs are terminated by four-jointed tarsi.

Termites are social insects living in rigidly organized societies that inhabit various types of nests. Each colony consists of several distinct castes that exhibit marked differences, both morphological and physiological. The colony is headed by a king and queen (the royal pair), the other castes being the workers and the soldiers. All have a specific function and specific duties to perform. Reproductive individuals are winged for a time but shed their wings following the nuptial flight.

Some termites feed on cellulose, in other words on wood or plant tissues, other species eat humus or are omnivorous. The digestion of cellulose is aided by hordes of micro-organisms called flagellates present in the termites' digestive tract. Food is procured by the workers which feed all the other castes in the colony.

The metamorphosis is incomplete. The queen is the mother of all the individuals in the colony.

In the tropics, where they are chiefly found, termites are of great economic importance. On the one hand they aid in the disintegration of dead plant tissues; on the other, they are destructive to wooden constructions and the like.

Of the more than 2,000 described species, only two are commonly found in southern Europe. They may, however, be introduced into areas where they were previously non-existent as witness occasional instances in some parts of central Europe. About 50 species live in North America and some do a lot of damage, but none makes the spectacular mounds characteristic of African and Australian termites. Australia supports about 200 termite species, some of them very large, but the most famous are the compass termites. These build huge elongated mounds up to 4 metres high, which are always arranged with their long axis running north/south. This directional clue is of great help to travellers in the Outback.

15. Order **Zoraptera** — zorapterans

The zorapterans are all minute insects, not more than about 3 millimetres long. Wings may or may not be present, and the antennae are either thread-like or bead-like. The insects live in decaying wood and under logs and stones, where they feed mainly on other small arthropods such as mites. Several species live in the southern United States and in most other warm parts of the world, but the insects have not been found in Europe. They are easily overlooked, but they are probably not common anywhere.

16. Order **Phasmida** — walking-sticks (stick-insects) and leaf-insects

The Phasmida are fairly large insects. The body is either elongate, cylindrical and covered with numerous spiny processes, or flat and green and reminiscent of leaves. Many are wingless, but some male stick-insects fly well with their large hind wings.

There are about 2,500 described species, distributed mainly in the tropics and subtropics. A few members of this remarkable order are to be found in the Mediterranean region of Europe, and several stick-insects also live in North America. Some large and very attractive species live in Australia. All stick- and leaf-insects are vegetarians and, because they have no particular requirements as to food or environment, some species are often kept as pets.

17. Order **Ensifera** — crickets and katydids

The members of this order are moderately sized insects often measuring about 3 centimetres in length. They also include a number of 'giants', however, measuring 5—7 centimetres in length (up to 12 cm in the tropics). The chief representatives of this order are crickets, bush-crickets or katydids (often called long-horned grasshoppers), and mole-crickets. Bush-crickets are often called wetas in New Zealand. The body is somewhat flattened in crickets and mole-crickets, and slightly compressed from side to side in many katydids. The head, bent downwards, is furnished with strong mandibles. The antennae are long, at least the same length as the body and often much longer. The insects usually have two pairs of wings, the fore wings generally thicker, leathery and narrower, the hind wings membranous and broad. Body and wings are generally greenish, brownish or greenish-brown. There are also short-winged (brachypterous) and wingless species in this group.

The hind legs differ in structure from the fore legs. The hind femora are very stout and long, and the legs are adapted for jumping. The tarsi are four-jointed in the bush-crickets, three-jointed in the others. The females have prominent ovipositors which are sabre-like in bush-crickets and needle-like in the other members of the group.

Many species are predacious and feed on other insects. The mole-cricket is omnivorous, while some other crickets are herbivorous.

Many crickets and bush-crickets produce shrill sounds which in some cases can be heard at great distances. Sounds are usually produced by the males, sometimes also by the females, by rubbing together the specially modified parts of the fore wings. The sounds, which are used mainly to attract mates, are picked up by tiny 'eardrums' on the front legs. Some species sing by day, and others by night.

The metamorphosis is incomplete. The females lay their eggs with the ovipositor either in the ground or in plant tissues. The nymphs, which emerge from the egg after varying lengths of time, shed their skins a number of times and greatly resemble the adults.

Crickets and bush-crickets are thermophilous (warmth-loving) insects which inhabit bushes, meadows and hillsides, forest clearings and paths, some occurring in the vicinity of human habitations, in households and in the greenhouses of botanical gardens and nurseries. Some also live in caves. In the wild, the insects are generally useful in that they destroy a great many insects that are often harmful to man.

There are more than 8,000 described species, most of which live in tropical and subtropical regions. More than 600 species occur in Australia. There are a good many in Europe and North America, and fifteen species are found in Britain, although most of these are confined to the southern areas.

The insects are dried for mounting in collections.

18. Order **Caelifera** — locusts and short-horned grasshoppers[*]

Until recently the locusts (Caelifera) and crickets and bush-crickets (Ensifera) were classed together in the same order — **Orthoptera** — **Saltatoria** — and this system is still widely used, but there are several differences between the two groups. Locusts and grasshoppers differ from crickets in body morphology and in their methods of producing sounds. Their diets are also different.

The body of the grasshopper is compressed from side to side, the mandibles are markedly

---

[*] True locusts are large, swarming grasshoppers, but the name is often used for any kind of grasshopper in the United States.

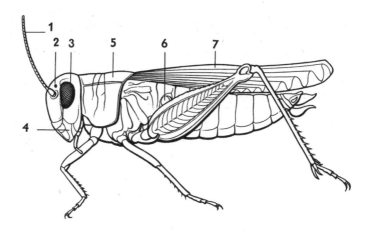

**13 Diagram of a Locust** (Caelifera):
1 — antenna 2 — ocellus 3 — compound eye 4 — mandible
5 — pronotum (shield over prothorax) 6 — tympanum 7 — wings

developed, the antennae are short — shorter than the head and prothorax combined, and the ovipositor is very short and often concealed. The tarsi are three-jointed.

The fore wings are hard and firm and the colour is generally nondescript, blending in well with the surroundings. The hind wings are broad, membranous and in many species brightly coloured — red, blue and yellow.

Grasshoppers produce sounds by rubbing the legs against the fore wings. The loudest sounds are produced by members of the family Acrididae, but these are not usually as loud or shrill as those produced by the bush-crickets.

In summer and autumn grasshoppers may be seen in open country — in meadows, forest margins, clearings, and the like. They are herbivorous and that is why some of the larger species are pests, chiefly in parts of the Near East where migrating species occasionally cause damage of catastrophic proportions. Locust invasions have been known since ancient times, and devastation of crops by locusts is one of the 'plagues of Egypt' referred to in the Bible. Mass invasions of locusts also appear in the annals of central Europe. As early as the sixth century A. D. old chronicles bear records of locust invasions into Europe. Locusts also figure in ancient cultures. They are depicted, for example, beside the bees and sacred scarabs of ancient Egypt.

It is estimated that there are some 7,000 species of grasshopper and locust in the world. Of this number, however, only about 80 are found in central and western Europe, and rather more in North America. Nearly 1,000 species live in Australia. True locusts occur mainly in the warmer regions.

Locusts and grasshoppers are dried for mounting in collections.

## 19. Order **Psocoptera** (Corrodentia) — psocids or book-lice

The members of this order, though common both in the wild and in human dwellings, are so inconspicuous that they generally escape notice. They are minute insects (1—4 millimetres long, up to 10 mm in the tropics) with soft skins and they are usually coloured yellowish or brownish; sometimes they have various markings.

The fairly large head bears mouthparts adapted for chewing, eyes, and antennae that are quite long and composed of as many as 50 segments. The prothorax is much smaller than the other thoracic segments. The wings, of which there may be two pairs, are usually longer than the body. In some species, however, they are short, in others mere scales, and in still others they are wanting altogether. They are usually transparent with darker patches on the fore wings. When at rest the wings are held roof-like over the body.

The Psocoptera feed on unicellular algae, moulds and other organic matter. They are thermophilous (warmth-loving) and therefore prefer drier situations. In the wild they occur in forests (under stones, under bark, amidst fallen leaves, and the like), on rocks, in birds' nests and in anthills; they also occur in storerooms, among old paper, hay and straw, and they get into zoological and botanical collections and the like and do a lot of damage. Some species spin a protective tissue of threads under which they hide.

The metamorphosis is incomplete. The eggs are laid in heaps. The nymphs shed their skin five to six times during development. Some species produce only a single generation a year, others two, and in rare instances as many as three.

Of economic importance are those species that occur in the vicinity of man. Most troublesome is the damage they cause to entomological collections: they bite off the hairs of prepared specimens and often reduce the bodies to dust.

There are more than 1,000 known species of which about 100 (a surprisingly high number) occur in central and western Europe. Many of these have been introduced from elsewhere, however, for it is very easy to transport these tiny insects unintentionally. There are about 150 species in North America, and 120 are known in Australia. A magnifying lens may be all that is needed to identify some species but many cannot be identified without a microscope. A collection of Psocoptera consists mostly of microscope slides.

## 20. Order **Mallophaga** — bird-lice or biting-lice

Most species of these wingless parasites measure from 1—5 millimetres in length but some species may measure up to 11 mm. The flattened body of bird-lice is generally oval, either broadly oval or longish. The colour is inconspicuous, generally yellow, yellowish-brown or brown. The head is fairly large in proportion to the body and clearly separated from the thorax. It is broader than the prothorax. Besides mouthparts fitted for chewing and small eyes, it is furnished with short antennae usually composed of three to five segments. The mesothorax is distinctly separated from the prothorax; the limits of the metathorax are difficult to distinguish. There are no wings. The legs are normally furnished with one or two claws.

The majority of biting-lice infest birds, but some are found among the fur of mammals such as cats, dogs, goats, sheep, cattle, horses, martens, roe deer and the like. They are not found on man. The parasites feed on feathers, hair, and dermal scales; only a few species actually feed upon the blood of their host. They cling to feathers and hairs with their mandibles. Bird-lice are often tied to a specific host species where their entire life cycle takes place. Some lice occur only on a certain part of the host's body.

Bird-lice are troublesome insects in that they infest and soil the feathers of domestic birds. They are particularly annoying when they occur in large numbers in poultry houses.

Of the more than 3,000 known species, some 700 are found in Europe, though it is estimated that this number may be much higher. About 200 species are known in Australia, while more than 300 have been discovered in North America, and it is certain that vast numbers still remain to be discovered on the birds of tropical regions.

A collection of Mallophaga consists of microscope slides.

21. Order **Anoplura** — sucking lice

The sucking lice are notorious insects, and some of them are important parasites of man. The body, measuring up to 6 millimetres in length, is flattened, oval and elongate, and coloured white or greyish white. The head is small but distinct and furnished with short antennae, consisting of five segments at the most, eyes and piercing and sucking mouthparts. The thoracic segments are fused. There are no wings, but the legs are often large and terminated by a claw. The claw, together with the opposed toothed projection of the tibia, forms an efficient organ for clinging to the hairs of the host.

Lice are ectoparasites of various mammals and they feed on the blood of their hosts. They attack man, rodents, dogs, horses, cattle, sheep, goats, roe deer, red deer and pigs. They are not known to affect cats, bats, hedgehogs or moles. Most are bound to a specific host species.

The metamorphosis is incomplete. The female lays large numbers of eggs commonly known as 'nits'. These are so firmly glued to the hairs of the host that even water will not wash them off. There are three nymphal stages. Development may be slow or fast, depending not only on the species but also on the temperature and other conditions.

Lice are a very unpleasant phenomenon in human society. Apart from the unpleasant feelings experienced by the infested person, one must not overlook the fact that lice also transmit various infectious diseases that until recently caused epidemics of typhus fever and relapsing fever.

There are some 400 known species and many more undoubtedly await discovery.

In most instances it is impossible to identify lice without the aid of a microscope. A collection of sucking lice is consequently composed of microscope slides.

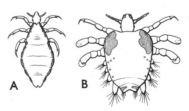

**14 Two of the commonest species of lice infesting man:**
*Pediculus humanus* (A) and *Phthirius pubis* (B)

22. Order **Thysanoptera** — thrips

Members of this order are minute insects measuring only 1—3 (up to 10) millimetres in length with elongate body coloured brown, black or yellow. The mouthparts are asymmetrical and adapted for piercing and sucking. The antennae have only six to nine segments. Most thrips can be recognized by two characteristic features: the featherlike shape of the wings (when present), and the protrusible, membranous pouch fitted into the end of each two-jointed tarsus.

Many species of thrips are wingless, but when present the wings are narrow and fringed with long hairs. Those on the hind or inner margin are generally longer and thicker than those on the front edge. The venation of all four wings is very simple.

Thrips generally feed on plant sap, which they suck from leaves and flowers with their specially fitted mouthparts; some species also suck the sap of fungi and lichens, or feed on pollen. A few feed on other thrips, aphids, and the like.

Thrips are generally found on plants, occurring mostly in the flowers and inflorescences (they are very plentiful, for instance, on dandelions and their relatives), under the leaf-sheaths of grasses (they are almost sure to be found under the leaf-sheaths of grain) and are also common on old mushrooms, amidst fallen leaves and the like.

The metamorphosis is incomplete. Females furnished with an ovipositor deposit their eggs in plant tissues, others conceal them in leaf-sheaths, flowers, and so on. The egg stage is followed by two nymphal stages very similar to the adult, and then by two or three quiescent stages which do not feed.

Thrips are of economic importance chiefly in the tropics and subtropics, but even certain European and North American species may be troublesome pests, particularly if they occur in large numbers on cereal crops. Infested plants suffer not only loss of sap but are also deformed in various ways, wilt, and even die.

There are some 4,000 known species distributed all over the world, even as far north as Greenland. About 300 are found in central and western Europe and there are about 600 in North America. A further 300 occur in Australia. They are divided into two sub-orders: the **Terebrantia** (with an ovipositor) and the **Tubulifera** (without an ovipositor).

A collection of thrips is composed of microscope slides.

23. Order **Homoptera** — cicadas, leaf-hoppers, aphids, scale-insects

The **Homoptera** were formerly grouped together with the **Heteroptera** in a single order known as **Rhynchota** or **Hemiptera**. This was based mainly on the arrangement of the mouthparts which are adapted for piercing and sucking in both groups. However, there are a great many differences between the two, both in structure and ecology, so that their separation into two distinct orders is fully warranted.

The Homoptera is a very varied order. Many of its members measure about 1 millimetre in length, whereas others may be several centimetres long. There is also great diversity in colouring, some species being a uniform colour whereas others are variously spotted or striped. All feed on plants.

The mouthparts are located on the underside of the head and bent backwards. They are formed for piercing and sucking and are very long in some species. Only very occasionally are they atrophied. The antennae vary in length and may be long and thread-like or reduced to mere stumps. The eyes, too, may be well developed or wanting.

In some species all three body sections — the head, thorax and abdomen — are clearly

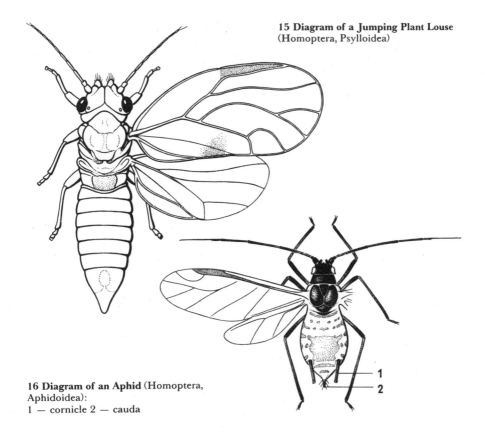

**15 Diagram of a Jumping Plant Louse**
(Homoptera, Psylloidea)

**16 Diagram of an Aphid** (Homoptera,
Aphidoidea):
1 — cornicle 2 — cauda

defined; in others they are partly or entirely fused so that the body resembles an elongate or broad sac (coccids or scale-insects). Most members of this order are winged, but some are wingless. The two pairs of wings are usually membranous and similar in structure, but the front ones are often tough and horny and marked with various patterns. Only the males among the coccids possess wings, and certain generations of aphids are wingless.

The legs vary in form and have one to three jointed tarsi. Sometimes they are reduced or wanting altogether, as in some female scale insects.

The Homoptera are important plant parasites, generally sucking up far more sap than they need. They are found on various plant organs, occurring even on the roots. Some species are not actively mobile in the adult stage; they attach themselves to some part of the plant and thereafter are unable to change their position (coccids).

Many aphids are born alive, but most Homoptera start life as eggs. The nymphs then undergo an incomplete metamorphosis with several skin changes. In many groups, however, the nature of the metamorphosis is not so simple. Male scale insects or coccids, for example, pass through two quiescent stages, called the prepupa and pupa, during which the wings develop. The wingless females do not pass through such stages. The little whiteflies, which are sometimes pests on cabbages and in greenhouses, also pass through a 'pupal' stage, although this is not quite the same as the pupa of a holometabolous insect. Many aphids have complex life cycles, with one or more parthenogenetic generations (females only) alternating with a sexual, egg-laying generation. Different parts of the reproductive cycle often occur on different species of foodplants.

As parasites, many species of Homoptera are detrimental to the plants on which they feed. Not only do they deprive the plant of nutrients by sucking the sap; they also inject toxic substances into the plant tissues and many carry serious virus diseases. They furthermore damage both cells and tissues with their probosces, and they excrete large amounts of a sugary deposit known as honeydew on to the plant leaves. Honeydew has a very damaging effect on the growth of a plant, for it hinders respiration and the plant becomes blackened with fungi that grow upon this secretion. Plants infested by a great number of Homoptera become weakened, wilt, and finally dry up. The Homoptera, chiefly aphids and coccids, are also troublesome parasites of greenhouse and house plants.

It is estimated that there are about 50,000 known species of Homoptera, of which some 5,000 are found in Europe, 2,000 in Australia and 6,500 in North America. These numbers, however, increase every year. The Homoptera are divided into two major sub-orders: the **Auchenorrhyncha,** which includes the cicadas, leafhoppers, froghoppers, and the thorn-like tree hoppers; and the **Sternorrhyncha.** The latter is a very heterogeneous group containing the aphids, the scale insects, the whiteflies, and the jumping plant lice (psyllids). A third sub-order, the **Coleorrhyncha,** contains just a few rare insects in Australia and other parts of the southern hemisphere.

Some of the larger Homoptera are dried for mounting in collections, but most of the smaller species are mounted as microscope slides.

## 24. Order **Heteroptera** — bugs

European Heteroptera grow to a length of about 2 centimetres but tropical species may measure more than 10 centimetres. The body is oval or elongate and usually dorso-ventrally flattened. The colours are most often inconspicuous — brown or grey, but some species are brightly coloured — very often red, green or brown — and decorated with patches or bands. The head bears greatly developed mouthparts fitted for piercing and sucking. The antennae have four or five segments. Besides compound eyes, there are also ocelli. Located behind the head is the pronotum, which may be variously shaped and is often large and broad, followed by the scutellum, which is clearly distinguishable and often quite large and shield-like.

Most bugs are winged, though some species may be wingless. The formation of the front wings is unusual: the basal two-thirds of the wing are thickened and leathery, and the terminal, or distal, portion of the wing is membranous. Because of their structure the front wings are termed hemelytra. The venation of the fore wings is an important diagnostic character in determining the various species. The hind wings are smaller and membranous. When at rest the hind wings are folded beneath the front wings flat on the body.

The legs have the usual number of segments and vary in length and structure according to the life habits of the given species, those of aquatic forms differing from those of terrestrial species.

**17 Diagram of a Bug** (Heteroptera):
1 — ocellus 2 — pronotum 3 — scutellum
4 — hemelytron 5 — thickened basal portion
of the hemelytron 6 — membranous tip of
the hemelytron

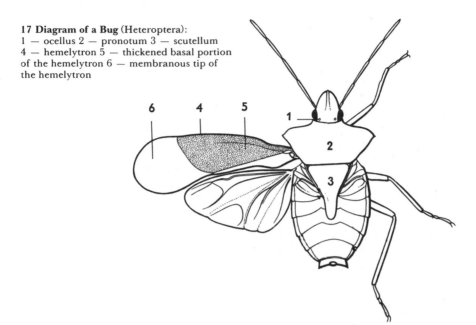

A characteristic feature of many Heteroptera are the stink glands which exude a fluid with a penetrating, disagreeable odour which takes a long time to disappear.

Bugs inhabit all kinds of situations, on land as well as in water. They may be found in forests, fields and meadows, and in the nests of birds and mammals. Most feed on plant sap which they suck with their specially fitted mouthparts. Some, such as the notorious bed bug, feed on blood while others are predacious and feed on various kinds of insects.

The metamorphosis is incomplete. During the course of development the individual passes through four or five nymphal stages, each increasingly more like the adult in appearance but smaller. The wings appear as wing-buds and become larger with each successive moult.

Bugs have a certain economic importance. Though quite a few are so-called 'indifferent' species, many are pests of cultivated plants, depriving them of nutrients by sucking their sap, damaging the plant cells and tissues with their probosces, injecting toxic substances into the plants and transmitting certain virus diseases. Bed-bugs which suck blood are troublesome insects in the home and in various lodgings. On the other hand, a great many bugs are beneficial insects in that they are predacious and feed on various noxious insects. For this reason they are sometimes used in the control of insect pests.

Bugs are divided according to their habitats into aquatic and terrestrial forms. They compose eight separate super-families.

The Heteroptera comprise some 58,000 known species. Of this number, over 3,000 are found in Europe, which is quite a high percentage, and about 4,500 occur in North America. Over 1,500 species are found in Australia.

Bugs are dried for mounting in collections.

41

## 25. Order **Megaloptera** — alderflies and dobson flies

The Megaloptera are moderate to large insects with a wing expanse ranging from 20—150 millimetres. The body is elongate with all three sections clearly defined. The colour is dark brownish-grey. The wings are broad and membranous, both pairs being about the same size. They are a dark colour and folded roof-like over the abdomen when at rest. Dobson flies have extremely large jaws projecting forward from the head on the male.

The alder flies and the much larger dobson flies are found near water, usually resting on some waterside plant and flying off heavily and rather weakly when disturbed.

The metamorphosis is complete. The female deposits several hundred or even a few thousand eggs on aquatic plants or on stones. The larvae are aquatic, spending two years feeding on various small animals they find on the bottom. Prior to pupation they leave the water and transform into pupae in earthen cells they dig in the banks.

There are a little over 200 known species, of which only two or three alder flies are found in central and western Europe. Other alder flies are found almost all over the world but the large dobson flies are found only in North America and Asia.

In collections some of the specimens are kept in glass tubes in 70 per cent alcohol; others are mounted on entomological pins.

## 26. Order **Raphidioptera** — snake flies

In older systems of classification the members of this order were grouped together with the Megaloptera and the lacewings (Planipennia) in the single order Neuroptera.

The Raphidioptera are strange-looking insects measuring some 8—18 millimetres in length, with a wing expanse of 12—38 millimetres. The flat and fairly large head bears mouthparts fitted for chewing. The prothorax is greatly elongate and can be raised up from the rest of the body. This, as well as the mobility of the head, plays an important role and stands the insect in good stead when it hunts for food.

The two pairs of wings are practically the same size, transparent and richly netted with longitudinal and cross veins, which is a characteristic feature of this order and of the lacewings. When at rest they are folded roof-like over the abdomen. Females are furnished with an ovipositor at the end of the abdomen.

Snake flies are predacious and feed on all sorts of insects, such as aphids, small beetles and the like. They may be seen from the early spring at the edge of woods, where they occur on felled logs, etcetera.

The metamorphosis is complete. The females deposit perhaps ten or fifteen eggs in cracks in bark. The larvae remain under the bark, their slender, elongate bodies enabling them to crawl through the corridors made by various insects that live under bark and upon which the snake fly larvae feed. Both the larvae and adults are beneficial because they destroy countless larvae of bark beetles and other pests. Unlike most pupae, snake fly pupae can crawl about, although they do not feed.

Fossil remnants of snake flies have been found both in Permian and Mesozoic layers, but there are 150 known species today, of which only about twenty are found in Europe. About 20 snake fly species live in North America, but the group is not found in Australia.

For mounting in collections they are either dried or put in alcohol in glass tubes.

## 27. Order **Planipennia** — lacewing flies and ant lions

This order includes species with a wing expanse of only several millimetres as well as ones with a wing expanse of 60—80 and even 150 millimetres. Many resemble the members of other insect orders, such as the dragonflies, mantids and caddis flies. Their colours are essentially brownish or green, although some of the nemopterons are brightly coloured. The antennae vary in length and are sometimes stout and clubbed.

All the members of this order possess four wings, which are usually of about equal size, membranous, in many cases transparent, and decorated either with green venation or yellow and dark markings. When at rest they are folded roof-like over the abdomen. Some Planipennia such as the ascalaphids are expert fliers, whereas the flight of others is weak and not prolonged (Osmylidae, Chrysopidae and others).

The members of this order are predacious, feeding on insects which they capture in flight or on plants. Some species also feed on honeydew, whereas others do not feed at all. The average lifespan of the adult is about four weeks, except for hibernating species. The insects can be found in almost any kind of habitat, from most stream banks to wooded hillsides and sand dunes. Green lacewings enter the dwellings of man.

The metamorphosis is complete. Females deposit their eggs either singly or in groups, the eggs of the green lacewings being stalked and cemented to the underside of leaves. The larvae are generally terrestrial and all are predacious. They feed on aphids and other small insects, piercing them and sucking up their body fluids with their powerful mandibles. They cover themselves with dust or the empty skins of their victims. They live under stones, in moss, or on leaves. The larvae of some ant lions live in pits which they dig in the ground, where they lie in wait for their victims. The only aquatic larvae are those of the family *Sisyridae,* which live in freshwater sponges; the larvae of the genus *Osmylus* are amphibious. When fully grown the larva pupates in a cocoon. In some species the development takes one

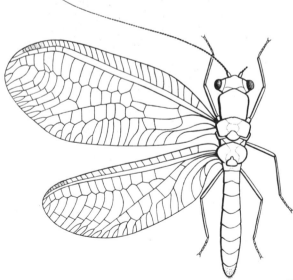

**18 Diagram of a Lacewing**

or more years, whereas some green lacewings produce two generations in a single year. As a rule it is the larva that hibernates, though sometimes it may be the adult. Adults of some green lacewing flies *(Chrysopidae)* fly into the rooms and attics of houses in the autumn and spend the winter there.

Most Planipennia are beneficial to man in that the adults and larvae feed on troublesome pests of field and forest, mostly aphids, and on the larvae of various Diptera. They therefore deserve our full protection.

They are very thermophilous insects and for that reason are most widely distributed in the tropics and subtropics. Of the 7,000 known species, some 200 live in Europe, and about 300 are known in North America. About 400 species live in Australia.

Specimens for mounting in collections are either dried or preserved in alcohol.

### 28. Order **Coleoptera** — beetles

The Coleoptera and Lepidoptera are the two insect orders which are of greatest interest to and most popular with nature lovers. Beetles are admired for their beauty of form, elegance of movement and remarkable life habits. They are furthermore comparatively easier to collect, prepare and identify than most other insects.

Morphologically beetles are a very uniform group, despite the fact that they exhibit marked diversity of shape. Little experience is needed to distinguish a beetle from other insects. The body is composed of three well-defined sections, though these are not precisely identical to the head, thorax and abdomen. They consist of the head, the scutum and the elytra. The scutum does not cover the entire thorax but only the first thoracic segment — the prothorax — the remainder (the mesothorax and metathorax) plus the abdomen being covered by the elytra. This may be more clearly seen by turning a beetle over on its back. The thoracic segments are easily distinguished by the points of attachment of the three pairs of legs.

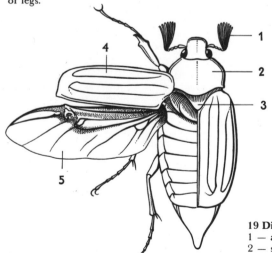

Beetles vary greatly in size. The smallest European species measure only a few tenths of a millimetre in length, while the largest European beetle measures 75 millimetres (including

**19 Diagram of a Beetle** (Coleoptera):
1 — antenna (in this case flabellate)
2 — scutum 3 — scutellum 4 — 1st pair of wings (elytra) 5 — 2nd pair of wings

44

the mandibles). Tropical species, however, are much longer and more robust. Even the form of the body cannot be described in one sentence. Most beetles have a long body but in many it is ovate or circular. It is usually more or less convex, as in ladybirds and leaf beetles, but frequently flat.

The body colouring also exhibits great diversity. Many beetles are sombre and inconspicuous, generally brown, grey or black; others are strikingly and beautifully coloured. Often they have a metallic sheen with green, gold, greenish-gold, purple, violet, blue-violet and other shades.

At the front end of the body is the well-defined head, usually roundish, triangular or oval, sometimes prolonged to form a long, sharp or blunt snout. It generally points straight forward (prognathous) or is bent downward (orthognathous). The mouthparts, located at the front, are adapted for chewing; some beetles have remarkably strong mandibles, often equipped with one or more teeth. The compound eyes are well developed. The ocelli, however, which are generally present in other insects, are absent, apart from rare exceptions. There are also some entirely blind beetles which live underground or in caves.

The antennae play an important role in the life of beetles and they exhibit great diversity of form. They may be filiform, moniliform, serrate, pectinate, clavate, geniculate or flabellate. They are generally composed of eleven segments, though sometimes they may have twelve or fewer joints. Most of the segments bear short or long sensory hairs and bristles. The antennae of some beetles are very short and hard to see, while in other beetles they may be as long as, or longer than, the body.

The scutum is always present and is often very striking. In some species it covers the head. It may vary in form and size and is either much narrower than, or of the same breadth as the elytra. It may be greater in length than width or vice versa, oval, elongate or angular, and with smooth or toothed margins. It is often covered with spiny processes.

There are usually two pairs of wings. The front wings are the thick leathery elytra. The hind wings are membranous and folded beneath the front wings. The elytra have no venation and meet in a straight line along the middle of the back. In many beetles the elytra are smooth, in others they may be covered with various ridges, pits or processes. In some species they cover the entire abdomen, in others they are shorter than the body. Most beetles have membranous hind wings which are fairly large with differing vein patterns. In some species the elytra are fused together at the line of junction, in which case the insects do not fly and have no hind wings. Several groups of beetles have no wings at all.

The legs are present in all beetles and their structure corresponds to the function they serve. Non-flying beetles have long legs adapted for running, others have legs fitted for scraping, swimming and so on.

Sexual dimorphism is very common among beetles, the males differing from the females in many respects. They may have various processes on the head or scutum *(Oryctes nasicornis),* stronger mandibles (stag-beetle), legs of different form (water-beetles, ground-beetles), antennae of different form (longhorn beetles, click beetles, Lamellicornia and others). There may also be differences of coloration between the sexes (longhorn beetles, Buprestidae). The most marked differences occur among the glow-worms, however, where the males have wings and the females are quite wingless.

Some beetles, such as death-watch beetles, longhorn beetles, water-scavenger beetles and bark beetles, produce quite audible clicking, ticking or chirping sounds. These are perceived through special auditory organs located in the legs. Some families exude foul-smelling fluids or haemolymph (ground beetles, water-beetles, blister-beetles, lady-bugs, potato beetles and others), while fireflies and glow-worms possess the power of producing light.

Beetles can be divided roughly into three groups according to the type of food they eat, namely carnivorous, herbivorous and omnivorous.

Beetles occur in all sorts of habitats: in forests, fields, gardens, meadows and hedgerows, in water and alongside water-courses, on sandy soils and in the desert, near human habitations and in households, storerooms, and the like. Some are found in lowland country, others only in the highest mountains, but many species are distributed from lowland up to mountain elevations. They occur in all zoogeographical regions and are found even beyond the Arctic Circle.

The metamorphosis is complete. The females deposit varying numbers of eggs, either singly or in groups, in all kinds of hiding places, under bark, in the ground, in wood, on plants. In many species the females deposit their eggs in special egg-cases (water-scavenger beetles, leaf-rolling weevils) or cover them with a protective layer. The larvae that emerge from the eggs show no resemblance to the adult. They cast off their skin several times before they pupate. The last larval instar often makes a cocoon. Many beetles emerge in the autumn but remain in their hideaway throughout the winter.

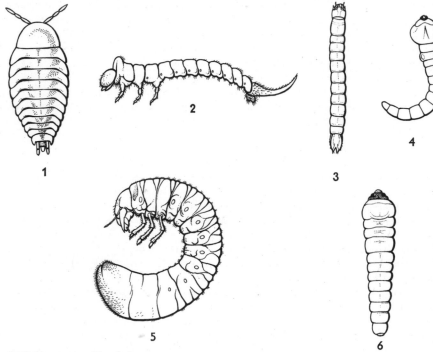

**20 Various types of beetle larvae:**
1 — Silphidae 2 — Lymexylidae 3 — Elateridae 4 — Buprestidae 5 — Scarabaeidae
6 — Cerambycidae

Some beetles, including the dung beetles, lay by stores of food for the larvae, while burying beetles are noted for the way the females care for the newly hatched larvae.

The larvae of beetles, just like the adults, feed either on animal matter, vegetable matter or both. The food they feed on, however, may be entirely different from that which forms the mainstay of the adults' diet.

Development in most beetles is slow, usually taking one year and in many cases even more. Wood-feeding beetles often take ten years or more to grow up. Only very occasionally are there two or three generations in a single year.

Beetles play an important role in nature. Though many are of no economic importance to man, there are countless others that are beneficial. These are primarily the predacious species that feed on various larvae or caterpillars, sometimes even the adults of those that are injurious to man. That is why many species of beetles, notably ladybirds and ground beetles, have been introduced to new territories, from the Old World to the New and vice versa, to help control certain insect pests. Beetles also help in removing the excrement of various animals as well as small dead animals, thus serving the role of scavengers. Some species are capable of pollinating plants. Their ranks, however, also include many pests of forests, fields, gardens and human dwellings.

As regards the number of species, beetles are not only the largest order of insects but of the whole animal kingdom. It is estimated that there are altogether some 350,000 to 400,000 species. In Europe, however, with some 20,000 species, they rank second to the Hymenoptera. There are about 30,000 species in North America and 20,000 in Australia. Beetles may be divided into three sub-orders: the **Adephaga,** which are carnivorous, **Myxophaga** (herbivorous), and **Polyphaga,** which are mainly omnivorous. The classification of beetles into families and superfamilies is still not finally settled.

Beetles are mounted in collections as dried specimens on entomological pins or on cards. Many species can be positively identified only by examining the copulatory organs under a microscope.

## 29. Order **Hymenoptera** — bees, wasps, ants and others

Members of this order show marked differences in size. Some measure only a few tenths of a millimetre in length, others as much as 60 millimetres.

Most have an elongate body with clearly defined head. In the sawflies (Symphyta) the abdomen is broadly attached to the thorax, but in others there is a stalk or waist (petiole) between the front and hind parts of the body.

The colours of many species are very obscure, mostly brown or black-brown (bees). Numerous species, however, are brightly coloured, often a combination of yellow and black (wasps), and still others have breathtakingly beautiful metallic colours (cuckoo wasps).

The mouthparts are adapted either for chewing or for licking and sucking. The compound eyes are usually composed of a great many small ommatidia. The antennae may be long and slender, short and thick, sometimes geniculate. The antennae of the males are usually longer than those of the females, and they often differ in shape as well.

As a rule, there are two pairs of membranous wings, the front wings being larger than the hind wings. They are scaleless but often covered with many fine hairs. Generally they are transparent; in some species brownish or violet.

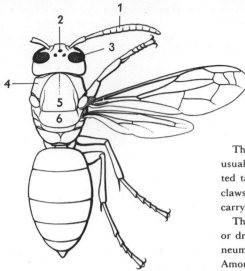

The legs are fitted for walking and all the usual segments are developed. The five-jointed tarsus is terminated by variously shaped claws. The hind legs of bees are adapted for carrying pollen.

The females of sawflies possess a saw-like or drill-like ovipositor, and the parasitic ichneumon flies also have drill-like ovipositors. Among the bees, wasps, and ants the ovipositor is modified to form a sting. The sting of some Hymenoptera is very painful.

Members of this order feed on leaves and flowers, pollen, nectar or various other insects. Their life habits are truly remarkable. Most species live solitarily, but many bees and wasps and all the ants form colonies composed of various, morphologically different castes. They congregate in nests which they make from paper, wax, mud and sand, or various bits and pieces. These nests are located underground, on or inside trees, under stones, on rocks and in man-made hives. The nests of some are truly remarkable constructions.

The Hymenoptera are found in meadows, steppes, forests and fields, as well as in gardens and human habitations. They occur on flowers and other plant organs, fly onto the walls of houses or into stacked wood, and run about in the grass.

The metamorphosis is complete. The larva which emerges from the egg may be caterpillar-like, with prolegs in addition to the three normal pairs of legs, or else — as is the case in most species — it may be legless. Many larvae feed on sweet juices, others feed on plant tissues, in most cases exclusively on leaves; still others are carnivorous. Some live in wood, where they bore a whole labyrinth of galleries, and the gall wasps induce plants to make characteristic outgrowths called galls.

The development of many species of Hymenoptera is extremely complex. Many females prepare a store of food for the future larvae, usually consisting of the larvae of other insects, or spiders which they immobilize and bring to the nest or to the spot where the nest is to be built. They then lay the eggs on top of the pile. Other species deposit the eggs directly on the host or in the body of the host, but without paralyzing it first. The larva feeds on it slowly and then pupates either on the exterior of its host or in its internal organs or tissues. The ichneumon flies are the best known of the insects which feed in this way. The larvae of the social bees, wasps and ants are incapable of feeding themselves and are dependent on workers for this service.

The larva moults a number of times before changing into a pupa (the quiescent stage), from which the adult emerges after a certain period.

From the viewpoint of man the Hymenoptera are without doubt the most important of the insect orders. Great numbers, more than any other insects, are pollinators. Many species deposit their eggs in insects that are enemies of man, thereby helping to maintain the balance of nature by regulating the number of insect pests. This feature of the Hymenoptera is being increasingly employed by man in the control of insect pests. The honey bee *(Apis mellifera)* is an important provider of honey and wax. Of course, even amongst the Hymenoptera there are many species whose larvae are herbivorous and feed on the leaves of various cultivated plants. Some of these are well-known pests of forests and orchards, but the usefulness of the Hymenoptera as a whole far outweighs any damage caused by their larvae.

It is estimated that there are more than 100,000 species distributed throughout the world; of this number more than 40,000 are found in Europe, thus making them the most numerous of the insect orders in that part of the world, followed by the beetles which, however, are universally the largest order of all. These figures are only rough estimates, for new species of Hymenoptera are still being discovered daily in various parts of Europe and the world. So far, about 16,000 species are known in North America and 9,000 in Australia.

The Hymenoptera are divided into two suborders: the *Symphyta* (sawflies), which have the abdomen firmly attached to the thorax, and the *Apocrita*, which have a petiole between the front and hind sections of the body.

A collection of Hymenoptera usually consists of dried specimens, but some are preserved in alcohol, especially the smaller ones.

30. Order **Trichoptera** — caddis flies

Caddis flies are closely related to moths, for which some species might easily be mistaken. They exhibit marked variation in size. Some species measure no more than a few millimetres; many others have a wing expanse of 50 and even 60 millimetres. The body is elongate and coloured yellow-brown or greyish. The antennae are filiform, the same length or several times as long as the fore wings. Besides compound eyes, there are usually also three ocelli. The mouthparts are fitted for licking and sucking so that these insects can imbibe only liquid food, but they rarely feed in the adult state, and the mouthparts are vestigial in some species.

All four wings are present, clothed with fine silky hairs or, very occasionally, with scales. The fore wings are larger and more brightly coloured than the hind wings, although none of the caddis flies are really colourful. When at rest the wings are folded roof-like over the abdomen. However, the wings are not much used for caddis flies only fly short distances. The legs are slender and the leg segments long. The tibiae may or may not have bristles.

The adults, if they feed at all, usually take nectar from flowers. They are found in the vicinity of water, either still or flowing water courses, on stones and on vegetation. Some species are diurnal, but many do not leave their hiding places until dusk or night time.

The females lay their eggs in a mass, enveloped in a gelatinous covering. These are either glued to plants or some damp support, or else deposited directly in the water. The larvae of caddis flies are known as caddis worms and they are readily distinguished. They may be of two types: stout and caterpillar-like (eruciform) in shape, or long and narrow and slightly flattened (campodeiform). Most larvae build a portable case in which the soft hind part of the body is concealed. The case may be woven entirely of silk fibres but other materials may also be used, e.g. grains of sand, small stones, pieces of water weed and even the shells of small molluscs. The materials used to build the case may aid in the identification of the species; many caddis worms, however, build the cases of whatever material is on hand. The larvae feed either on plant matter or small animal life (plankton) and the larvae of other insects. The larvae of some caddis flies build nets in which they catch food carried along by the current. Pupations also takes place in a case. This may be the old larval case fitted and adapted for the purpose, or an entirely new case.

Caddis flies are distributed throughout the world, their range extending far to the north. There are approximately 6,000 known species, of which some 400 are found in Europe. Nearly 1,000 occur in North America, with a further 270 or so in Australia. Identification of certain of the larger species is not difficult, but many others can be identified only by microscopical examination of the copulatory organs.

Specimens in collections are either mounted dry or in alcohol in glass tubes.

31. Order **Lepidoptera** — butterflies and moths

Butterflies and moths are studied and collected mostly by amateurs, who have contributed greatly to the existing knowledge about their distribution — mainly in Europe.

There are immense differences in size between the smallest and largest species. Whereas the smallest — the pygmy moths of the family Nepticulidae — have wing spans of only 2 — 3 millimetres, the largest — the Indian atlas moth and some of the birdwing butterflies of the New Guinea regions — measure more than 300 millimetres from wing tip to wing tip. The fore wings of the largest European species (*Saturnia pyri*) measure 120 — 140 millimetres from wing tip to wing tip.

The body is clearly divided into three distinct sections: the head, thorax and abdomen. In some species it is slender, in others quite stout. It is usually covered with a thick or thin covering of hairs and sometimes scales.

The head is furnished with antennae, eyes and mouthparts. The antennae may be composed of merely a few, or a great many, segments. The shortest are found in the family Hepialidae, the longest in the family Adelidae. Those of butterflies and a few moths are club-shaped, while those of other moths may be thread-like, bristle-like or serrate. In the males they are often pectinate or bipectinate (comb-like with teeth on one or both sides). The form of the antennae is an important distinguishing characteristic aiding the identification of both sex and species. The antennae may, furthermore, be smooth or covered with fine hairs. The mouthparts of most species form a proboscis that is spirally coiled beneath the body. In many it is extremly long and can, when uncoiled, easily reach to the very bottom of a trumpet-shaped flower. Only primitive species (family Micropterygidae) have the mouthparts adapted for chewing.

There are usually two pairs of wings which are the pride and glory of butterflies and moths, although in the females of certain species the wings are reduced or entirely absent. The wings are membranous and, though in some families they are almost the same size, in most the hind wings are much smaller than the fore wings. Each part of the wing has

**22 Diagram of Lepidoptera:**
1 — costal margin of the wing
2 — inner margin of the front
wing 3 — outer margin of the
wing 4 — apex 5 — anal angle

a specific name: the section where it is joined to the body is called the wing base and the three margins are termed the costal margin, outer margin and inner margin. The angle between the costal margin and the outer margin is the apex of the wing and that between the outer margin and the inner margin is the anal angle. In most species both sides of the wings are covered with layers of minute scales set close together and partly overlapping. A single scale measures 0.07 — 0.4 millimetre in length and its structure is very complex. It is like a tiny flat box, either hollow or filled with plasma. The upper surface is richly and finely sculptured with longitudinal and transverse ridges (striae). Scales differ in shape; they may be simple, merely slightly prolonged, or broad and with variously branched outer surfaces. Scales contain pigments and the upper layers determine the coloration of the wings. In many species, however, the colour is produced by the diffraction of light by the striae (so-called physical or structural colours). In some species one may come across dark, so-called melanic forms in which there is an excessive development of dark pigment; in others, the spring generation is coloured differently to the autumn one.

The wings of many species, chiefly the wings of males, may have scented scales that serve as the outlets of scent glands. These scent glands sometimes occur in patches. Some scales are sensory and detect changes in air currents and pressure.

Very occasionally, as in certain hawkmoths and the clearwing moths of the family Sesiidae, the wings may be transparent. Such species then resemble various bees and wasps.

The wings are generally entire but in some families they are split by longitudinal fissures into fine plume-like divisions, as in the delicate plume moths of the families Orneodidae and Pterophoridae. At other times the wings may have long or short fringes of fine hairs. The venation is concealed by the scales and is easily visible only in species with transparent wings.

Some members of this order are superb fliers, whereas others have a slow and vascillating flight. Without a doubt the hawkmoths are capable of the swiftest and most prolonged flight. Poor and slow fliers are, for example, the apollo butterflies and burnet moths. Some species fly in a straight line, whereas others fly a zig-zag course. The way in which the fore and hind wings are joined is important in flight. In most of the Lepidoptera the hind wings

51

have a frenulum, or little bristle, which fastens into the retinaculum, or hook, located under the fore wing, thus holding the two together. In a number of families, such as the Hepialidae, the inner margin of the fore wing has a posterior, finger-like lobe, termed the jugum or yoke, which projects beneath the costal margin of the hind wing. In other species that are not provided with such structures, there is simply a large overlap of front and hind wings. When not in use the wings of most butterflies are held vertically over the body, while most moths hold theirs flat or roof-like over the abdomen.

The legs are developed but are of little importance as a means of locomotion, serving primarily for climbing short distances or for holding on to a support while resting. In some families, the segments are reduced and in certain instances some legs are entirely atrophied. In some Lepidoptera the middle and hind pair of legs have sensory organs or cells that serve as organs of taste.

Sexual dimorphism or dichroism occurs in many forms. In the females of some species the wings are absent or else are reduced to small scales (some Geometridae). The form of the antennae is markedly different in the males and females (e.g. family Saturniidae). There are also frequent striking differences in the colouring of the males and females, the former being as a rule more brightly coloured.

The males of many blue butterflies (Lycaenidae), for example, are bright blue, whereas the females are often brown.

It is not commonly known that the Lepidoptera are also able to produce various sounds — stridulating, drumming and squeaking. Sounds are perceived by special auditory organs located on various parts of the body.

The proboscis enables butterflies and moths to partake only of liquid food. The adults generally visit flowers to suck their nectar. Some species need water for their existence and may be encountered in great numbers round puddles of forest trails. Others are attracted to decaying matter. The Satyridae (the browns or satyrs) are fond of alighting on the skin of man which they 'taste'. Many species, however, do not feed at all.

Butterflies and moths are to be found in practically all types of situations, both natural and man-made. They are particularly fond of resting on flowers and plants on which the larvae feed. They may be seen on stones, fences, telegraph poles, and also pressed close to the bark of trees and branches. They frequent the margins of forests and forest clearings, flit along pathways, and are also seen in fields, meadows and gardens. Many species are fond of damp localities and are found in peat moors and alongside ponds, rivers and streams. They may also be encountered in the vicinity of man — in city streets, in houses, warehouses and food stores.

As to their vertical distribution, butterflies and moths may be found from lowland to mountain elevations and sometimes even on high mountains. Many species require warmer conditions and thus are found only on sun-warmed hillsides and in steppe country in the lowlands. Some fritillaries, browns and apollo butterflies, on the other hand, prefer cold and high mountain peaks and are never seen in lowland country.

In temperate climates the greatest numbers of Lepidoptera are on the wing in the spring and summer months; some do not appear until autumn and quite a few are about even in winter. Some species, including most of the butterflies, are fond of bright sunshine, while others like the dusk of late afternoon and early evening; many moths are active only when darkness falls.

52

Many members of this order are migratory. As a rule they journey from southern parts to more northerly regions, where they produce a new generation and then die. Some of their offspring may then fly south again. Non-migratory species living in temperate climates hibernate in various stages of their development.

The metamorphosis of Lepidoptera is complete. The larvae, known as caterpillars, as well as the pupae are fairly easy to identify. The eggs are deposited singly or in groups (in rows and rings) on vegetation, wood and in various places of concealment including provisions and clothing. The caterpillars, which emerge from the eggs after varying lengths of time, have distinct mandibles with which they begin to chew their food. There are three pairs of thoracic legs, and the abdominal segments bear several pairs of so-called prolegs, the anal pair being known as claspers. Caterpillars are usually cylindrical and frequently covered thickly with hairs. Many are strikingly coloured. The caterpillars of some species of **Notodonta** (prominent moths) have a peculiar shape, while the larvae of hawk moths (family Sphingidae) have a horn or tubercle on the abdomen.

Caterpillars live on various plant parts, but generally feed on the leaves. Some simply nibble the leaves, others make mines inside them (family Lyonetiidae). Less common are larvae that bore in wood (carpenter moths — family Cossidae) or live in anthills (certain gossamer-winged or blue butterflies — Lycaenidae). Most caterpillars live on land, though a few are known to live in water. Only a few, such as the larvae of the bagworm moths (Psychidae), construct protective sacs of bits of plants. The rest rely on camouflage or irritating hairs to protect them.

The larvae of many species are solitary but some are gregarious and live in communities within a silken web (families Yponomeutidae, Thaumetopoeidae (processionary moths) and others).

After a certain period the caterpillar changes into a pupa. Most butterfly pupae are naked, but many moth larvae spin cocoons or else burrow into the soil before pupating.

Moths and butterflies are not only beautiful creatures that decorate our woodlands, fields, meadows and gardens, they are also important pollinators of plants, like the Hymenoptera. Some, such as the silkworms (family Bombycidae), are important in Europe and the Orient

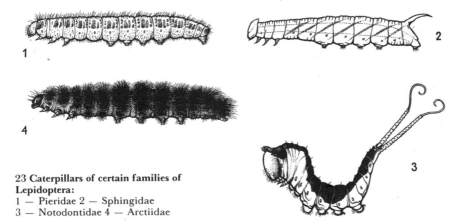

23 **Caterpillars of certain families of Lepidoptera:**
1 — Pieridae 2 — Sphingidae
3 — Notodontidae 4 — Arctiidae

in the commercial production of silk. The caterpillars of other species feed on weeds and are thus beneficial to man. Their numbers, of course, also include many injurious species. The adult itself (the imago) may be a useful pollinator, but its larva often feeds on plants cultivated by man. Several species are well-known forest pests (Lymantriidae, Thaumeto-poeidae and others); others are pests of gardens (Pyralididae, Pieridae and others), of houses (Tineidae), etc. Both adults and larvae, however, have many natural enemies which prevent their overpopulation. These may be birds or mammals, other insects that feed on the eggs and larvae (Coleoptera, Hymenoptera), or fungus and bacterial diseases that deplete their numbers.

At a rough estimate there are some 140,000 species distributed throughout the world. The largest and most beautifully coloured are found in the tropics and subtropics. As regards number of species, the Lepidoptera rank second after the beetles worldwide, but in Europe they rank third, after the Hymenoptera and Coleoptera. There are well over 6,000 species in Europe, but only about 380 species are butterflies. There are more than 11,000 species of Lepidoptera in North America and about the same number in Australia, and again most of them are moths.

The order Lepidoptera is divided into two sub-orders: the **Zeugloptera** (including only the family Micropterygidae) and the **Glossata.**

Specimens are dried for mounting in collections.

## 32. Order **Mecoptera (Panorpata)** — scorpion flies

Besides minute species (2.5 millimetres long), this order includes also species that measure about 20 millimetres in length and have a wing span of up to 40 millimetres (up to 54 mm in Australia). The body is generally long and narrow and coloured brown. The head is prolonged into a deflexed beak, at the end of which are situated the mouthparts adapted for chewing. The eyes are usually large and the antennae long.

All four wings may be present, in which case they are practically the same size, membranous and covered with dark spots. In some species, however, the wings are mere stumps. The flight is vascillating and not prolonged. The legs are well developed, and sometimes they are long and adapted for catching prey (Bittacidae). Members of the family Boreidae can jump and are sometimes called snow fleas.

The males of some species have a pair of clasping organs on the last abdominal segment.

The Mecoptera feed mainly on decaying plant and animal matter but the Bittacidae are predacious and capture living insects.

They inhabit meadows, forest clearings and thickets, and are often also found alongside watercourses. Boreidae may be encountered from October until April on snowfields.

The eggs are either laid in the ground, just below the surface, or scattered freely on vegetation (Bittacidae). The larvae live in the ground, in sand, and in undergrowth. They pupate underground.

The Mecoptera were living as long ago as the Permian. Many species exist now only as fossil remnants and these are divided into several sub-orders. Of the 350 or so known species, about 15 are found in Europe and there are about 75 in North America. Only 20 species are known in Australia.

## 33. Order **Diptera** — true flies or two-winged flies

Members of this order exhibit great uniformity in form as well as in the arrangement of the wings. However, some species, such as the hover-flies (Syrphidae), the bee-flies (Bombyliidae) and others resemble other insects — mostly Hymenoptera.

The smallest dipterans (the gall-midges — Cecidomyidae), measure less than 1 millimetre, while the largest are about 3 centimetres long (the robber-flies — Asilidae, the horse-flies — Tabanidae, and the typical crane-flies — Tipulidae).

The body of the Diptera is sometimes elongate and slender (typical crane-flies and mosquitoes), sometimes short, broad and stout (house-flies and horse-flies). The colouring shows marked diversity. Many species are grey, greyish-brown, rufous or some other sombre hue, whereas many others are very brightly and strikingly coloured (Syrphidae, Trypetidae and certain blowflies).

The body is divided into three sections. The head bears a pair of antennae, compound eyes, ocelli and mouthparts. The antennae may be long, sometimes longer than the body (**Nematocera**) or short (**Brachycera**). The eyes of many species are large and often brightly coloured as in the horse-flies. Most members of this order have wings. The first pair are membranous, usually transparent; the second pair are thread-like appendages known as halteres. The fore wings usually have only a few veins. When not in use they are generally held horizontally, but in some groups they are folded roof-like over the abdomen (the moth-flies — Psychodidae). The Diptera also include several wingless species such as the bee-lice (Braulidae) and bat-ticks (Nycteribiidae), as well as ones with rudimentary wings (the louse-flies — Hippoboscidae). Some species, such as hover-flies and mosquitoes, make a penetrating sound in flight.

The legs have the usual number of joints. They may be stout and covered with hairs, or very long and slender. Organs of taste are located in the tarsi.

Diptera eat all sorts of food. Many species suck the sweet nectar of flowers; predacious species, such as robber-flies and empis-flies, (Empididae), capture insects. There may even be differences in diet between the sexes, with the males feeding on nectar and the females sucking blood (mosquitoes — Culicidae, horse-flies — Tabanidae). Some species are partial to foul-smelling, decaying plant or animal matter.

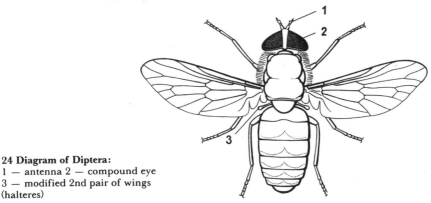

**24 Diagram of Diptera:**
1 — antenna 2 — compound eye
3 — modified 2nd pair of wings
(halteres)

**25 Head of a male mosquito**
(genus *Aedes*)
1 — antenna 2 — palp
3 — proboscis

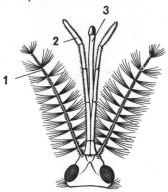

The Diptera are common insects found in widely varied situations. Often we are not even aware of their presence, whereas at other times they are extremely noxious. Many species live in woodlands where in summer you can see hover-flies hanging suspended in the air, horse-flies, mosquitoes and countless others. Pastures are also frequented by horse-flies, and the banks of ponds, lakes and watercourses by mosquitoes, black-flies (Simuliidae) and others. They are likewise plentiful in fields and gardens and many Diptera are synanthropic species which live in the neighbourhood of man (house-flies — Muscidae, blow-flies — Calliphoridae, fruit-flies — Drosophilidae, and others). They are on the wing chiefly in the warmer months but many small species fly in the winter; the wingless genus *Chionea* is occasionally encountered on snow.

The metamorphosis of the Diptera is complete. Most species are oviparous and the eggs are deposited on the ground, on vegetation, on water, in decaying organic matter, and also in wounds. Some species produce active larvae or pupae. The larvae are generally cylindrical or carrot-shaped, legless and with a delicate skin. They live in the ground, under bark, in decaying matter, in foodstores, in fruit (Trypetidae), in the bodies of various higher animals (Oestridae and Gasterophilidae), in the bodies of other insects (Tachinidae), and under the

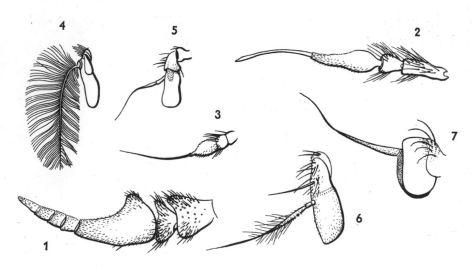

**26 Antennae of various dipterous insects:**
1 — Tabanidae 2 — Bombyliidae 3 — Platypezidae 4 — Syrphidae (not always plumose)
5 — Scatophagidae 6 — Sarcophagidae 7 — Hypodermatidae

skin (Oestridae), or in galls (Cecidomyiidae). Most live on land, but the larvae of many families live in water (Culicidae, Chironomidae, Simuliidae, some Stratiomyidae and others).

Prior to pupation, the larvae of some species abandon the place where they passed the larval stage and often burrow in the ground, whereas others pupate directly where they have lived as larvae. In the more specialized Diptera the pupal stage is passed within what is termed the puparium, the last larval skin which becomes hard and barrel-like and serves as a cocoon.

The Diptera are a very important order of insects which includes many beneficial as well as injurious species. Beneficial species are the robber-flies (Asilidae), tachina-flies (Tachinidae) and hover-flies (Syrphidae). Many species are troublesome insects, for example, the horse-flies, mosquitoes, black-flies and others, whose females all suck the blood of man and animals. The Trypetidae infest cherries, the Cecidomyiidae deform the leaves and annual shoots of plants, and the larvae of Mycetophilidae (fungus gnats) are found on mushrooms. Also damaging are the Oestridae, Gasterophilidae and Hippoboscidae, whose parasitic members attack our domestic animals. Flies may also transmit diseases and, as hosts of disease-causing parasites and viruses, they are of particular importance in the tropical and subtropical regions of the world where they infect both man and animals. Mosquitoes and other flies transmit diseases such as sleeping sickness, yellow fever, malaria and many others.

It is estimated that, worldwide, the Diptera number nearly 100,000 known species, of which over 15,000 are found in Europe. Some 16,000 are known in North America, and over 6,000 in Australia.

The order is divided into three sub-orders: the **Nematocera, Brachycera** and **Cyclorrhapha.**

Specimens are usually dried for mounting in collections, but the minute species are kept in alcohol or mounted on microscope slides.

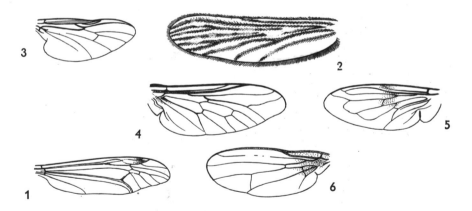

**27 Various types of wings of dipterous insects:**
1 — *Tipula* 2 — *Anopheles* 3 — *Bibio* 4 — *Tabanus* 5 — *Volucella* 6 — *Psila*

## 34. Order **Siphonaptera** — fleas

Members of this order are easily recognized at first glance. The body is greatly compressed from side to side and usually measures no more than 2—4, occasionally as much as 6, millimetres in length. The colour is generally rufous, black or yellowish-brown. The body segments are equipped with rows of backward-turned spines. The legs are covered with bristles.

The anterior part of the head bears mouthparts adapted for piercing and sucking. Small eyes are usually present and behind these, in small depressions, are situated the short and stout antennae.

All fleas are wingless. The legs are strong and fitted for running and leaping. Fleas are parasites well adapted for life in the feathers of birds and the fur of mammals. They feed on blood. Some species are monophagous (feeding on a single kind of host), but most are polyphagous and will suck the blood of many different kinds of animals. They can go without food for many days.

Fleas undergo a complete metamorphosis. The females lay as many as several hundred pearly white eggs, most of which fall into the nest or sleeping quarters of the host where the larvae later develop. They have mouthparts adapted for chewing and feed on particles of animal and vegetable matter they find in the nest. They also feed on bits of fur and feathers. The larvae of the cat and dog fleas commonly thrive under carpets and in similar situations in houses where the hosts live. When fully grown the larva spins a cocoon in which it pupates.

In Europe fleas are merely annoying pests of man and animals. In the tropics and subtropics, however, they are dangerous insects as they are carriers of bubonic plague and other diseases.

There are about 1,600 described species of which some 100 are found in Europe and 250 in North America. About 70 are known in Australia. Many more will certainly be discovered.

Accurate identification of most species is possible only with a well-prepared microscope slide.

## 35. Order **Strepsiptera** — twisted-winged insects or stylopids

Until recently these insects were classified as a sub-order or family of the Coleoptera. As an independent order they were classed next to the Hymenoptera by some authorities, whereas others classed them next to the Coleoptera. However, their relation to the other insect orders still remains unclear.

The Strepsiptera are small insects, measuring about 3—5 millimetres in length, and are distinguished by marked sexual dimorphism. They are all parasites of bees, wasps, homopterans and various kinds of cricket. The body of the adult male is elongate. The antennae are often rather stout and composed of three to five segments, some of which are furnished with a lateral prolongation. The eyes do not resemble compound eyes but look more like a cluster of simple eyes. The wings are very unusual. The fore pair are small, elongate and hard, scale-like appendages; the hind wings are large, membranous and furrowed with reduced venation. The female remains a parasite all her life and in the adult state she resembles a segmented sac, usually legless, without any trace of wings, blind and lacking both antennae and mouthparts. It is enclosed in the skin of the last two developmental stages and usually sticks out between two abdominal segments of the host insect. All that may be seen is the front end of the female's body. Infested insects are termed stylopized insects, the term being derived from *Stylops* which is the most common genus of these parasites.

As the mouthparts are greatly reduced the adult insects do not feed — the males do not live more than a few hours, anyway.

The development of the Strepsiptera is very complex. Basically they undergo a complete metamorphosis. The larva is born active. As it resembles the larva of the blister-beetles, it is also called a triungulin. It is carried by its mother's host (a stylopized bee or wasp) to a flower where it hops off and waits until another bee or wasp appears; attaching itself to the new arrival it is carried off to the latter's nest, where it enters the body of one of its larvae. The development of the two sexes is different. All the stages of the female's development take place within the body of the host where the adult female remains, whereas the adult male leaves the host and flies off.

There are some 400 known species, but the insects are rarely seen. About 25 species are found in central and western Europe. About 60 are known in North America, and a further 100 in Australia.

A collection of these insects is composed of microscope slides.


# Basic Key to the Orders of Insects


In view of the vast number of existing species of insects, it is no easy task to identify the individual species. It is far easier to determine the order to which a given insect belongs.

The following key to the orders has been tried and tested many times in the field. Like all keys, it consists of a clue and its alternative; thus, when faced with the task of identification, it is recommended that both possibilities are checked and a decision made in favour of one or the other. If the clue or its alternative does not yield the name of the order to which the insect belongs, then it is necessary to continue in accordance with the number indicated in the extreme right-hand column until the name is arrived at.

*Example:* Take any 'housefly', of which there are always plenty about, and determine the order to which it belongs.

Clue 1 has as its alternatives: 'wingless' or 'winged'. In our case the insect is winged and so we turn to No 26, our next clue, which has as its alternatives: 'with one pair of wings' or 'with two pairs of wings'. Our specimen has one pair of wings and so we continue on to No 27, from which we select the alternative, for our fly has developed front wings and hind wings that are thread-like organs, and turn to No 28. The wings of our specimen are membranous and so we look up No 31. Of the two possibilities we select the alternative again, because the wings are small, which leads us to the final clue — No 32b, which tells us that the given fly belongs to the order Diptera because the alternative clue applies.

The Grylloblattodea and the Zoraptera, both very rarely found, are not included in the following key.

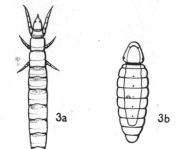

3a

3b

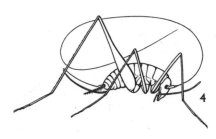

4

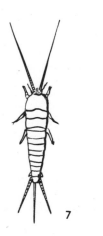

7

## KEY

1 Insect wingless or with only vestigial wings    2

— Insect winged    26

2 Antennae absent    3

— Antennae present, even if reduced    4

3a Fore legs facing forward; body slender elongate; colourless or yellowish; about 2 mm long. Insects live in soil . . .
. . . Order **Protura** (telson-tails)

3b Not only antennae but also eyes, legs and mouthparts are absent. Body cylindrical. Insects live inside the abdominal segments of other insects.
. . . Order **Strepsiptera** (twisted-winged insects), females of family Stylopidae

4 Hind legs have stout femora and are modified for jumping. Body laterally flattened. Large-sized insects that live in the open (not parasitic). Often found in garden hothouses. Nocturnal . . .
. . . Order **Ensifera** (crickets and bush-crickets)

— Hind legs resemble other pairs (with the exception of the parasitic fleas — see number 15)    5

5 Conspicuous terminal appendages    6

— Terminal appendages absent or else short and inconspicuous    10

6 Appendages long and filiform or lamellate, stout    7

— Appendages forming pincers    9

7 Three terminal appendages. Body narrowed towards the hind end. Smaller, quick-running insect. Some species mainly found on stony slopes (order **Archaeognatha**), in vicinity of man (nocturnal insects in bathrooms and larders) or in anthills (order **Zygentoma**)

— Two terminal appendages    8

8a  Body elongate, narrow, yellowish. In-
    sects live under bark and in soil . . .
    . . . Order **Diplura,** family Campodei-
    dae (two-pronged bristle-tails)
8b  Body broad and flat, with conspicuous
    flat shield that covers the head.
    Mouthparts adapted for biting. Larger,
    mostly dark-coloured bodies. Insects
    run swiftly. Long, many-jointed anten-
    nae. Sexual dimorphism: female with
    rudimentary wings, male four-winged.
    Often in vicinity of man. Nocturnal . . .
    . . . Order **Blattodea** (cockroaches)
9a  Tarsi with 3 segments. Larger insects
    . . . Order **Dermaptera** (earwigs)
9b  Tarsi with 1 segment. Small insects
    with soft non-pigmented skin. Only
    last abdominal segment and appen-
    dages sclerotized and coloured dark.
    Live in soil. In central Europe only
    rarely found, more abundant in sou-
    thern Europe . . .
    . . . Order **Diplura,** family Japygidae
    (two-pronged bristle-tails)
10  Special springing organ under the hind
    end of body. Abdomen with 6 segments
    at the most. Body 0.3 — 6 mm (excep-
    tionally also larger). Usually inconspi-
    cuous in colour — bluish-grey, grey,
    whitish or yellowish, but sometimes
    also with bright pattern. Live mostly in
    damp localities, in soil, fallen leaves,
    plant debris, moss, under stones, tree
    bark, etc. Almost everywhere abundant
    (also on snow) . . .
    . . . Order **Collembola** (springtails)
—   No springing organ. If the insect jumps
    then only with the aid of the legs  11
11  Body stick-like, reaching several cen-
    timetres in length, head very small. Not
    found in cooler areas such as northern
    Europe. Often kept as pets or laborato-
    ry animals . . .
    . . . Order **Phasmida** (walking-sticks)
—   Body of a different shape  12

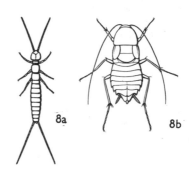

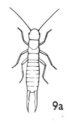

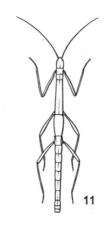

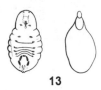

**13**

**14**

**15**

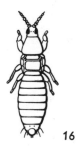

**16**

12 Head prolonged into a beak with chewing mouthparts at its end . . .

. . . Order **Mecoptera** (scorpion flies)

— Head not prolonged into a snout, mouthparts of various types 13

13 Insect covered with a small waxy chitinous scale or with a casing, or itself assumes a scale-like form which is immobile in the adult stage. Scale mostly roundish, elongate or pear-shaped and very inconspicuous in colour (greyish, brownish, or even whitish). The insect's body mostly coloured yellow, white or carmine-red. (Male is winged; see number 32) . . .

. . . Order **Homoptera** (scale insects) (super-family *Coccoidea*)

— Insect is mobile 14

14 Tarsi of forelegs swollen and with glands that secrete silken fibres. Insects live in tubes spun of silk. Found only in warmer parts of world — southern Europe, southern U.S. and tropical regions. Only few species. (Male is four-winged; see number 34) . . .

. . . Order **Embioptera** (web-spinners), female

— Tarsi without spinning glands 15

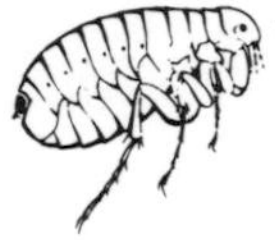

15 Body conspicuously laterally flattened, several mm long, with numerous thick hairs. Antennae very short. Mouthparts piercing-sucking. Most species inconspicuously coloured (brown, brownish-black, yellowish). Insects move by jumping. Parasites on mammals and birds; suck blood . . .

. . . Order **Siphonaptera** (fleas)

— Body not much laterally flattened 16

16 Tarsi has a protrusile bladder. Minute insects usually coloured ·black or yellow. Live in flowers, under leaf sheaths, etc. . . .

. . . Order **Thysanoptera** (thrips)

— Tarsi without protrusile bladder 17

17 Head conspicuously large    18

— Size of head proportional to other body parts    21

18 Mouthparts adapted for piercing. Legs with strong tarsal claws for clinging to hairs. Body 1 — 5 mm long, soft, hairy, mostly whitish to brownish. Head smaller than thorax. Parasitic on mammals ... Order **Anoplura** (sucking lice)

**18**

— Mouthparts adapted for chewing    19

19 Eyes absent. Antennae not longer than head and thorax. Body very soft, light-coloured. Insects live in colonies consisting of several distinct castes. Individual castes morphologically and biologically different (see number 54 — winged individuals). Live on wood ...

... Order **Isoptera** (termites), workers and soldiers.

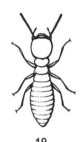

**19**

— Eyes usually present, though they may be very small    20

20a Antennae short, prothorax distinct. Insects greatly flattened and found mostly in feathers of birds, less frequently in the fur of mammals ...

... Order **Mallophaga** (bird lice)

20b Antennae long, filiform. Large head on short neck, body often flattened and soft, only several mm long. Mouthparts adapted for biting. Insects live among dried materials and in zoological collections. (Many species winged, see number 52) ... Order **Psocoptera** (psocids or book lice)

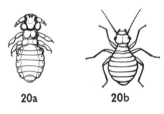

**20a**          **20b**

21 Body covered with scales. Wing vestiges present. Robust, haired insects. Some species occur early in spring, others in late autumn. (Almost all species four-winged, see number 46) ...

... Order **Lepidoptera** (moths), females of the family Geometridae

— Body without scales    22

**21**

**22**

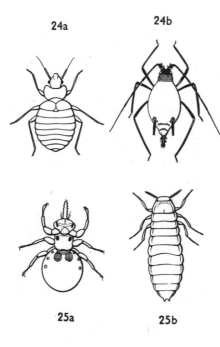

**24a**           **24b**

**25a**           **25b**

**27**

22   Hind end of body joined to the front end by a slender pedicel. Colour dark or yellow. Usually live in colonies . . .
     . . . Order **Hymenoptera,** family Formicidae (ants)

—   Hind end of body broadly joined to the front, or if narrow-waisted, without a distinct pedicel   23

23   Tarsus usually 2- to 3-segmented   24

—   Tarsus usually 5-segmented   25

24a  Body flat, brownish. Parasitic on warm-blooded animals. (Most members of this order four-winged, see number 38) . . . Order **Heteroptera,** family Cimicidae

24b  Body usually convex with delicate skin. Antennae often long. Plant parasites . . . Order **Homoptera** (aphids and scale-insects)

25a  Antennae short. Legs usually with distinct claws. Found mostly in the fur of mammals, sometimes on snow . . .
     . . . Order **Diptera** (flies)

25b  Body soft, resembling a larva. Light organs on body underside. (Most species four-winged, see number 41) . . .
     . . . Order **Coleoptera** (beetles), females of family Lampyridae (glow-worms)

26   Only one pair of wings fully developed. Sometimes the fore wings but usually the hind wings form wing vestiges, or are missing completely  27

—   All four wings well developed   33

27   Front wings reduced to small flaps or club-like appendages; hind wings large compared with size of body, folded like a fan . . . Order **Strepsiptera** (males)*

—   Front wings developed; hind wings, if present, are small scales or pin-like appendages   28

---

*   In the tropics occur long, stick-like creatures in which the front wings are no more than small flaps: hind wings large and fan-like when extended . . .
    . . . Order **Phasmida** (stick insects)

28  Wings hard, elytra-like    29
—   Wings membranous    31
29  Hind legs adapted for jumping with stout femur. Larger insects. Found on plants . . .
    . . . Orders **Ensifera** and **Caelifera**
—   Hind legs resembling other pairs    30
30  Caudal end of body with pair of strong appendages resembling forceps. Front wings elytra-like and very short.
    . . . Order **Dermaptera** (earwigs)
—   Caudal end of body without forceps-like appendages. Front wings, forming elytra, are large and well developed and usually cover the abdomen . . .
    . . . Order **Coleoptera** (beetles)

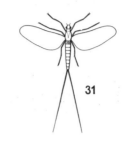

31

31  Wings conspicuously large, richly veined and held vertically when at rest. End of body has 2 or 3 long filaments . . .
    . . . Order **Ephemeroptera** (mayflies)
—   Wings usually small    32
32a Wing venation greatly reduced. Second pair of wings transformed into halteres. Eyes usually simple. Mouthparts atrophied . . . Order **Homoptera** (male scale insects)
32b Wing venation comparatively complex. Second pair of wings transformed into halteres. Eyes usually large, compound, often conspicuously coloured (red, green, or striped). Mouthparts present . . . Order **Diptera** (flies)

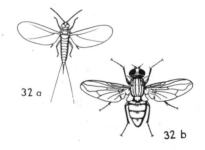

32 a

32 b

33  Wings narrow, heavily fringed and featherlike. Insects small, either yellow or a dark colour. Live in flowers and on plants. . . . Order **Thysanoptera** (thrips)
—   Wings not fringed with fine hairs    34

33

34  Tarsi of forelegs swollen with special silk-producing glands. All 4 wings the same size . . . Order **Embioptera** (web-spinners), males
—   Tarsi of forelegs without swollen silk-producing glands. Wings of equal size or different    35

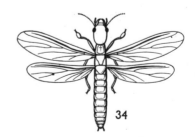

34

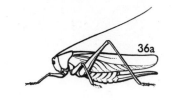

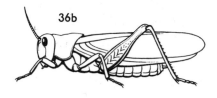

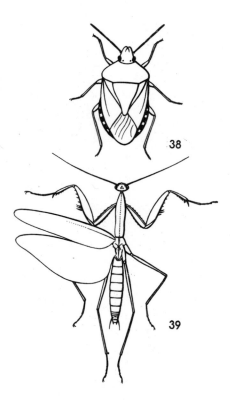

35 Hind legs with stout femora. Mostly large insects, move by jumping. Front wings narrower and harder than hind wings, which are folded beneath the front pair    36

— Hind legs usually not much different from other pairs    37

36a Antennae at least the same length or longer than the body, with more than 30 segments (excepting mole-crickets in which the front legs are very stout and used for digging). Tarsi with 3 or 4 segments. Females with variously long and strong ovipositors ...

... Order **Ensifera** (crickets and bush-crickets)

36b Antennae short, no longer than head and first thorax segment, with less than 30 segments. Tarsi with 3 segments. Mouthparts with large mandibles. Most species brownish, underwings often conspicuously coloured (red, blue, yellow). Found on grass, mostly in summer and autumn ...

... Order **Caelifera** (locusts or short-horned grasshoppers)

37 Front and hind wings differ conspicuously in anatomy and quality    38

— Front and hind wings differ only slightly in quality or not at all. They may differ in size    43

38 Front wings leathery at the base with membranous tip (hemelytra). Piercing mouthparts. Body green, brown or multicoloured. Insects usually found on plants, some also in water, often emitting a disagreeable odour ...

... Order **Heteroptera** (true bugs)

— Front wings leathery all over and much thicker than hind wings    39

39 Front legs raptorial, long, with spines. Large insects ...

... Order **Mantodea** (mantids)

— Front legs not raptorial    40

40 Wings folded roof-like, often strikingly coloured. Tibiae of hind legs often spiny, long. Insects move by jumping. Head bent down and backwards. Piercing and sucking mouthparts. Insects found on plants ... Order **Homoptera** (super-family *Cicadoidea*)

— Wings not folded roof-like. Move by jumping only occasionally 41

41 Hind end of abdomen without appendages. Front wings hard and thickened elytra meeting in a straight line along middle of back, usually, but not always, covering whole body. Hind wings membranous, folded beneath the elytra. Besides pigmented individuals, also metallic-coloured ones are known. Many species are deep black. Small, about 1 mm to several-cm-long insects. Live on plants, under bark of trees, under stones, in caves, in water, many also in vicinity of man, in households ... Order **Coleoptera** (beetles)

— Conspicuous terminal appendages 42

42a Terminal appendages resembling forceps. Elytra small and hard leaving hind part of body exposed. Membranous hind wings folded underneath front wings. Live in various shelters (often under stones, tree bark, in flats, near water)...
... Order **Dermaptera** (earwigs)

42b Terminal appendages long, outward-spreading. Membranous hind wings covered by thicker front wings. Antennae long. Fast runners. Larger insects, some living in woods, others in vicinity of man (flats, larders, bakeries, hospitals)... Order **Blattodea** (cockroaches)

43 Head prolonged into a deflexed beak with biting mouthparts at the end ...
... Order **Mecoptera** (scorpion flies)

— Head not prolonged into a deflexed beak 44

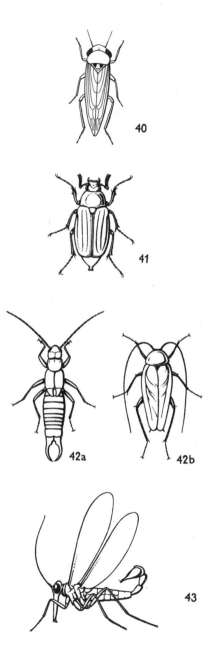

40

41

42a   42b

43

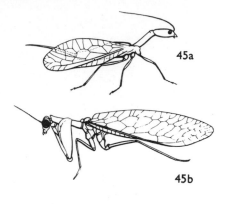

**45a**

**45b**

**46**

**49**

44 Prothorax conspicuously elongate, several times longer than its width   45
— Prothorax not conspicuously elongate   46
45a Front legs resemble the other pairs of legs. Head flat, mobile . . .
  . . . Order **Raphidioptera** (snake flies)
45b Front legs raptorial . . .
  . . . Order **Planipennia,** family Mantispidae (mantis flies)
46 Wings covered with numerous, small, variously coloured scales. Sexual dichroism and dimorphism is not rare. Mouthparts (when present) in form of a slender, coiled tube under head. Insects usually found on flowers, or at rest on tree trunks, etc. . . .
  . . . Order **Lepidoptera** (butterflies and moths)
— Wings without scales   47
47 Wings transparent or variously coloured   48
— Wings covered with a whitish, waxy powder. Insects small or minute   56
48 Hind end of body with 2 or 3 long, thread-like appendages   49
— Terminal appendages absent or else short and thick   50
49 Terminal appendages long and slender, many-segmented and about twice as long as the body. Antennae very short, front legs longer than two other pairs (in males longer than in females). Body very soft. Wings held upright when at rest. Insects often found in large numbers near water . . .
  . . . Order **Ephemeroptera** (mayflies)
— Two terminal appendages. Hind wings larger than front wings. Folded flat over the body when at rest . . .
  . . . Order **Plecoptera** (stoneflies)

50 Antennae short, almost invisible. Body very long (25 mm or more), often blue, yellow, green or red with black stripes. Head large, wings of almost equal size. ...Order **Odonata** (dragonflies and damselflies)

— Antennae comparatively long   51

51 Wings usually densely covered with fine hairs, less often with scales (of different type than those of butterflies). Front wings usually smaller than hind wings and may be thicker...
   ...Order **Trichoptera** (caddis flies)

— Wings not densely covered with hairs, membranous, transparent, variegated or dark. Venation complex or simple   52

52 Tarsi with 1 to 3 segments. Wings of varying size; venation simple.
   (a) Mouthparts adapted for piercing and sucking, situated below the body and pointing backwards. Some species with so called cauda on end of abdomen and two siphunculi on the sides. Insects parasitic on plants ... Order **Homoptera** (super-family *Aphidoidea*)
   (b) Mouthparts adapted for chewing. Small or minute insects with soft body. Large head with conspicuously long antennae. Wings held rooflike when at rest...
   ...Order **Psocoptera** (psocids)

— Tarsi with 4 to 5 segments   53

53 All 4 wings of about equal size   54

— Hind wings smaller than fore wings. Insects of varying size, sometimes conspicuously striped, robust or slender. In some species the hind end of the body is joined to the front end by a pedicel. Some species with ovipositor. Certain groups live in colonies (wasps, bees, bumblebees, ants). Insects are often pollinators ... Order **Hymenoptera**

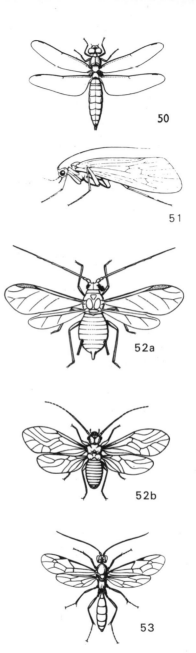

50

51

52a

52b

53

54

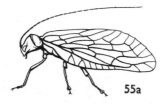

55a

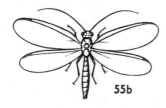

55b

56

54  Wing venation consisting mostly of longitudinal veins. Wings folded flat over the body when at rest. Antennae not longer than head and thorax. Social insects that form castes. Most individuals are wingless (see number 19) Feed on cellulose . . .

. . . Order **Isoptera** (termites), males and females

—  Complex wing venation consisting of numerous longitudinal and cross veins. Wings folded roof-like when at rest. Antennae thread-like or club-like    55

55a  Mouthparts facing forward. Wings dark brown. Antennae long, filiform. Insects found in the vicinity of water . . .

. . . Order **Megaloptera**

55b  Mouthparts bent downward. Wings transparent, greenish, brown or variegated, less often covered with yellow and black spots. Antennae either filiform or club-like. Often in households in winter . . .

. . . Order **Planipennia** (lacewings)

56  Antennae with 7 segments, tarsi with 2 segments. Wing venation very simple. Mouthparts adapted for piercing and sucking. Small insects with white wings. Found mostly on the underside of leaves of trees and shrubs . . .

. . . Order **Homoptera,** (super-family *Aleyrodoidea*)

—  Antennae with at least 14 segments. Tarsi 5-segmented. Wing venation comparatively complex. Mouthparts adapted for chewing . . .

. . . Order **Planipennia,** Coniopterygidae

# Insects and Man

Insects are of great importance to man. There is no need to give examples from the past, for the present day and age with its great advances in the science of entomology provides us with more than enough. Gone are the days when insects were creatures that interested only amateurs, for whom collecting them was a pleasurable pastime. Nowadays special scientific institutes throughout the world are concerned with their classification and the study of their life habits as well as the damage they cause. Insects have become a factor of which the national economy must take note.

Insects are generally divided into three groups from the viewpoint of their relationship to man, namely beneficial insects, pests and indifferent insects which are neither beneficial nor injurious but have their place in nature's scheme of things.

Insects are useful in many ways. They pollinate plants; are a source of honey, wax, silken fibres, shellac and dyes; act as scavengers by removing decaying matter; and feed on pests and their larvae. For many of their products, such as silk, dyes and shellac, man now has synthetic substitutes, but as pollinators and in the biological control of insect pests they stand unchallenged. Man has nothing that could replace them in these functions.

The pollination of flowers by insects is often referred to as symbiosis, for they are so interdependent that one could not exist without the other. If flowers were to vanish from the face of the earth, so would tens of thousands of insect species: and, vice versa, if pollinators did not exist then the world would be deprived of a great many species of plants.

Insect pollinators are many and they belong to several orders. Heading the field are the **Hymenoptera,** which are attracted to flowers by the sweet nectar and pollen grains upon which they feed. Next come butterflies and moths which suck only nectar, for which purpose they have a proboscis of varying length (in hawk moths it is up to 80 millimetres long). Butterflies are attracted by the bright colours of the flowers by day and they are very important pollinators. Most moths fly at night and they are attracted to flowers not only by their colouring (they visit mainly those that are of a light hue) but also by their fragrance — many flowers emit scent only at night.

Other important pollinators include two-winged flies (**Diptera**), such as the hover-flies, bee-flies (Bombyliidae), March-flies (Bibionidae) and thick-headed flies (Conopidae).

Beetles (**Coleoptera**) and other smaller orders also play a role as pollinators of certain flowers. Best fitted for this role are the longhorn beetles (Cerambycidae) and certain of the lamellicorn beetles, such as *Trichius fasciatus,* and various chafers, such as the rose chafer, *Cetonia aurata.*

The honey-bee (*Apis mellifera*) has been known for ages past for its product — honey. However, it is not the only species that produces honey. Many other species of bees, as well as bumblebees, which nest in the ground fill their cells with honey, but they consume it themselves as food. Only the honey-bee makes honey in large quantities which can be taken regularly by man, who has cultivated it for this purpose for centuries and does so to this day in all parts of the world.

The honey-bee produces not only honey but also wax which is secreted by the wax glands. In this it is not alone. Even greater quantities of wax are excreted by the coccid, or scale insect, known as pe-la (*Ericerus pela*) of China. The male larva of this coccid produces a quantity of wax equal to the volume of a hen's egg. In China it is an article of commerce.

Also well known for its service to man is the silk-worm (*Bombyx mori*) which spins a large white or yellow cocoon of silken fibres prior to pupation. Silk-worms were reared for their fibres in China as long ago as 3,000 B. C., the system of rearing them and obtaining the silk being a well-guarded secret. In spite of this, the silk-worm made its way to Greece in the sixth century A. D. and later to France where it was raised on a large scale. The silken fibre that forms a single cocoon measures about 2,000 metres in length, but somewhat less than half that may be used commercially.

The silk-worm, however, is not the only producer of silken fibres. *Antheraea pernyi* is one of the giant silk moths, with a wingspan of 180 millimetres. Its larvae eat oak leaves, and they are reared for silk production in China and in the U.S.S.R. The cocoon is about three times as heavy as that of the silk-worm, although it does not contain as much unbroken silk. Weighing nearly as much is the cocoon of *Antheraea yamamai* which is reared mainly in Japan and Korea.

Though silk has nowadays been replaced in large measure by synthetic fibres, the silk-worm and giant silk moths are still raised commercially in many parts of Asia.

Scale insects are the source of shellac and dyes. Species that excrete the resinous substance from which shellac is prepared are found in India, Africa, tropical America and Australia. They live on the branches of tropical trees which in time become covered with a thick coat of this substance excreted by the young larvae. This is collected and then processed for commercial purposes.

Scale insects or coccids are also a well-known source of dye, the best known being *Dactylopius cacti* of Mexico. This insect produces a crimson dye — cochineal — which was once used to colour fabrics. The use of these dyes was very widespread. In Europe, too, there are many species that produce red dye, but they have always been of far lesser importance.

Insects are also important as scavengers. Many species feed on decaying animal and vegetable matter and contribute to its disintegration. Generally this is done by larvae, but sometimes also by adult insects. This function is filled primarily by the beetles (earth-boring dung-beetles, rove-beetles, burying-bettles, carrion-beetles and others), the larvae of **Diptera**, springtails, etc.

Of great value in maintaining the balance of nature are the predatory insects that feed on the hordes of caterpillars, aphids, flies and other species that would otherwise strip the vegetation and play havoc with our farm animals and us. Such beneficial insects include the **Coleoptera, Hymenoptera, Planipennia, Odonata** and others. Predacious insects are an invaluable help to man in the biological control of pests, without any direct intervention on his part.

Among beetles, the most important agents are the ladybirds (Coccinellidae), the ground-beetles (Carabidae), the rove-beetles (Staphylinidae), the carrion-beetles (Silphidae), Nitidulidae, the checkered beetles (Cleridae) and others. Ladybirds play an important role wherever aphids or scale insects occur. Some eat only certain species. The larvae of many are even more predacious than the adult beetles and consume far more food. Of great value are the common seven-spot ladybird (*Coccinella septempunctata*), the two-spot ladybird (*Adalia bipunctata*), the eyed ladybird (*Anatis ocellata*) and others.

The predacious ground-beetles of greatest value are those that inhabit fields and woodlands. Important in forests are all species of the genus *Calosoma*; in fields the larger species such as *Carabus auratus, Carabus granulatus, Carabus ullrichi, Carabus cancellatus, Feronia vulgaris* and others which avidly hunt the larvae of various pests, including the Colorado potato beetle.

Among the **Hymenoptera,** some of our most powerful allies in the fight against insect pests are the ichneumon flies. The eggs of these insects are deposited either on or inside the body of the victim. The larvae that hatch from the eggs feed on the body content of the host. As the eggs of various ichneumon flies are deposited in various injurious larvae, the number of beneficial species is quite large. Many limit their choice of host to a certain group; for example, the larvae of beetles, the caterpillars of butterflies and moths, coccids and aphids; others, however, have no particular preferences. Ants, too, are of considerable value in the biological control of injurious insects, especially the wood ant (*Formica rufa*), in the vicinity of whose nest one will practically never find any larvae or smaller insects. There is no doubt that this insect deserves the protection it is accorded by law in many countries. Many species of Hymenoptera are so small that they generally escape notice, but their numbers include a great many common and widely distributed species parasitic upon aphids, coccids and various larvae. If you bring home a branch infested with European fruit scale or some other scale insect and put it into a large glass bottle, in all probability within a short time several small chalcid wasps will emerge. These tiny insects grow up inside the scale insects and destroy them.

Besides the **Coleoptera** and **Hymenoptera,** which include the greatest percentage of beneficial insects, certain other orders also include species or whole groups that feed on various pests. This applies first and foremost to many **Planipennia,** better known as the lacewing-flies (family Chrysopidae and the Hemerobiidae). These are predacious and feed on soft-bodied insects, generally aphids and their larvae. Also beneficial are snake-flies (**Raphidioptera**) and their larvae. The adults inhabit wooded areas, and the flat larvae seek their victims under bark and moss. They are of far less importance than the lacewings in that they are not sufficiently numerous to be of any great value.

The true bugs (**Heteroptera**) also include several predacious species which pursue, pierce and suck up the body content of many insects. One species was introduced into Europe in an attempt to control the Colorado potato beetle, a pest which came originally from North America.

The word 'flies' generally calls up visions of annoying house-flies, mosquitoes, gadflies, gnats, midges and other such insects which attack and bite man. This order, however, also includes many predacious species which feed on various injurious insects. These beneficial flies are mostly members of families such as Tachinidae, Asilidae and Syrphidae.

# Insect Pests

The damage caused by insects in the past is well documented, and they still cause great damage every year in all parts of the world. Pests are found in all sorts of habitats, in woodlands, fields, gardens and greenhouses, in grainstores, foodstores and fabrics, as well as in collections of all kinds. Some species are notorious vectors of dangerous diseases affecting man and animals. Insects, therefore, can seriously affect agriculture, forestry, industry and also hygiene.

Some pests are found only in certain areas, whereas others (cosmopolitan species) have a worldwide distribution. These found their way to various parts of the world by ship, rail and air in cargoes of plants or other goods. As a rule, the pests soon became adapted to their new environment and, relieved of their natural enemies, began to multiply very rapidly.

Every cultivated plant has its insect pests. Some insects feed only on a single type of plant; others, however, often have no special preferences and inhabit many, even unrelated, plant species. The latter insects are the most dangerous.

Some insects are injurious only at a certain stage of their development, usually the larval stage; others, however, are pests both in the larval and adult stage.

The most serious pests of agriculture and forestry are locusts (**Caelifera**), thrips (**Thysanoptera**), **Homoptera,** certain beetles (**Coleoptera**), the caterpillars of certain butterflies and moths (**Lepidoptera**), certain sawflies ( **Hymenoptera, Symphyta**), termites (**Isoptera**) and bird-lice (**Mallophaga**). Damage to stores of foodstuffs, fabrics, leather and similar goods is caused mainly by certain families of beetles and the larvae of certain tineid moths.

Important species in the field of hygiene are disease vectors which suck the blood of man and animals and infect them with parasitic protozoa and various other micro-organisms. This group includes chiefly some of the two-winged flies (**Diptera**), the fleas (**Siphonaptera**) and the sucking lice (**Anoplura**).

A general summary of all the damage caused by insects would touch upon all fields of human activity. Insects eat the leaves of plants or else bore mines or bite holes in them; feed upon or damage flowers, fruits and stems; tunnel in bark, sapwood and phloem; burrow in and destroy living as well as dead wood — furniture, wood flooring, art treasures and so on; spoil stores of grain, foodstuffs, spices, fabrics, leather and often also plastics; annoy man and his animals, sometimes also endangering their health.

Man is thus forced to wage war on insects as the occasion demands.

## Insect Control

Insects may be controlled by mechanical, chemical and biological means, the various methods frequently being combined to achieve better results.

The simplest form of control is by mechanical means. On small plots of land, pests can be collected by hand and destroyed, and farming by crop rotation is also very effective. This form of control is simple, inexpensive and not in the least injurious to human health, which cannot be said of chemical control.

In chemical control use is made of various pesticides that kill insects in a number of different ways. Contact pesticides are absorbed through the insect's skin; systemic pesticides are absorbed into the tissues of plants which, in consequence, become poisonous to the insects that feed on them. Some years ago the discovery of DDT seemed to have opened the way to entirely new methods of insect control. At that time, however, no one guessed what effects its widescale use would have. Two decades showed that not only did it have a damaging effect on nature but on the human organism as well, and so its use has been banned in the developed countries.

Chemical factories are continually developing new types of pesticides and publishing pamphlets and other promotional material concerning their use and toxicity. A pesticide should be applied only after thorough deliberation and study of the entire habitat where the preparation is to be used. In many cases the ill-considered use of pesticides has had dire results. Besides eradicating the pest, their application has affected all the other beneficial creatures in the habitat and upset the balance of nature. In addition, many insects have become immune to certain pesticides.

The third method is biological control, which applies knowledge of various predacious insects and their habits. In nature, constant war is being waged between the various insect species, and knowledge of the laws that govern this fact has been used to man's benefit. This method pits one species (the predacious) against the other (the injurious). It could in many instances be used in place of chemical control or in conjunction with it (so-called integrated control which is winning an increasing number of adherents).

Biological control undoubtedly has a great future, but it is not as simple a method as it might seem at first glance. It does not consist of merely introducing any kind of beneficial species to gardens or forests infested by a pest, but is based on a thorough scientific study of the particular pest and its enemies, feeding habits, number of generations produced in a single year, lifespan and other relevant factors. Only when all these important facts are known is it possible to determine which species of insect will be suitable for the given purpose, and will bring about the desired control.

Biological control is a comparatively recent method. It was first tried in the United States more than a hundred years ago, but its more widespread use is of recent date.

Most widely used in biological control are **Coleoptera** and **Hymenoptera.** Heading the list of the first group are the ladybirds (family Coccinellidae), which were the first to be used in the control of insect pests. One of the best-known species, used for over a century, is *Rodolia cardinalis.* This small ladybird is a native of Australia and was first used in California in the second half of the nineteenth century, when a great part of the area was infested by the cottony cushion scale (*Icerya purchasi*), which proved so destructive to citrus plantations that it was necessary to fell and burn trees on huge tracts of land. Scientists discovered that in its native Australia the damage caused by this scale was comparatively small, and that its numbers were held in check by this particular ladybird. This species was therefore brought to California, where it was bred in insectaria and then successively introduced into the infested orchards. Within a short time the number of scales was reduced to such a degree that they were no longer dangerous pests. Nowadays, *Rodolia cardinalis* is distributed throughout the tropical and subtropical regions of the world, being reared in insectaria and introduced wherever the cottony cushion scale occurs in damaging numbers.

In recent years ladybirds have become the focus of widespread interest. Scientists are studying their life-styles and determining their winter quarters, and fruit-growers collect them and introduce them to their gardens.

Attempts have also been made to breed ground-beetles, chiefly certain larger species. Their use in the biological control of insect pests has also brought good results. Hymenoptera reared in insectaria include first and foremost the tiny chalcid wasps, such as *Prospaltella perniciosi.* They have been used with success on many occasions in the control of aphids and scale insects (Diaspididae).

# Collecting and Preserving Insects

Collecting insects is becoming an increasingly popular pastime and there is no doubt that it is a worthwhile pursuit. The collector who makes a collection for his own pleasure can also help in solving a number of entomological problems. He establishes a picture of the existing structure of the insect population in the area where he does his collecting, and this is of particular importance wherever the countryside is undergoing great changes. Collectors take part in the study of the entomofauna of large cities, register migratory species and, sometimes, even help in solving important problems in the control of insect pests.

Every collector must be heedful of nature and of the insects he collects, taking care not to damage the locality where the given species occurs. If he takes up large samples of material (such as leaf litter and decaying matter), he should take pains to leave the locality as he found it.

Nature is nowadays undergoing such marked changes within short periods, in a way never experienced before in the history of mankind, that the collector is thus also its protector, seeing that no abuse of it is caused by his hobby and observing the laws and regulations laid down for the protection of nature and the landscape by the governments of all cultured nations. He is acquainted with the lists of protected animals and plants, and does his best to protect them.

## Collecting Equipment

The collector will need general equipment, plus several special items for collecting certain types of insects, for not all can be collected by the same method.

Standard equipment includes killing jars of different kinds, various nets, an aspirator, glass tubes filled with alcohol, a magnifying lens and, sometimes, bait and light traps.

The *killing jar* is a wide-necked glass bottle with a well-fitting cork stopper. It is recommended that several of these bottles should be taken when collecting specimens. In the case of larger bottles, an opening is drilled in the cork stopper through which a glass tube fitted with a small stopper is then inserted. Pieces of tissue or coarse wood shavings should be placed inside the bottle.

The *net* may vary in pattern but it is usually circular and generally has a collapsible frame. The handle is attached firmly by means of a screw. The net bag can be made of various kinds of material, depending on the type of insects to be collected (flying, crawling or aquatic insects).

For butterflies and moths the net should be about 30 centimetres across and 60 centimetres long. The material must be light and not too closely woven, to allow for the rapid passage of air. This is very important when collecting, for closely woven material exerts a resistance as it is swept through the air.

The sweeping net which is used for collecting insects such as beetles, bugs, cicadas, grasshoppers, locusts, flies and Hymenoptera consists of a strong linen bag narrowing towards the end and reinforced with a stout hem at the rim to prevent the frame wearing through the material. The net is swept to and fro in front of the collector in a figure-of-eight pattern as he walks along. The sweeping motion must be vigorous to prevent the captured insects escaping. The net should be examined at frequent intervals to remove unwanted insects such as bees and bumblebees, as well as caterpillars or slugs which might damage the collected material. If the net contains only a small number of specimens these may be taken out on the spot with the aid of an aspirator. If there are a large number they should be transferred to a linen pouch and examined and sorted at home.

For catching aquatic insects the net must be of very permeable material, otherwise collecting would be a very difficult task as water exerts a large resistance. In shallow water, in streams and in springs, the collector can also use a wire-mesh sieve.

The *aspirator* is used to remove insects from the net as well as for collecting. It consists of a thick-walled, hollow glass cylinder of varying width, plugged at both ends by bored stoppers in which short glass tubes are inserted. Fitted on the outer end of one tube is a narrow rubber tube, the inner end covered with a piece of fine muslin. Collecting with the aspirator is simple and fast work. The lower end of the instrument is placed close to the insect which is drawn up inside the aspirator by the collector sucking on the tubing at the other end. The insect is then shaken out directly into the killing jar.

When the collector has gained some experience he will eventually add to his equipment a sifter and a beater, with the aid of which he will be able to collect species that are difficult or impossible to obtain by other means.

A *sifter* consists of a sturdy cloth bag with a circular wire frame at one end, and another sewn in part way down at right-angles. Stretched on the lower frame is a wire mesh. The bottom of the bag is tied with a purse string. The upper part of the bag is filled with rotting wood, leaves, litter, moss, etc. When it is shaken larger particles are held back by the mesh, while insects and smaller particles fall through into the bottom of the bag. At intervals the bottom of the bag is opened and the collected material put into cloth bags to be taken home and examined at leisure. The debris and litter remaining in the top part of the sifter should be put back in place so as to leave the spot as it was.

A *beating tray* resembles a large upturned umbrella with a hole at the bottom opening into a wide-mouthed bottle, preferably plastic. The collector holds the tray in one hand and beats the vegetation with a soft rubber truncheon, thus dislodging the insects. The beating tray must be shaken continually so that the insects caught in it cannot fly off. The collected specimens may be picked over on the spot or else put in a cloth bag for closer examination later.

Another thing the collector must do, no matter where or what he intends to collect, is to insert *a slip of paper with pertinent information* about the locality and date of capture into the collecting jar along with the specimen(s). He should never depend on his memory!

*Soft forceps* will come in good stead when collecting insects that live under bark, under stones, in decaying matter or on dung.

*Glass tubes* of different sizes filled about two-thirds with 75 per cent alcohol are another basic item of equipment.

A *magnifying lens* with ten-fold magnification is very useful when out collecting. It is preferable to wear this on a piece of string tied round the neck.

## Baits and Traps

If the collector is able to remain in a given locality for some length of time, then he can use traps for catching insects. This method is mainly used for beetles. Good for the purpose are open tin containers sunk in the soil up to the rim and baited. They should be covered with a slanting roof to keep out rain. The bait — a piece of cheese, a piece of carrion, mushrooms or fruit — is placed on a piece of moss in the bottom of the trap. Some insects are attracted to carrion, others to the sweet juice of fruit. The catch is usually quite varied and must be sorted frequently, otherwise the captured specimens might devour one another. Another type of trap is one containing formaldehyde in which the insect drowns. This method, however, is not recommended as frequently a great many common and often beneficial species, which the collector already has in his collection, are killed unnecessarily.

Butterflies and moths, certain beetles, Hymenoptera and two-winged flies that are fond of sweet substances are attracted to 'sugar', a bait consisting of a mixture of various sweet and aromatic substances, for example apples stewed in dark beer, sweet syrup combined with honey, and fruit juices. A streak of bait (about 1 decimetre wide and 3 decimetres long) is painted on tree trunks, thick branches or rocks, always on the leeward side. Many interesting species may be collected by this means.

A large number of species are attracted to light. An ordinary bulb in a room or porch will attract many moths, which fly in through an open window. However, to catch other species the collector must take the light out into the field. This may be an electric, kerosene or spirit lamp, depending on the circumstances. Very good results are obtained with an ultra-violet lamp, but in this case care must be taken to shield the eyes. The collector can also take with him a white sheet which is attached to branches with clothes' pegs and illuminated by the light of the lamp. Light traps also yield good results, and simple portable traps with ultra-violet lamps are now available.

## Killing and Preserving

Wood shavings or pieces of tissue in the killing jar are soaked with a killing agent. Ethyl acetate is widely used for this purpose nowadays, but this is a very volatile substance and therefore only a few drops are put in the jar. The jar must be recharged from time to time, particularly on hot days. Small insects are tossed into the killing jar through the tube inserted in the stopper.

Formerly, cyanide mixed with plaster of paris to form a layer on the jar was used as a killing agent. This, however, is a very dangerous substance and in several instances a broken killing jar has been the cause of tragic death.

Ethyl acetate is used to kill beetles, bugs, cicadas, Hymenoptera, Diptera and other insects. The insects are dead and ready for treating within a few hours (the time depends on the size of the insects and the concentration of the vapours in the jar). If the insects cannot be treated immediately after they have been brought home, they should be placed between layers of soft tissue or coarse wood shavings where they soon dry. Such specimens must be moistened (relaxed) before being treated.

Lepidoptera should be killed as soon as possible after capture, otherwise the wing scales may be damaged. In the case of butterflies, all that needs to be done is to place the wings vertically with upper surfaces touching and lightly pinch the thorax. Moths are put into the killing jar together with the net. Killed butterflies are put in previously prepared packets (small envelopes) for the journey home. Other Lepidoptera must be pinned in the field before taking them home. Diptera, or at least members of certain families, should also be pinned as soon after killing as possible. If this is not done, the numerous bristles, important in identification, will be broken off as the flies are shaken about.

Some insects are preserved directly on the spot in 75 per cent alcohol. For this purpose the collector should always take with him several different-sized glass tubes. Aphids, coccids, mayflies, stoneflies, certain Planipennia, wingless insects and various larvae are preserved by this method.

## Preparation of Insects

There are many methods of preparing insects, some of which are used for only certain groups. Most insects are preserved simply by drying. A less common, and far more complicated, method is preparing insects in cavity slides for use with microscopes. However, even drying does not always follow a standard procedure. Much has been written about preserving insects, and the collector will find detailed information about the various methods in many books on the subject.

## Equipment

There are several basic items every collector must have for preserving and mounting insects. These include setting needles, forceps, several fine brushes, a suitable holder, strips of polystyrene, a setting board, pins, cards, a good glue, a pinning block and a strong magnifying lens or binocular stereoscopic microscope.

Setting needles are of two kinds — straight and curved — and can easily be made by inserting a straight or slightly bent entomological pin into a holder, preferably a soft elder branch.

Forceps are also of two kinds— sharp forceps for pulling out and arranging the legs and antennae, and soft forceps for lifting and transferring the insects.

Brushes are very useful and necessary, particularly when preparing very small specimens. When moistened, the brush forms a sharp tip with which the legs and antennae of the smallest specimens are easily spread out.

The holder is merely a piece of glass slide glued to a small wooden stick. It is held in the left hand and is used to hold the specimen steady while preparing it.

The collector should have several strips of polystyrene, about 1—2 centimetres thick, on which to pin specimens. It is recommended that they be wrapped in a piece of white paper so that they do not crumble when pins are pushed in and pulled out.

For setting the wings of butterflies and moths, dragonflies and damselflies, certain Planipennia, grasshoppers and locusts, the collector must have a special setting board. This consists of two smooth boards of soft wood, cork or polystyrene fixed side by side, either level or slightly tilted towards the centreline which forms a groove of varying width and height; the bottom of the groove is lined with a layer of cork or polystyrene. The width of the groove may be permanently set or else regulated by means of a screw. Setting boards are of various lengths and widths (depending on the type of insect).

Pins are used to pin larger specimens. These are not ordinary pins but specially manufactured entomological pins, either of stainless steel or with a black japanned finish. 'English' pins come in various lengths and thicknesses, each suitable for a particular kind of insect. 'Continental' pins come in standard lengths and in various thicknesses designated by numbers. Size 0 is rather slender and suitable for most flies. Size 3 is a stout pin ideal for bees, grasshoppers and large moths.

Cards are used for mounting small insects, especially bugs and beetles. These cards are of good-quality white cardboard and come in a number of sizes and shapes. As a rule they are rectangular with sharp or rounded corners. Cards may also be pointed or perforated; these are used for special purposes. A good, water-soluble glue should be used for sticking the insects to cards so that the specimens can be lifted up again without difficulty if necessary.

A pinning block is essential to ensure that all specimens, both pinned and glued to cards, are at the same height. The block consists of three graded steps with holes 10, 21 and 25 millimetres deep. The pinned specimen must be moved to the desired height immediately after pinning, for once it has dried it can no longer be moved. This is done by inserting the head of the pin on which the specimen is mounted into the 10-millimetre hole and then moving the insect with the aid of forceps until its back touches the block. The height is measured from the pinhead and not from the point of the pin because insects are not all equally stout. In the case of carded specimens the distance is measured from the pin point. The card should be at a height of 25 millimetres, the data label at a height of 21 millimetres.

A good entomological lens fitted on a stand, or else a binocular stereoscopic microscope, not only makes the process of preparing insects easier and quicker but also reduces eye strain. Everybody for whom insect collecting is a serious pastime and not a passing whim, should purchase at least a school microscope which will not only be an invaluable aid in preparing specimens but will also reveal many interesting features of the smaller insects which otherwise escape notice.

Larger insects are generally pinned; smaller insects are carded. However, it is not possible to say exactly which insects should be pinned and which carded, for much depends on the collector's preference. Some pin even small beetles, such as ladybirds and leaf beetles, whereas others card beetles as large as rove-beetles and lamellicorn beetles.

In direct pinning the pin is inserted straight through the insect. In beetles it is inserted into the front part of the right elytron; in bugs into the right-hand side of the scutellum; in other insects such as dragon-flies, two-winged flies, moths and butterflies, and Hymenoptera, into the centre of the thorax; in cockroaches into the centre of the scutum. Each specimen should be set to the appropriate height as soon as the pin is inserted. Then the antennae, wings and legs are arranged in the desired position, with the pin on which the specimen is fixed inserted in a strip of polystyrene about 2.5 centimetres thick.

Far more complicated is the preparation of insects with large or showy wings, such as Lepidoptera, dragonflies, lacewings, grasshoppers and locusts. This is done with the aid of a setting board. The body of the insect, e.g. a butterfly, is placed in the groove on a wad of cotton so that it remains at the required height. Then the wings are spread out on the board and covered with a sufficiently broad strip of cellophane. After that they are arranged in the desired position with the aid of a setting needle (the usual practice is to arrange the wings so that the hind edge of the front wing is at right angles to the body) and secured in place with pins inserted round the margins. All this must be done with great care so that the wings are not damaged. Lepidoptera, dragonflies and certain other insects are set on both sides — all four wings are spread out. Grasshoppers and locusts, however, may be set only on one side, the wings on the other side remaining folded. The reason for setting the wings is to display the colouring, which is often quite striking, particularly in some grasshoppers.

When dealing with stout-bodied specimens it is sometimes necessary to remove the internal organs and in their place put a wad of cotton soaked in a setting solution. Stout-bodied Lepidoptera, such as hawk moths and giant silk moths, are regularly prepared in this way, as are certain beetles, grasshoppers, locusts and dragonflies.

Besides large insects, small Lepidoptera, Diptera and other insects are also sometimes pinned. However, their bodies are extremely delicate and so standard-size entomological pins cannot be used for the purpose. Very fine, short, headless pins are used instead. Such a pin is passed through the body of the insect and stuck into a strip of elder pith or polyporous which is then attached to the collection box with a stouter pin.

Most small insects, as has already been said, are carded, the card being held in place in the collection box with the aid of a pin inserted at the edge. Before sticking the insect to the card it is necessary to stretch out the legs and antennae with the aid of a needle and brush. Then a small drop of glue is put on the card and the prepared specimen is carefully transferred to it with the aid of soft forceps or moistened brush. Just the right amount of glue should be applied so that the specimen is not submerged in it, and with a little practice the collector will soon know how much. Usually only the position of the insect is arranged at first, as it is necessary to wait at least half an hour or more until it adheres to the card before arranging the legs and antennae. These are arranged differently than in pinned specimens. In carded specimens the antennae are spread out in front and the legs extend sidewards from the body — the front legs pointing forward, the middle and hind legs towards the rear.

Some insects have important identifying characters on the underside of the body which would be obscured by the normal method of carding, thus making it necessary to lift up the specimen for purposes of identification. In such cases special perforated cards are used, the insect being stuck to the card so that the respective characters are visible through the hole in the card. Insects whose identifying characters are located on the front end of the body are stuck to the point of a triangular piece of card with the front part of the body hanging free. If the prepared insect on the card is sufficiently dry and ready for putting in the store box, it should be moved to the desired height with the aid of the pinning block.

Each mounted insect must have a data label, for otherwise the specimen is worthless from the scientific point of view. This is a cardboard label bearing pertinent data such as where and when it was found, the collector's name and, if desired, further information such as the host plant of the insect (important in the case of plant parasites), the elevation above sea level of the locality of capture, whether the insect was raised from a larva or pupa, and any other relevant details. Because there is not enough room on the data label for all this information it should be entered in a journal kept for this purpose.

Data labels, which should not be larger than the cards on which the insects are mounted, should be at a uniform height (21 millimetres) whenever possible.

Mayflies, stoneflies, caddis flies, lacewings, snake flies and others may also be mounted as dry specimens, and usually are for exhibition purposes. However, the soft bodies shrivel on drying, thus making the specimen worthless for scientific purposes, including correct identification of the individual. For this reason such insects are kept in glass tubes containing 70 — 75 per cent alcohol, from which they may be removed for examination and then put back again. Naturally, these glass tubes must also be provided with data labels.

Many species of insects can be preserved in cavity slides for use with microscopes, without which the collector would be unable to distinguish the identifying characters of the given individual. This method is used for coccids, aphids, whiteflies, fleas, sucking lice, bird-lice, thrips and others. In general these are small, unattractive insects that are rarely of interest to the amateur collector and are studied only by scientific laboratories and museums, which alone possess the special equipment required for microscopic preparation.

Insect larvae are not set as a rule, but kept in small glass tubes filled with 75 per cent alcohol or other preservative. In former times they were often preserved by drying but this has been abandoned in most cases today. Larvae, too, must have data labels.

Dry specimens, even those that have been stored for a number of years, are mounted in the same way but must first be moistened (relaxed) so that the appendages are not damaged. This is done in one of two ways. Insects whose bodies are not covered with hairs or scales may be immersed for one or two days in 5 per cent acetic acid. Insects thickly covered with fine hairs or scales (butterflies and moths, caddis flies, bumblees, bees and others) are relaxed by another method: the bottom of a glass dish is covered with sterilized moist sand topped by a piece of filter paper on which is placed a drop of creosote or phenol or several thymol crystals to prevent mould. The insect is placed on the paper and covered with a glass dish (its rim must be submerged in the sand). The length of time the specimen is left in this moist atmosphere depends not only on the size but also on the type of insect. If only a few specimens are being relaxed at one time, a layer of moist filter paper may be used instead of sand.

## Establishing a Collection

Mounted and properly labelled, insects are put in special entomological boxes. These come in standard sizes and are supplied by special dealers. Such a box is covered with a layer of cork or polystyrene on the bottom and is provided with a tight-fitting lid to prevent the entry of dust or insect pests. Some collectors have special entomological cabinets with glass-covered wooden drawers made to order for their collections.

At the beginning it is not necessary to classify the collected material, but as the collection grows larger it is time to consider the matter. At first they should be arranged according to families; later, also according to genera and species. This, however, requires a certain degree of experience in identifying insects on the part of the collector.

There is plenty of time for a final, definitive arrangement of the collection. The collector must also decide what kind of collection he wishes to have — whether he will specialize in the study of the insect population of a given area, or whether he will specialize in one particular family or group of insects to which he will add both by his own efforts in the field and by trading with other collectors.

## What Dangers Threaten Insect Collections?

Every collection, even the smallest, may be attacked by insect pests or damaged by some other means — sunlight, dust, damp or changes in temperature. Insects exposed to the sun's rays and ordinary daylight soon change colour. Damp is very dangerous and can completely destroy an entire collection for it is conducive to the spread of mould which covers the mounted specimens with a white coat. Mould is very difficult to remove even from hard, sclerotized insects such as beetles, earwigs and long-horned grasshoppers; butterflies and moths and other insects with a soft cuticle can be written off entirely when they become mouldy. The collection should always be stored in a place which is not subject to marked changes in temperature (hot in summer and freezing in winter).

Heading the list of insect pests that may cause irreplaceable damage are small beetles, several species of tineid moths, and book-lice. Most serious of the beetle pests are members of the family Dermestidae. Until recently, *Anthrenus museorum* was considered the chief pest of collections, but evidence has proved that *Anthrenus verbasci* causes the greatest damage. Two other serious pests are *Anthrenus scrophulariae* and *Anthrenus fuscus*. All four are small beetles which in their adult stages are not dangerous as they feed on flowers. It is the small and thick-haired larvae, known as woolly bears, that feed upon dry insect specimens and reduce them to fine rufous dust. Other pests belonging to this family are *Attagenus pellio* and the larder beetle *(Dermestes lardarius)*. Both are larger than the *Anthrenus* beetles.

The larvae of the common clothes moth *(Tineola biselliella)* occasionally damage collections of Lepidoptera, constructing tubular cases of the mounted specimens' hairs, bristles, etc. However, being omnivorous, they also feed on other materials besides collections.

Psocids, or book-lice, are further annoying pests of entomological collections. These are such minute insects that they often entirely escape notice. They feed on the surface of the insects' bodies and soil the data labels.

It is necessary, therefore, to check the collection at frequent intervals. Small collections are much easier to keep in good condition than large museum collections. A very simple method of disinfecting a collection is to put paradichlorbenzene crystals in a muslin bag and pin it into one corner of the box. The fumes ward off insect pests and also protect the specimens from mould.

To safeguard the collection it is also necessary to put specimens received from other collectors into 'quarantine' for a certain period, i.e. in a special box containing disinfectant.

# Rearing Insects

In this section it is not our aim to discuss how to raise bees, silkworms or other useful insects for the purpose of controlling pests but how to breed insects simply for the fun of it. Nature lovers generally rear butterflies and moths or stick insects.

The rearing of caterpillars has a long-standing tradition and good and well-established methods. Butterfly collectors take caterpillars home not only to observe them but also to acquire adult specimens with undamaged wings.

To rear larvae successfully it is necessary to provide them with the correct food. Many are not particular, but some species feed only on a single kind of plant and if this is not available they will eat nothing else and die.

Larvae are often reared in special cages consisting of a wood or metal framework with sturdy top and bottom, enclosed on three sides with wire mesh or fabric such as nylon and with a glass door on the fourth side. Much simpler cylindrical cages can, however, be made with cake tins and muslin. The bottom of the cage is covered with a layer of soil and sand, which is important for pupation. Some larvae eat only fresh vegetation; others prefer plants that are slightly wilted. Fresh plants keep best and last longest if put in a glass tube filled with water. The mouth of the tube, however, must be plugged with tissue paper so that the larvae can't climb inside and drown. It is recommended that each species be reared separately; rearing several together can pose a number of problems. Some larvae require greater moisture; others a higher temperature. Detailed information on how to rear the various types of larvae is outside the scope of this book, and the collector must learn by experience.

It is essential to ensure the utmost cleanliness, for larvae, like all living things, are prone to disease.

After a time the larva grows to a certain size and begins to change its life habits. Often it crawls round and round the cage and stops eating. It has entered the stage that precedes pupation. Some larvae pupate on bark, others under bark, in the forks of branches and very often in soil at various depths. For this purpose the cage should be provided with a sufficiently deep layer of soil or sand, and twigs or pieces of bark should also be made available.

Some species of larvae may be raised successfully without a cage, directly on the host plant. The best conditions for this are in the garden, greenhouse or a special plot. All that needs to be done is to put a piece of wire mesh or synthetic fabric round the plant and, if the larvae live on branches, to wrap a piece of fabric round the branch to prevent the larvae from crawling off. Larvae move to another spot when they have consumed the greater part of the leaves.

Rearing larvae in summer is usually no problem. It is far more difficult in winter when most efforts meet with failure, for the collector cannot provide the conditions of the natural environment.

Many collectors prefer to rear pupae they have found in the wild. This is far easier than raising larvae, and the surprise on seeing the adult when it emerges is usually far greater because pupae are much more difficult to identify than larvae.

Rearing butterflies and moths from the egg is also interesting. The eggs found in the wild are put, together with a piece of the host plant, into a laboratory dish and when they hatch the larvae are transferred either to small boxes or glass tubes and later to a cage. For beginners, however, rearing insects from the egg is difficult for it requires a certain amount of knowledge about the life habits of the larvae, chiefly what kind of plants they feed on.

The collector should keep a detailed journal about the course of the process. This should include information on the time and number of moults, the foodplants, atmospheric moisture, temperature, lifespan, pupation, emergence of the butterfly and any other relevant data.

Beetles are reared less often than caterpillars. However, there are many species besides the meal worm *(Tenebrio molitor)* that provide the collector who raises them with much enjoyment. Aquatic beetles are fairly easy to rear. All that is necessary is to put them in a glass aquarium of any size, provided with a little sand and a few plants. Beetles must be given the proper food — animal food in the case of predacious diving beetles, or an ample supply of aquatic plants in the case of water-scavenger beetles. Less suited for longer-term observation are the larvae of diving beetles. When rearing these it is generally forgotten that they do not pupate in water, and many collectors disappointedly fish out from the aquarium dead larvae that were unable to pupate as the only place where they can successfully complete their development is in soil in banks. Because it is impossible to provide the larvae with these conditions they should be released or returned to their natural habitat after the collector has completed his observations.

The larvae of caddis flies make interesting additions to insect life in an aquarium. These remain on the bottom and are interesting because of the remarkable cases they construct of various materials — bits of wood and leaf, small stones and even bits of mollusc shells.

Suitable and rewarding subjects for rearing at home are the large species of ground-beetles. The author himself raised a number of species for many years. They do well in insectaria which should be provided with some forest soil, a clump of moss, some leaves and a stone or piece of old wood. Beetles are best raised singly, for then there is no danger of their attacking one another. Feeding ground-beetles is no problem for they eat all kinds of animal food — earthworms, snails, various larvae, beetles and other insects, pieces of meat and, in the autumn, even sweet fruit.

Beetles that have died can be treated and put in the collection, even though they show signs of age such as segments missing from the antennae or tarsi.

Other very good subjects are the larvae of longhorn-beetles, though rearing them requires a little more patience as their development takes several months; so also are ladybirds as all that is necessary in this case is a constant supply of fresh aphids. Beetles are easily reared from pupae, for their development is rapid.

Stick insects, or phasmids, are good and easy subjects to raise at home, for they require practically no effort. All you need to do is to put them in a cage, an aquarium or simply a glass jar and provide them with food, of which there is a sufficient supply even in winter. The leaves of ivy or Bergenia satisfy some species, while most of the other commonly reared species will eat bramble or rhododendron. Phasmids grow fairly rapidly and do not have a quiescent stage. They lay numerous eggs, without mating in many species, and, although the eggs may take several months to hatch, it is very easy to rear generation after generation.

# PLATES

Sub-class: **Endotropha**

Order:    **Two-pronged Bristle-tails — Diplura**

Family:    **Campodeidae**

**1.** *Campodea fragilis* Mein. 3.5 mm. Has two caudal setae shorter than the body. Blind, like all the other species. Lives in damp, humus-rich soils under stones, old logs. Also occurs abundantly in anthills. Distribution: cosmopolitan.

Order: **Springtails — Collembola**

Family: **Onychiuridae**

**2.** *Tetrodontophora bielanensis* Waga. 6—9 mm. A large, robust species. Fond of damp situations; frequent in foothill and mountain forests where it occurs gregariously on tree stumps, in moss, on fungi, etc. Also found in caves and abandoned mines. The dark blue colouring fades after death. Distribution: central Europe (Carpathians, Sudeten), Yugoslavia.

**3.** *Onychiurus armatus* Tullb. 2.3—3 mm. Abundant under stones, in moss, in soil and in caves from lowland to mountain elevations. Distribution: cosmopolitan.

Family: **Poduridae**

**4.** *Podura aquatica* L. 1.1—1.5 mm. Very common on and around lakes and ponds, chiefly during spring thaws. Also occurs abundantly on the surface of puddles on forest rides. Found from lowland to mountain elevations of about 2,500 metres. Distribution: all Europe, Siberia, North America.

Family: **Isotomidae**

**5.** *Isotomurus palustris* Müll. c. 3 mm. Marked variability in colouring and markings. Body green or yellowish with violet band down the middle and dark patches on the sides (several colour forms have been described). Abundant in damp places from lowland to mountain elevations. Distribution: all Europe and North America, probably cosmopolitan.

Family: **Tomoceridae**

**6.** *Tomocerus flavescens* Tullb. 4—4.5 mm. Abundant under stones, logs and under bark, from lowland to mountain elevations. Distribution: Europe, North America.

Family: **Sminthuridae**

**7.** Lucerne Flea — *Sminthurus viridis* L. 2 mm. Coloured either greenish or yellowish. Occurs in meadows, fields and parks where it is often very plentiful. Distribution: cosmopolitan.

Sub-class: **Ectotropha**

Order:    **Zygentoma**

Family:    **Lepismatidae**

**8.** Silver-fish — *Lepisma saccharina* L. 7—10 mm. Synanthropic in cooler regions (i. e. occurs in human habitations), but in warmer parts, including southern Europe, it lives in the open. Found in households, warehouses and libraries. Active at night when it emerges from its hiding places; runs very rapidly. May sometimes cause damage where it occurs in large numbers. Distribution: cosmopolitan.

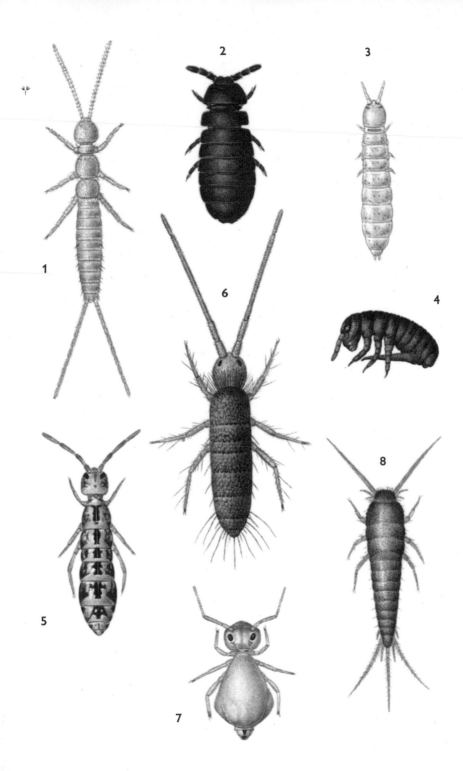

Order:     Mayflies — Ephemeroptera

Family:     Siphlonuridae

1. *Siphlonurus lacustris* Eaton 11 — 14 mm + cerci 16 — 22 mm. Occurs from May to August at higher elevations (400 — 900 metres). Female lays as many as 2,500 eggs. Nymphal development takes place by the banks of slow-flowing foothill and mountain streams. Distribution: most of Europe and Asia Minor.

Family: Baetidae

2. *Cloëon dipterum* L. 6 — 8 mm + cerci 8 — 17 mm. Has two generations a year (May to June, August to September). Females occur in large numbers near water, males fly to forests far from water. Nymphs emerge from the eggs as soon as they are laid. They live in ponds, pools and small puddles as well as in ditches. Distribution: Europe, Siberia, Japan.

Family: Oligoneuriidae

3. *Oligoneuriella rhenana* Imh. 9 — 16 mm + cerci 3 — 13 mm. Occurs in July and August in swarms above the surface of larger rivers. Not active until late afternoon. Nymphs frequent clear rivers and streams. Distribution: Europe (absent from Scandinavia and Great Britain).

Family: Heptageniidae

4. *Heptagenia sulphurea* Müll. 7 — 12 mm + cerci 13 — 23 mm. Occurs from May to July, sometimes as late as August. Nymphs frequent running water from lowland to hilly country. Found on stones and submerged wood. Distribution: Europe (mostly central and northern), western Asia. (Illustration shows the nymph.)

Family: Ephemerellidae

5. *Ephemerella ignita* Poda 6 — 9 mm + cerci 6 — 9 mm. On the wing June to September, often in large groups. Nymphs inhabit only running water from lowland to hilly country. Distribution: mainly central and western Europe, absent in the south.

Family: Leptophlebiidae

6. *Habrophlebia lauta* Eaton 5 — 7 mm + cerci 6 — 11 mm. Occurs in midsummer. Active in daytime as well as at night. Nymphs frequent running water in foothills and mountains. Distribution: chiefly central and northern Europe, absent from the south and from Great Britain.

Family: Polymitarcidae

7. *Ephoron virgo* Oliv. 10 — 18 mm + cerci 13 — 35 mm. Occurs above water on August evenings, often in large swarms. Adults are strongly attracted to light — in the vicinity of rivers, even to lights in cities. Nymphs inhabit larger rivers. Distribution: much of the Palearctic, absent from the British Isles.

Family: Ephemeridae

8. *Ephemera danica* Müll. 15 — 24 mm + cerci 14 — 40 mm. On the wing May to August (most abundant in June). Nymphs frequent still or slow-running water. Distribution: almost all Europe.

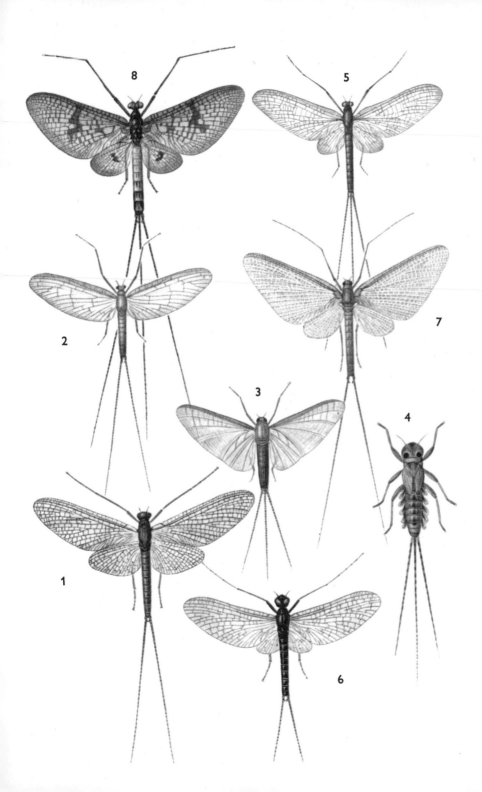

Order: **Dragonflies and Damselflies — Odonata**

Family: **Agriidae**

1. *Agrion virgo* L. 50 mm, wingspan 70 mm. May be seen May to September in slow flight above brooks or resting on the nearby vegetation. Male's wings have a blue-green sheen. Abdomen terminated by two pairs of prominent appendages that serve as copulatory organs. Female's wings are pale brown, transparent, with a whitish patch resembling a pterostigma near the apex of each front wing. Development of this (and the following) species takes two years. Female deposits about 300 eggs in the tissues of various aquatic plants such as *Sagittaria, Butomus, Sparganium, Batrachium,* etc. Nymphs live in water and are easily identified by the terminal appendages which are triangular in cross-section, and the antennae which have the first segment longer than all the others. The full-grown nymph climbs up out of the water onto a plant where it changes into the adult. Distribution: much of Europe, including the Mediterranean region; northern Asia.

2. *Agrion splendens* Harris 50 mm, wingspan 70 mm. Also found in the vicinity of flowing water. Male recognized by the blue or blue-green band of varying width on the front and hind wings. Wings of females are pale green and transparent. Distribution: much of Europe, Middle East, north Africa.

Family: **Lestidae**

3. *Lestes sponsa* Hansemann 35 mm, wingspan 40—45 mm. Sexes differ in colour. Male's body is a metallic green with bluish powdery dusting, female's is coppery. Pterostigma on the wings is dark. Adults occur June to October near stagnant water, occasionally flying quite far from water. Female deposits her eggs in various aquatic plants, assisted by the male who clings to her tightly with his anal claspers. Eggs overwinter. Nymphs emerge in April. They have three leaf-like 'tails', the same as other related species. Distribution: central and northern Europe and northern Asia, from British Isles to Japan.

4. *Lestes viridis* v. d. L. 45 mm, wingspan 60 mm. Wings are a metallic green with pale-ochre pterostigma. Adults occur July to October in the vicinity of ponds, which they often leave. Female deposits about 200 eggs in branches of trees and shrubs growing near water. Eggs overwinter and hatch in spring. Nymphs need aquatic environment. Development takes one year. Distribution: Europe (except the northern part), Asia Minor, Middle East, north Africa.

Family: **Platycnemidae**

5. White-legged Damselfly — *Platycnemis pennipes* Pallas 35 mm, wingspan 45 mm. Greatly resembles members of the family Coenagrionidae in form but easily recognized by the enlarged, spiny tibiae, chief distinguishing character of this family. Adults fly from mid-May to mid-September near slow-flowing and stagnant water. Development from the egg to the emergence of the adult takes one year. Nymphs hibernate. They are readily recognized by the three pointed 'tails'. Distribution: almost all Europe (absent from far north and the Iberian Peninsula), Middle East.

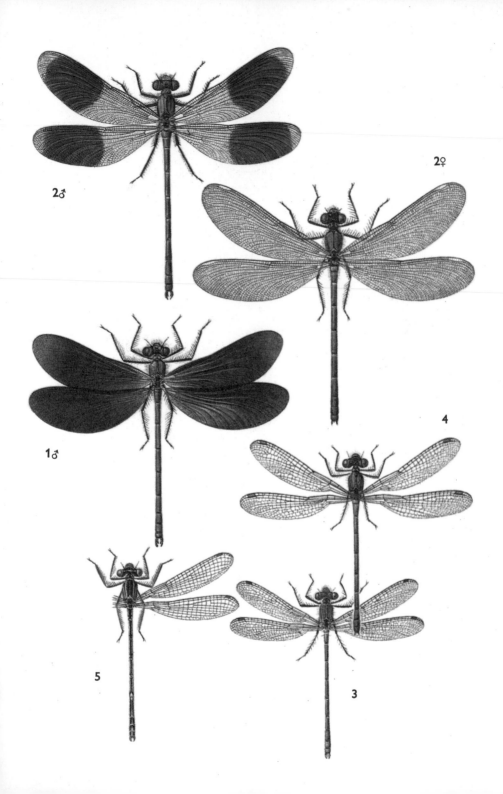

2♂

2♀

1♂

4

5

3

Family: **Coenagrionidae**

**1.** *Pyrrhosoma nymphula* Sulzer 35 mm, wingspan 45 mm. Abdomen mostly red with black pattern. Occurs abundantly from late April to early August on slow-flowing and stagnant water. Female is accompanied by the male when depositing the eggs. Development takes one year. Distribution: Europe, Asia Minor.

**2.** *Coenagrion puella* L. 35 mm, wingspan 45 mm. One of the commonest damselflies in Europe. Resembles many other related species, recognized by the markings and appendages on the abdomen (males) and by the markings on the abdomen and shape of the prothorax (females). Males of this species have dark markings on the second abdominal segment that look like a horseshoe placed open end forward. Occurs abundantly May to September on still and slow-flowing water. Development takes one year. Distribution: most of Europe, Middle East, north-west Africa.

Family: **Aeschnidae**

**3.** *Aeschna juncea* L. 70 — 80 mm, wingspan 90 — 105 mm. Two colour forms in females exist, one practically identical with the male (dark abdomen with pale-blue and yellowish markings), the other with yellow dorsal patches and green patches on the sides of the abdomen. Adults fly from June to October, occurring not only along streams but also in forest clearings and on forest rides. Female deposits the eggs in various peat-moor and aquatic plants. Development takes four years. Nymph resembles those of related species; it is elongate with large eyes, long legs and only short 'tails' at the end of the abdomen. It generally frequents the water of peat moors. Distribution: regarded as a boreoalpine species, found in lowland country in northern Europe and Asia and in the mountains and heathlands further south.

**4.** *Aeschna cyanea* Müll. 65 — 80 mm, wingspan 95 — 110 mm. One of the commonest members of the family. Occurs from June to November by stagnant water, which it often leaves to travel, frequently visiting even cities. Eggs are laid in late autumn in living and dead plant tissues. They hatch in spring. Nymphs develop until autumn and then hibernate. Adults emerge the following summer. Development takes two years. Distribution: almost the whole of Europe except the north (even mountain elevations), Asia Minor, north Africa.

**5.** Emperor Dragonfly — *Anax imperator* Leach 70 — 80 mm, wingspan 95 — 110 mm. Best flier of all the Odonata and one of the best in the whole class of insects. Male's abdomen is bright blue with dark markings, female's blue-green with brown markings. Like the preceding species, it also frequently travels far from water. Eggs are deposited in aquatic plants and in remnants of these plants, and hatch two to four weeks later. Nymphs hibernate and adults emerge the following summer. Distribution: from Europe to central Asia, and Africa.

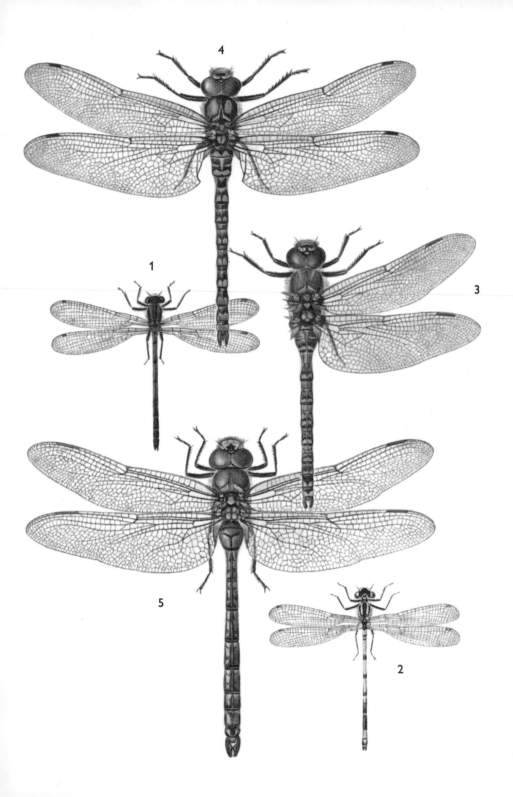

## Family: **Gomphidae**

**1.** *Gomphus vulgatissimus* L. 45—50 mm, wingspan 60—70 mm. One of several species with green and black markings. Adults may be seen from May to June, not only near water but often also on forest rides, clearings and meadows. Female lays about 500 eggs. When doing so she submerges the abdomen in water and releases a cluster of eggs. Nymphs emerge after three to four weeks but the development takes a long time. They hibernate thrice before changing into the adult. Distribution: almost all Europe.

**2.** *Onychogomphus forcipatus* L. 45—55 mm, wingspan 55—75 mm. One of the rarer species. Male distinguished by the prominent abdominal appendages shaped like forceps. Adults occur in the vicinity of streams and rivers from May to July. Distribution: central and northern Europe (not the British Isles).

## Family: **Cordulegasteridae**

**3.** *Cordulegaster boltoni* Donovan 70—85 mm, wingspan 90—105 mm. Easily recognized by its size and conspicuous black and yellow markings. Occurs mainly by hill streams, rarely in lowlands. Adults are on the wing from June to August. Little is known yet about the habits of this beautiful species. It is thought that development takes as long as five years. Distribution: much of Europe.

## Family: **Corduliidae**

**4.** *Cordulia aenea* L. 50—55 mm, wingspan 65—75 mm. Distinguished by metallic green colour and glowing green eyes. On the wing from May to August near water of various kinds, often also visiting forests. Female deposits the eggs in batches in water, flying back and forth over the surface before submerging the tip of her abdomen. The eggs fall to the bottom. Nymphs emerge after about three weeks, but their development is slow, taking two to three years. Distribution: Europe, Asia (as far as the Amur), north Africa.

**5.** *Somatochlora metallica* v. d. Lind. 50—60 mm, wingspan 70—75 mm. Distinguished by its prevailing metallic green colour. Female may also be metallic blue. She has a fairly long ovipositor extending straight downward. Found mostly in mountain regions (in the Alps as high up as 1,400 metres); less frequent in the lowlands. On the wing from May to mid-September near slow-flowing and stagnant water. Fond of peat moors; may also be seen on forest rides. Flies also at dusk. Female lays more than 500 eggs during July and August. Nymphs emerge after four to six weeks, but eggs laid in August do not hatch until the spring. Nymphs inhabit still water throughout their development, which takes two to three years. When fully grown they measure up to 25 mm in length. Distribution: Europe (mainly central and northern; less common in France and Great Britain), western Asia (as far as Tomsk).

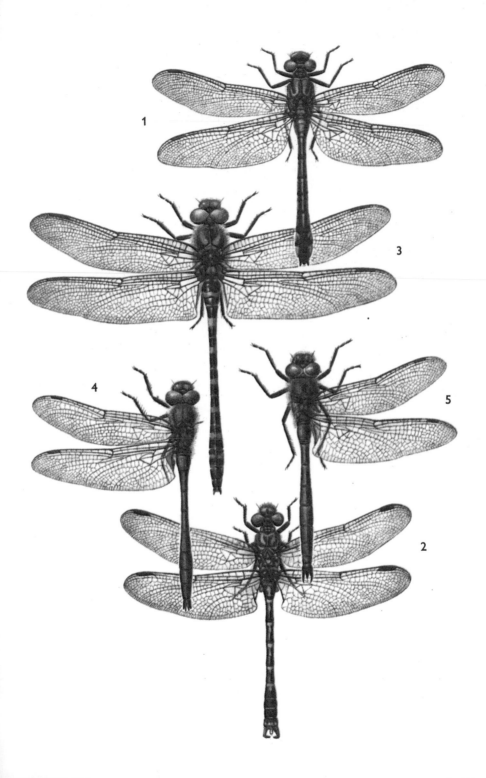

## Family: **Libellulidae**

**1.** *Libellula quadrimaculata* L. 40—50 mm, wingspan 70—85 mm. Name derived from the four spots located one on the node of each wing. Certainly one of the commonest of dragonflies. Favours stagnant water where it may be seen from May to August. Eggs are deposited freely in water in batches. First small nymphs appear within two to three weeks, but otherwise development is slow. Nymphs are stout, and after two years, having hibernated twice, change into the adults. Distribution: Europe, Middle East, north-central Asia, North America.

**2.** *Libellula depressa* L. 40—45 mm, wingspan 70—80 mm. Easily recognizable by the broad and flattened abdomen with its pale blue dusting in the male. Occurs abundantly from May to August round smaller bodies of stagnant water. Development is the same as in *Libellula quadrimaculata*. Distribution: Europe, Middle East.

**3.** *Sympetrum flaveolum* L. 35 mm, wingspan 50—60 mm. A common species of summer and early autumn. Does not keep to water but often visits fields. Female lays the eggs assisted by the male, sometimes also by herself. Eggs deposited while the weather is still warm hatch before the winter; those deposited later wait until spring. Development takes one year. Distribution: Europe, Middle East, the whole of northern Asia. Migrates north in spring.

**4.** *Sympetrum sanguineum* Müll. 35—40 mm, wingspan 50—60 mm. Occurs abundantly from end June to October on stagnant water. Development is the same as in *S. flaveolum* and likewise takes one year. Distribution: Europe, Middle East. Nymphs associated with reedmace and aquatic horsetails.

## Order: **Stoneflies — Plecoptera**

## Family: **Nemouridae**

**5.** *Nemoura cinerea* Retz. 4—6.8 mm, length of front wing 5—7.9 mm. One of many central European species that are very similar and difficult to identify, particularly the females. Male is recognized by the abdominal cerci with two spines at the tips. This species occurs abundantly from April to September by stagnant and running water. Distribution: central and northern Europe (Norway, Finland), Iberian Peninsula.

## Family: **Perlidae**

**6.** *Perla bipunctata* Pict. 18—30 mm. One of the large stoneflies. Distinguished by the black or light-coloured patch between ocelli and by the colour of the underside of head. Thorax is darker than abdomen. Adults fly from May to July, the larval stage is passed in rivers. Found in mountainous regions. Distribution: most of Europe.

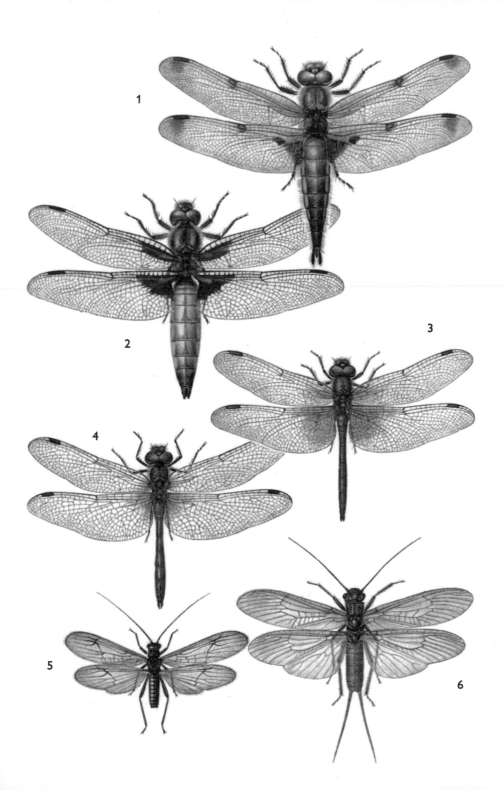

Order: **Earwigs — Dermaptera**

Family: **Labiduridae**

**1.** *Labidura riparia* Pall. 13—30 mm. Favours damp, sandy situations, such as are found alongside rivers and on the seashore, where it bores tunnels in the sand. A thermophilous, nocturnal insect found from May to November. In summer the female deposits several tens of eggs in an underground cavity. She broods over them, licking and cleaning the eggs, thus protecting them from attack by fungi as well as enemies. She also cares for the young nymphs which later scatter and bore their own tunnels. Nymphs usually change into adults before the winter and then hibernate deep in the sand. Diet consists of various dead as well as live insects. Distribution: cosmopolitan. In Europe it occurs mainly in the south.

Family: **Labiidae**

**2.** Small Earwig — *Labia minor* L. 5—9 mm. A common species (unlike *L. riparia*). Occurs from spring until autumn (October) in fields, meadows, forest margins and hothouses. One of the few earwigs that fly readily. Distribution: most of Europe (as far as Sweden), most other continents.

Family: **Forficulidae**

**3.** *Forficula auricularia* L. 14—23 mm. A very common and well-known insect. Nocturnal. Often large numbers may be found under stones, under logs and in old rags in the vicinity of man. Female deposits several tens of eggs in an underground chamber between November and March. As is the earwigs' habit she cleans them constantly and remains in the chamber even when the young nymphs have emerged. The earwig feeds on plant and animal matter; in autumn it may often be found on fallen fruit. Because it also feeds on aphids it may be considered to some degree a beneficial species. It occurs from lowland to mountain elevations. Distribution: cosmopolitan.

**4.** *Chelidurella acanthopygia* Géné 9—18 mm. Shortened elytra. Occurs abundantly from spring until autumn. Found under stones and amongst fallen leaves. Distribution: Europe (not the British Isles).

Order: **Praying Mantids — Mantodea**

**5.** Praying Mantid — *Mantis religiosa* L. 40—75 mm (the female larger than the male). Distinguished by the form and function of the front legs, which are excellently fitted for seizing prey. Adults found from August to autumn on sunny, grassy or shrub-covered areas. During the day they sit waiting for prey — flies, wasps, locusts, grasshoppers, bees and other insects. Eggs are laid in oothecae; female produces several during her lifetime. The ootheca is a case about 4 centimetres long made of light, spongy material which protects the eggs from cold and also from some enemies. The eggs pass the winter inside the case. Distribution: warm parts of southern Europe (reaching as far north as Poland, but not Britain), Asia and Africa; introduced into North America and Australia.

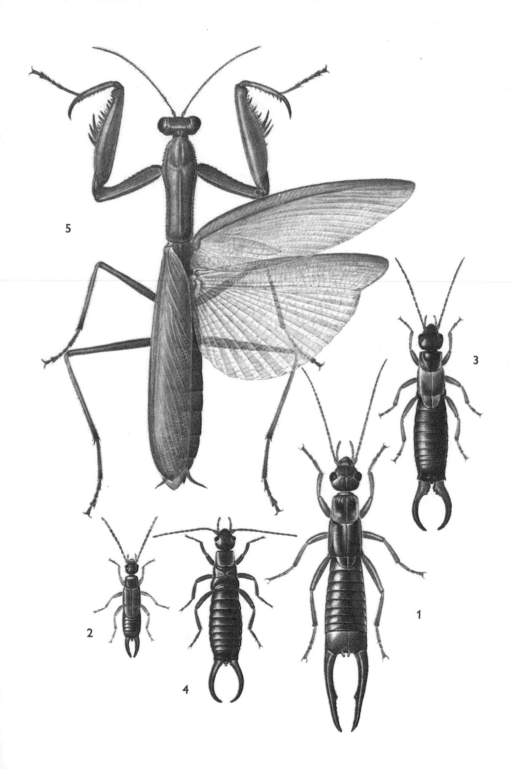

Order: **Cockroaches — Blattodea**

Family: **Blattidae**

**1.** Dusky Cockroach — *Ectobius lapponicus* L. 7 — 10 mm. An extremely mobile species of forest and rough grassland. Eggs are laid in oothecae about 3 mm long with horizontal stripes. Distribution: southern England and most of Europe, from northern Italy to Lapland, and as far as western Siberia.

**2.** German Cockroach — *Blattella germanica* L. 10.5 — 13 mm. Found in the temperate zone, mostly in human habitations which are heated in winter. A common and troublesome insect in flats, baths, hotels, bakeries, hostels, etc. In the tropics and subtropics it lives in the wild. Female lays the eggs in an ootheca which she carries about with her for a time. Distribution: cosmopolitan. Probably a native of southern Asia introduced by man to all parts of the world.

**3.** Common Cockroach — *Blatta orientalis* L. 18 — 30 mm. Marked sexual dimorphism. Male has wings that cover most of the abdomen; female has only two wing stumps. A nocturnal species, hiding in cracks during the day. Occurs in human habitations, bakeries, hotels, barracks, etc., where it finds suitably warm conditions. Also found on rubbish dumps. Nowadays on the decline. It contaminates and destroys foodstuffs and may also carry disease germs. Female lays eggs in an ootheca about 7 — 12 mm long. Adult stage is preceded by six larval stages. Distribution: cosmopolitan; its land of origin is not known. In Europe its range extends from the Mediterranean to the north, excepting the polar regions.

**4.** American Cockroach — *Periplaneta americana* L. 27 — 34 mm. One of the larger cockroaches. Female has shorter wings than the male. Omnivorous and thermophilous. In the subtropics and tropics it lives in the wild; in Europe in warehouses, greenhouses and the like. Female lays eggs in an ootheca which is flat and about 9 — 11 mm long. She conceals it in the ground or in some other hiding place. Distribution: cosmopolitan. It is common on ships and came originally from southern Asia.

Order: **Termites — Isoptera**

Family: **Rhinotermitidae**

**5.** *Reticulitermes flavipes* Kollar. Lives in colonies consisting of various different castes — workers, soldiers and reproductives. Feeds on cellulose (wood) and is therefore injurious. The species was described in 1837 after individuals found in the greenhouses of the Schönbrunn in Vienna; recently discovered in several places in western Germany (Hamburg) where it has acclimatized and forms colonies. It is raised also in laboratories for experimental purposes. Distribution: North America (USA, Canada), western Europe (introduced).

Order: **Stick Insects — Phasmida**

Family: **Bacteriidae**

**6.** Laboratory Stick Insect — *Carausius morosus* Brun. Watt. 80 mm, wingless. Resembles a dry twig in form and colour. Though not found in Europe, it is commonly raised in laboratories and also kept as a pet. Has great powers of regenerating lost limbs, particularly during the period when it can still moult. Male is extremely rare. Reproduction is parthenogenetic (without fertilization). Eggs are spherical and equipped with a small 'cap'. Distribution: comes from southern Asia, but established in several warmer parts of the world.

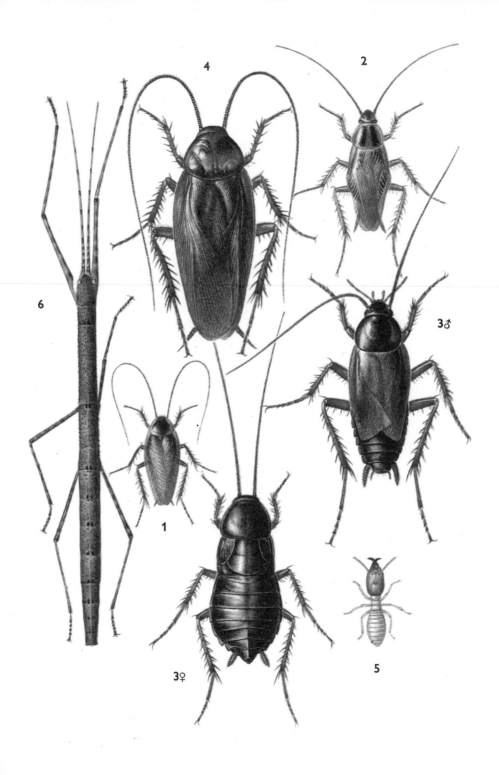

Order: **Crickets and Bush Crickets — Ensifera**

Family: **False Katydids — Phaneropteridae**

1. *Isophya pyrenea* Serv. 16 — 26 mm. Generally rare, though sometimes locally abundant on certain hills from June to September. Mainly found on mountain and hill pastures. Feeds on leaves. Female has a broad, sabre-like ovipositor with which she lays several eggs (each about 4 mm long) under the surface of the ground. Distribution: southern and central Europe.

Family: **Cone-heads — Conocephalidae**

2. Short-winged Cone-head — *Conocephalus dorsalis* Latr. 12 — 18 mm. Moisture-loving. Occurs in damp meadows and on vegetation of stagnant and running water. Feeds on plants and various insects. Male produces high shrill notes. Distribution: Europe, including southern Britain.

Family: **Bush Crickets — Tettigoniidae**

3. Great Green Bush Cricket — *Tettigonia viridissima* L. 28 — 42 mm. Occurs from July to October in meadows, fields, forests and often even in villages. A good flier but flies only short distances. Feeds mainly on various insects (flies, caterpillars, small Lepidoptera, etc.) but also nibbles plants. Males are tireless singers that stridulate both in daytime and at night. In former days they were kept as pets. Female lays as many as 100 eggs which do not hatch until spring. Distribution: all Europe, Asia Minor, Siberia, north Africa.

4. Wart-bites — *Decticus verrucivorus* L. 24 — 44 mm. Several green and brown colour forms exist. Found from June to September in fields and heathlands, both dry and damp. Feeds on living and dead insects and plant tissues. In former times country folk used it to bite out warts (hence its Latin and English names). Males produce a very shrill chirp. Female lays eggs underground. Distribution: Europe, Siberia.

Family: **Ephippigeridae**

5. *Ephippigera ephippiger* Fieb. 22 — 31 mm. A thermophilous bush cricket very common on bushes and rough ground in southern Europe. Rarer in central Europe where it is considered a relic that survived from the warm post-Ice Age. Both sexes stridulate. Distribution: central Europe (only locally), southern and western Europe, southern parts of the U.S.S.R.

Family: **Wingless Camel Crickets — Raphidophoridae**

6. Greenhouse Camel Cricket — *Tachycines asynamorus* Adel 13 — 19 mm (female's antennae up to 80 mm; male's about 75 mm long). Both sexes wingless. Representative of the superfamily **Gryllacridoidea**. Polyphagous: feeds on small insects, mostly aphids, as well as young germinating seedlings. In some places regarded as a pest, but in others a beneficial insect because it eats aphids. Probably comes from China, whence it spread throughout the world. In Europe it has become a synanthropic species (found in the vicinity of man). Found throughout the year, often in large numbers, in the greenhouses of botanical gardens and nurseries.

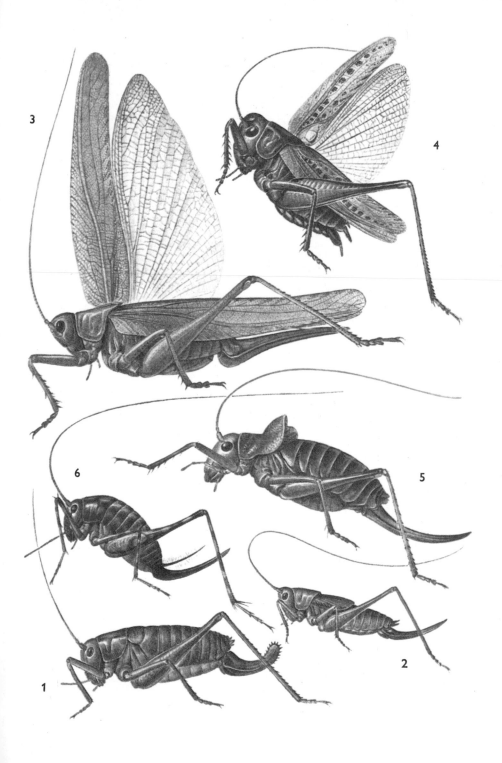

Family: **True Crickets — Gryllidae**

**1.** Field Cricket — *Gryllus campestris* L. 20—25 mm. Adult found from May to July in underground chambers which it excavates in sandy banks, grassy hedgerows, pine forests, etc. Very thermophilous. Eats plant and animal food. Males are noted for their musical notes which may be heard from May to late June; this is their courting song. About a week after mating female lays her first eggs. She continues to lay eggs even when the first ones have hatched. These young crickets live gregariously but before the onset of winter each excavates a separate chamber in which to hibernate. Distribution: Europe (central and southern, including southern England), western Asia, north Africa.

**2.** *Acheta frontalis* Fieb. 11—13 mm, found from May to August in vineyards, on sunny slopes, edges of forests, etc. Generally wingless or else with only short wings. Distribution: central Europe, the Balkans, eastern Europe to the Caucasus and the Urals, Asia Minor.

**3.** House Cricket — *Acheta domestica* L. 16—20 mm. Nocturnal. In central and northern Europe it is synanthropic, occurring in houses, bakeries, hospitals, etc. It is raised for food in zoos. Thermophilous. In summer found also in the wild, but in winter it is able to survive only indoors or on refuse tips. Feeds on various plant and animal remnants. Males produce a musical chirp in the evening and at night. Distribution: probably a native of western Asia and north Africa: now cosmopolitan through human activity.

**4.** Wood Cricket — *Nemobius sylvestris* Bosc. 7—10 mm. Adult found from June to September in woodlands with quantities of fallen leaves. Males stridulate loudly. Feeds on plant and animal matter. Eggs are laid just below the surface of the soil. They hatch in spring and the nymphs take a further year to grow up. Distribution: Europe (the northern limit runs through central Europe), north Africa.

Family: **Ant-loving Crickets — Myrmecophilidae**

**5.** *Myrmecophila acervorum* Panz. 2—3.5 mm. First captured in the vicinity of Dresden, where it was described in 1799. Lives as a guest in anthills; reproduction is parthenogenetic, the male being extremely rare. Distribution: central and southern Europe (absent in the north and in certain parts of western Europe), north Africa.

Family: **Tree Crickets — Oecanthidae**

**6.** Italian Cricket — *Oecanthus pellucens* Scop. 9—15 mm. Occurs from July to October on flowers in very warm situations; feeds on various parts of flowers. Males stridulate from dusk into the night — their song carries far. Eggs are generally deposited in the stems of the grapevine and many other plants. Distribution: central and southern Europe, western and central Asia, north Africa.

Family: **Mole Crickets — Gryllotalpidae**

**7.** *Gryllotalpa gryllotalpa* L. 35—50 mm. Found from April to October in underground corridors in meadows and gardens. Feeds on various insects, often quite large ones such as cockchafer grubs. Plant food is eaten only when its usual fare is not available. Female deposits several hundred eggs in an underground chamber and broods over them as well as the newly emerged nymphs. Development takes two years. Distribution: Europe, western Asia, north Africa.

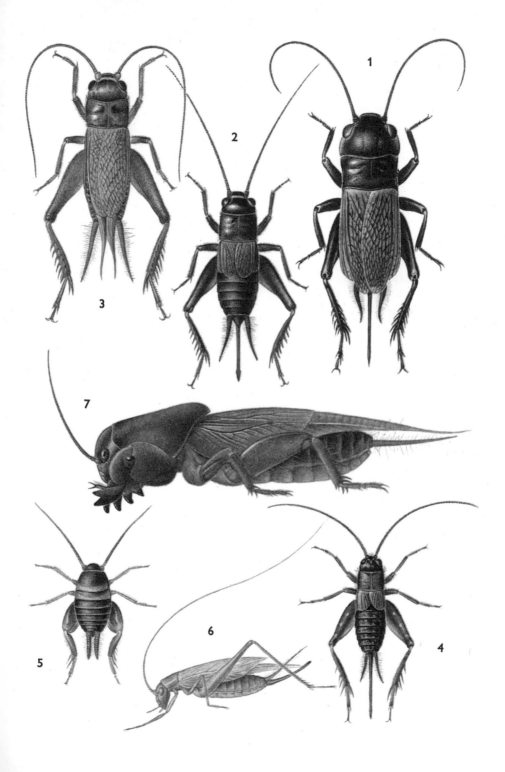

Order: **Locusts or Short-horned Grasshoppers — Caelifera**

Family: **Ground Hoppers — Tetrigidae**

**1.** *Tetrix subulata* L. 7—10 mm. Found in abundance from spring till autumn. Found in damp meadows (specially along water courses) and in forests and damp heaths. It is a plant-feeder and good flier. Occurs not only in lowlands but also at mountain elevations (up to 1,000 metres). Distribution: all Europe, temperate Asia, north Africa, and North America (possibly introduced).

Family: **Catantopidae**

**2.** *Miramella alpina* Koll. 14—31 mm. Has many forms, including one with short wings (f. *brachyptera*). Flies from June to September, mostly in alpine meadows. One of the relics of the fauna inhabiting central Europe as long ago as the Ice Age. Distribution: Europe, from the west through central Europe eastward.

**3.** *Calliptamus italicus* L. 14—34 mm. Occurs from July to September, sometimes as late as October, on dry meadows, fallow ground, etc. Population explosions, during which the insect built up to such numbers that it caused damage in fields, were more frequent in the past than they are now. Distribution: Europe (chiefly central and southern), Asia Minor, Middle East (Syria), north Africa.

Family: **Acrididae**

**4.** *Psophus stridulus* L. 23—32 mm. When resting it is quite inconspicuous in the wild. Both sexes produce grating sounds in the grass; most often heard, however, is the song of the male in flight when one can also see the bright red hind wings with a dark patch at the apex. In cold weather and in the evening the male flies without singing. The scientific name is derived from the grating sounds that are so characteristic of the species. Found from June to October, chiefly in meadows and clearings in hilly country. Distribution: Europe (absent from Scandinavia and Great Britain), Siberia.

**5.** Migratory Locust — *Locusta migratoria* L. 33—60 mm. Occurs in several geographical races throughout its extensive, worldwide range. Ssp. *migratoria* is found in Europe, central and western Asia. Each race has two phases that differ in form, colour and habits: the migratory phase *(gregaria)* and the sedentary phase *(sedentaria)*. Under certain specific conditions the sedentary phase changes into the migratory and vice versa. The occurrence of two phases, however, is not restricted to this species but is known in several other locusts also. The migratory locust was formerly a greatly feared pest even in central Europe. History records countless invasions by swarms of these locusts which had catastrophic results for they devoured all the crops. The migratory phase came to central Europe from the Danube River region, where conditions were conducive to the overmultiplication of the species. Nowadays, this locust is no longer a problem in Europe. However, it is a dangerous pest in the tropics and subtropics, where, along with other species, it causes grave damage to agriculture. Distribution: southern and central Europe, much of Asia and Africa, Madagascar.

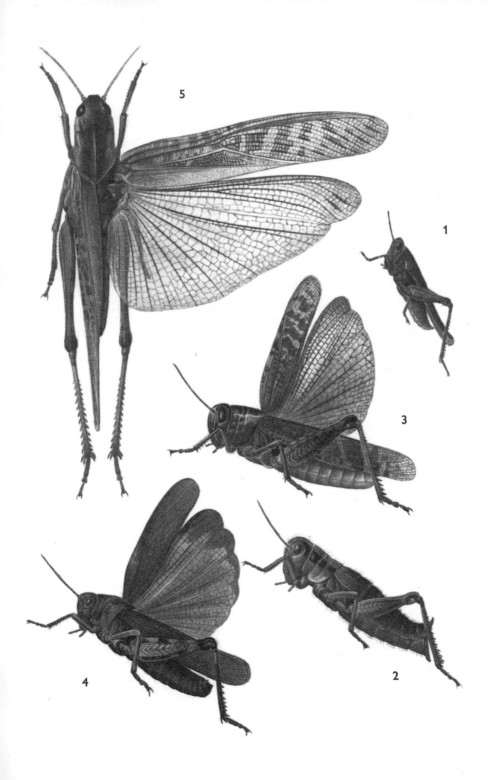

Family: **Acrididae**

**1.** *Oedipoda coerulescens* L. 15 — 28 mm. Very inconspicuous when sitting in the wild, for the colour of the body and elytra blends perfectly with the surroundings. The coloured hind wings, however, are clearly visible in flight. They are usually pale blue with a dark band, but may be yellow or even pinkish in some individuals. Quite abundant in certain localities from July to September. Favours dry situations — steppes, heaths, dry sunny slopes with sparse vegetation, abandoned quarries, etc. Fond of places with sandy soil. Feeds mostly on grasses. Distribution: Europe (as far as southern Sweden; absent from Great Britain), Asia Minor, Middle East (Syria), north Africa.

**2.** *Oedipoda germanica* Latr. 17 — 28 mm. Hind wings usually red with a black band on the margin. In some individuals the hind wings may be yellow or blue. Adults occur from July to September in dry and warm localities such as heaths, sunny slopes, steppes, localities with sandy soil, edges of vineyards, etc. It has become quite rare in some parts of Europe but elsewhere is still fairly common. Distribution: Europe (northern limit passes through central Germany), western Asia.

**3.** Stripe-winged Grasshopper — *Stenobothrus lineatus* Panz. 16 — 25 mm. Noted for its great variability of colour. Individual deviations are described as colour forms. Adults abundant from July to September. Found from lowland to mountain elevations, mostly in dry meadows, forest rides, heaths, etc. Male produces very delicate sounds that are not very loud. Distribution: Europe (as far as southern Sweden, but including only southern England), western Asia and Siberia.

**4.** Common Green Grasshopper — *Omocestus viridulus* L. 13 — 24 mm. One of the species that exhibit the greatest variation in colouring. Common from June to September in damp as well as dry meadows and from lowland to mountain elevations. Most plentiful in foothills. Distribution: Europe (absent in the south), Siberia.

**5.** *Chorthippus biguttulus* L. 13 — 24 mm. Occurs abundantly from June to October in drier localities where it finds ample food. Found in lowlands, hilly country and mountains. Both males and females stridulate; their distinctive song can be heard from summer until autumn. Female lays eggs in an ootheca which she usually hides in the ground. Distribution: Europe (less plentiful in southern than in central Europe and absent from the British Isles), Siberia, north Africa.

**6.** Mottled Grasshopper — *Myrmeleotettix maculatus* Thunb. 12 — 16 mm. Occurs in large numbers from June to late autumn (October) in drier meadows, sand dunes, steppes, heaths and forest clearings. A very variable species, found in lowlands and foothills as well as mountains. Both male and female stridulate. Distribution: Europe (north as far as Lapland, south to the northern parts of the Balkans), Asia Minor, Siberia.

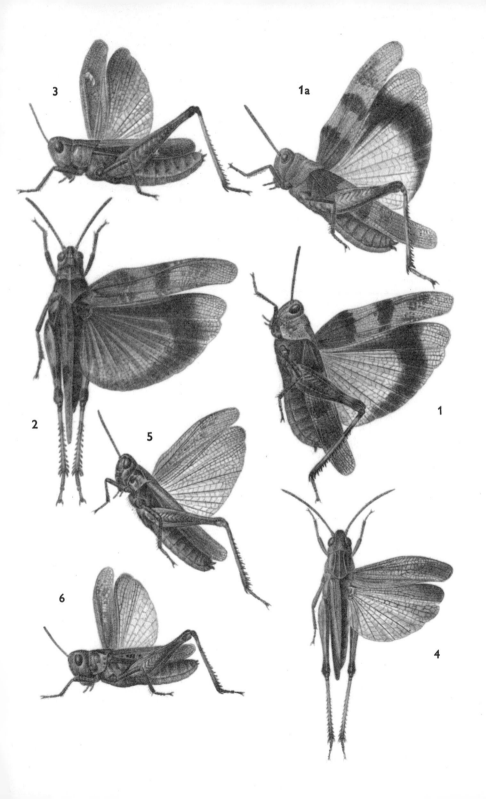

Order: **True Bugs — Heteroptera**

Family: **Cydnidae**

**1.** Negro Bug — *Thyreocoris scarabaeoides* L. 3 — 4 mm. Found on vegetation in dry meadows, on sunny slopes, sand dunes, etc. Common on buttercups. Adult hibernates. Eggs are laid in May. Both sexes stridulate. Distribution: Europe (to southern Sweden and Finland), Asia Minor, north Africa.

Family: **Scutelleridae**

**2.** European Tortoise Bug — *Eurygaster maura* L. 8.3 — 11.3 mm. Great variability in colouring, ranging from pale-grey to black. Occurs most abundantly in dry localities. Adults hibernate. Eggs are laid mostly in wild grasses but nymphs often damage the leaves and spikes of cereal crops. Adults are polyphagous and feed on both monocotyledonous and dicotyledonous plants. Occasional pest. Distribution: Eurasia, north Africa.

Family: **Pentatomidae**

**3.** *Graphosoma lineatum* L. 9 — 11 mm. Often plentiful on flowering Umbelliferae, chiefly in warm localities. Distribution: southern and central Europe, Asia Minor, Middle East.

**4.** Bishop's Mitre — *Aelia acuminata* L. 7 — 9.5 mm. Lives on various wild grasses and cereal crops. Adults hibernate until April. Eggs are laid on grass blades. Development lasts until August when the young adults emerge. Occasional pest. Distribution: Eurasia, north Africa.

**5.** *Stollia venustissima* Schr. 5 — 6 mm. Found mostly in damp localities. Abundant throughout most of the Palearctic region.

**6.** *Palomena viridissima* Poda 12 — 14 mm. Found on Umbelliferae, shrubs and trees. Similar to the green shield bug *(P. prasina)* in appearance and habits. Adults emerge in late autumn and hibernate. Distribution: Europe (absent from Great Britain and rare in the north), much of Asia including northern India.

**7.** Brassica Bug — *Eurydema oleracea* L. 5 — 7 mm. Marked colour variability. Metallic green or blue with red, yellow, orange or whitish spots. In spring adults emerge from their winter shelters and appear in large numbers, mostly on Cruciferae. Eggs are laid at the end of May. Older nymphs are found in summer, mostly on members of the carrot family. Distribution: Europe, Siberia, Middle East.

**8.** Forest Bug — *Pentatoma rufipes* L. 13 — 16 mm. Found mostly in forests on various trees — chiefly oak, birch and alder. Often sucks up body fluids of dead insects, mainly caterpillars. Occurs also on fruit trees in gardens. Nymphs are yellow with dark spots. Eggs laid in August. Nymphs hibernate. Distribution: Europe, Asia Minor, northern Asia.

**9.** *Picromerus bidens* L. 11 — 14 mm. Found in deciduous forests. Feeds on the caterpillars of Lepidoptera and the larvae of Colorado beetles and is thus very important as a predator. Eggs are laid on leaves. They overwinter and hatch in spring. Adults occur from July to August. Distribution: much of the Palearctic.

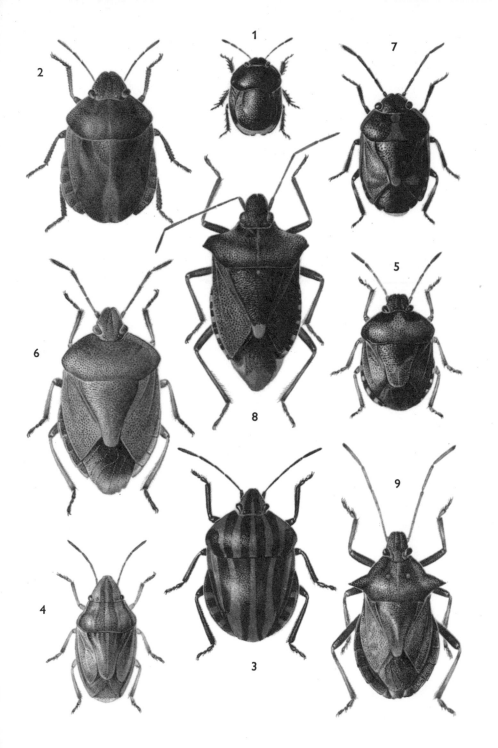

Family: **Acanthosomidae**

1. *Elasmucha ferrugata* F. 7.5 — 9 mm. Occurs mainly at higher elevations on blueberry and blackberry bushes, roses, broad-leaved trees and conifers. Adults hibernate. Eggs are laid in batches of about 35 on the underside of leaves. Female broods over the eggs as well as the first nymphal stages which live gregariously. Distribution: mainly western and central Europe (absent in Scandinavia and very rare in Britain), northern Asia.

Family: **Squash Bugs — Coreidae**

2. *Coreus marginatus* L. 12 — 14 mm. Very common, chiefly on sorrels, docks, blackberry, groundsel, etc., by waterside or in damp meadows and edges of fields. Adults hibernate. Eggs are laid in May. Distribution: Europe, Asia Minor and central Asia.

Family: **Rhopalidae**

3. *Corizus hyoscyami* L. 8 — 10 mm. Occurs mostly on Compositae but has also been found on many other plants such as mullein, oak, hazel, tobacco, sugar beet, etc. Adults hibernate. Eggs are laid at the end of June or beginning of July. Nymphs are full-grown by the end of August. Distribution: all Europe, Asia Minor, Middle East, north Africa.

Family: **Ground Bugs — Lygaeidae**

4. *Lygaeus saxatilis* Scop. 10 — 11 mm. A strikingly coloured and pretty bug. Locally abundant, chiefly at the edges of fields and meadows in warmer localities. Sucks on various plants. Distribution: much of Europe (absent from the north and Great Britain), Asia Minor, Middle East, north Africa.

5. *Geocoris grylloides* L. 4 — 5 mm. Favours warm and sunny situations where it is found in grass and amidst leaves. Distribution: Europe (absent from Spain, Great Britain, Norway and Balkans), central to northern Asia.

6. Nettle Ground Bug — *Heterogaster urticae* F. 6.5 — 7 mm. Widespread in warm localities. Nymphs as well as adults feed on nettles *(Urtica)*. Adults hibernate, emerging as early as March. Eggs laid in summer at the base of the host plant, sometimes also on the leaves or plant stem. They are covered by a protective layer secreted by the female. Adults emerge from September and in late October start making ready for hibernation. Distribution: the whole of Europe, Asia Minor, Middle East, north Africa.

7. *Rhyparochromus pini* L. 6.5 — 8.5 mm. Usually common in coniferous woods under leaves, among moss or under stones. Common also on heaths. Adult hibernates. In March or April you often come across groups of several individuals. The new generation of adults emerges in August. Distribution: Europe, all the way to the north, and Palearctic regions of Asia.

8. *Trapezonotus arenarius* L. 4.5 — 5 mm. Found on fallow land, sand dunes, in dry forests, heaths, etc. Adults hibernate and emerge from their shelters in early spring. The new generation is fully developed in August. Distribution: the Palearctic.

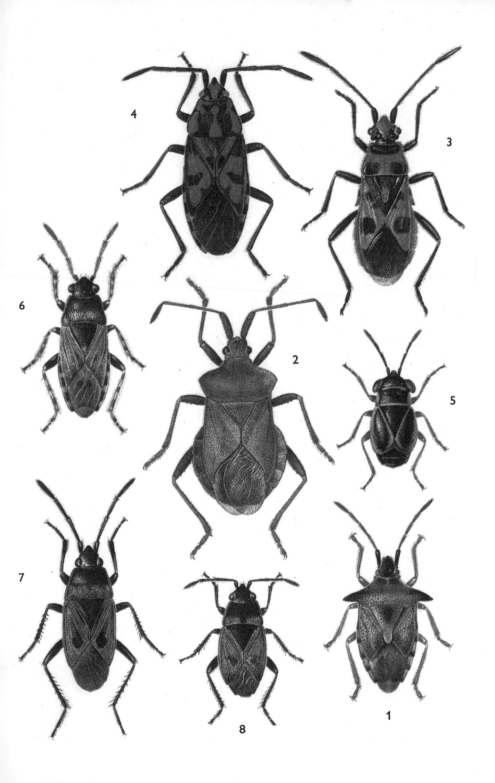

## Family: Pyrrhocoridae

1 Firebug — *Pyrrhocoris apterus* L. 7 — 12 mm. Often very plentiful even in late winter at the base of lime, horse chestnut and locust trees in tree avenues and parks. A common inhabitant of cemetery walls and graves; found near water. Always occurs in groups. Adults of the new generation emerge beginning August. This bug feeds on plant juices as well as sucking up the fluids of dead and live insects. Distribution: all Europe (but very rare in Britain), Asia Minor, Middle East, Siberia, India, north Africa, central America and elsewhere.

## Family: Beet Bugs — Piesmidae

2. *Piesma quadrata* Fieb. 2.5 — 3.5 mm. Originally it fed on wild Chenopodiaceae but after 1900 it began feeding on cultivated sugar beet and has become an occasional pest in certain areas, though elsewhere its occurrence is only sporadic. It has one or two broods a year. Adults hibernate. Female lays about 150 eggs in succession. Distribution: mostly central and northern Europe, especially in coastal and saltmarsh areas.

## Family: Stilt Bugs — Berytidae

3. *Neides tipularius* L. 9 — 11 mm. Found in dry situations — sandy localities, heaths, forests, dry meadows, etc. Adults hibernate. Female lays fairly large eggs (1.1 mm) in April and May. Adults of the new generation emerge in July to August. Distribution: all Europe (as far as central Sweden and Finland), Transcaucasia, Turkestan.

4. *Berytinus minor* Herr. Schaeff. 5 — 6 mm. Occurs in dry localities where it has one or two broods a year. Adults hibernate. Distribution: much of the Palearctic.

## Family: Flatbugs — Aradidae

5. Pine Flatbug — *Aradus cinnamomeus* Panz. 3.5 — 5 mm. Lives on various species of pine, mostly on 10 — 20-year-old diseased trees. Found also on spruce. Occurs on branches and under bark. Distribution: all Europe.

## Family: Barkbugs — Aneuridae

6. *Aneurus avenius* Duf. 4.5 — 6 mm. Common under the bark of decaying deciduous shrubs and trees, chiefly willow, oak, beech, birch, elder, privet, etc. Distribution: Europe (except the southern parts and the Balkans), Middle East.

## Family: Lace Bugs — Tingidae

7. Spear Thistle Lace Bug — *Tingis cardui* L. 3.3 — 3.8 mm. Found on various thistles (*Carduus, Cirsium*). Adults hibernate amidst leaves. Eggs are laid in the leaves of thistles. Young adults may be seen as early as late July. Distribution: Europe (as far as Lapland), Asia Minor, northern Asia, north Africa.

8. *Stephanitis pyri* F. 3 — 3.3 mm. Lives mostly on fruit trees (pear, apple, cherry, walnut), where it sucks sap from the leaves. Distribution: much of Europe (absent from Great Britain), Middle East, central Asia, north Africa.

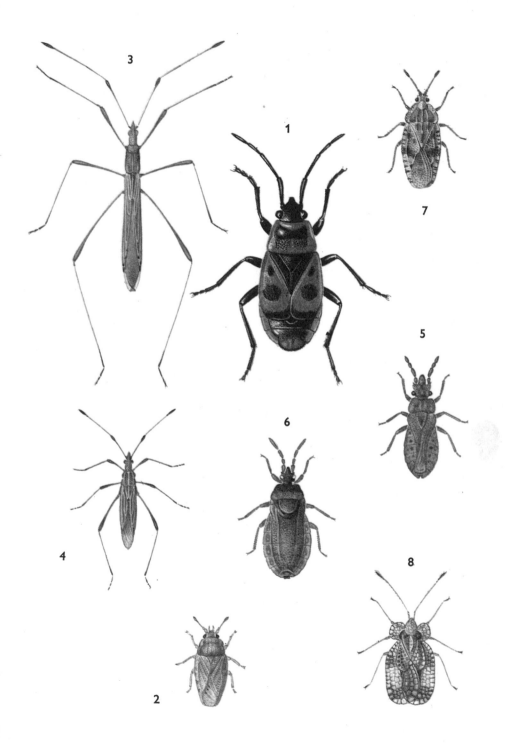

Family: **Assassin Bugs — Reduviidae**

**1.** *Empicoris vagabundus* L. 6 — 7 mm. Occurs in damper localities on deciduous as well as coniferous trees, in buildings and in their vicinity. Adults hibernate. Eggs are black and laid during May. A new generation of insects emerges in July. Besides plant food it also eats small arthropods. Distribution: much of Europe (to central Scandinavia and Finland), northern Asia.

**2.** *Rhinocoris iracundus* Poda 13 — 18 mm. Found in warm, sunny situations, where it is locally abundant. It rarely flies. Distribution: much of Europe (absent from British Isles).

**3.** Heath Assassin Bug — *Coranus subapterus* Deg. 9 — 12 mm. Found in sandy localities, sand dunes, heaths, etc., where it feeds on small arthropods (spiders and insects). It has two forms: short-winged (brachypterous) and long-winged (macropterous). Adults are most plentiful from July to October. Eggs overwinter. Distribution: Europe as far north as central Scandinavia.

Family: **Damsel Bugs — Nabidae**

**4.** *Himacerus apterus* F. 8 — 10 mm. Inhabits margins of deciduous and coniferous forests. Adults most plentiful in August; sometimes they may still be seen in October. Eggs hatch in May to June. Nymphs and adults feed on small arthropods (aphids, etc.) Distribution: much of Europe, as far as Latvia.

**5.** *Nabis rugosus* L. 6 — 7 mm. Very plentiful. Commonest is the short-winged form. Adults hibernate under grass. Distribution: the Palearctic.

Family: **Blood-sucking and Bed-bugs — Cimicidae**

**6.** True Bed-bug — *Cimex lectularius* L. 3.5 — 8 mm. Found primarily in and around human habitations. Active at night, concealing itself under pictures, in crevices and other places during the day. Feeds on blood. If undisturbed will suck up as much as twice its body weight, swelling in size proportionally. Feeds primarily on man, also on mice, poultry and other vertebrates. Female deposits some 100 — 200 eggs over a period of several weeks or months. First, however, she must suck her fill of blood. In heated flats development takes place even in winter. If the temperature drops below 13°C development is halted. Bed-bugs have a lifespan of several months. Distribution: cosmopolitan, introduced by man to all parts of the world.

Family: **Flower Bugs — Anthocoridae**

**7.** *Orius niger* Wolff 1.9 — 2.1 mm. Common in dry localities where it preys on mites and small insects (aphids, thrips, etc.). Adults hibernate. Distribution: the whole of Europe, Asia Minor, Middle East, Siberia.

**8.** Common Flower Bug — *Anthocoris nemorum* L. 3 — 4.5 mm. Very common bug. Found in hardwood forests and gardens. Preys on and sucks the bodies of Homoptera, primarily aphids and scale insects, or mites. Sometimes also sucks the sap of leaves. Adults hibernate and may be found on catkins as early as March. Eggs are laid on underside of leaves. In some areas two and sometimes even three generations occur. Distribution: practically all Europe, Asia Minor, northern Asia, north Africa.

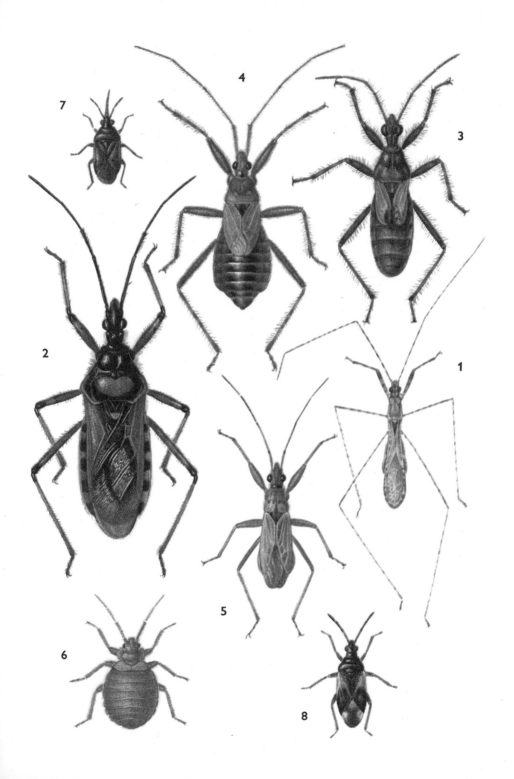

Family: **Leaf Bugs — Miridae**

**1.** *Phytocoris tiliae* L. 6.1 — 6.9 mm. Lives on various deciduous trees, chiefly oak, lime, ash, apple, etc. Adults are most abundant in summer. Eggs overwinter. Predacious. Feeds on small caterpillars and the larvae of other insects, mites, etc. Distribution: Europe (except the Far North), north Africa.

**2.** Lucerne Plant Bug or Alfalfa Bug — *Adelphocoris lineolatus* Goeze 6 — 8 mm. Common on Leguminosae and Compositae growing in sunny situations. Sucks on young leaves, stems, flowers and unripe fruit. Adults occur from July to September. Eggs overwinter. In eastern Europe it has two broods a year. Regarded as a pest. Distribution: the whole Palearctic region, North America.

**3.** *Calocoris biclavatus* H. Sch. 5.6 — 7.6 mm. Found from June to September on various herbaceous and woody plants, e.g. blueberry, blackberry, willow-herb, alder, hazel, birch, etc. Eggs overwinter. Distribution: central and northern Europe (absent from Great Britain), the Alps.

**4.** *Lygus pratensis* L. 5.8 — 6.7 mm. One or two generations a year. Adults hibernate and emerge in early spring (March, April). Lives on various shrubs and trees and on heather. A very abundant species found in widely varied localities. Distribution: the Palearctic region.

**5.** Meadow Plant Bug — *Leptopterna dolobrata* L. 7 — 9.7 mm. Occurs in grassy places including fields of grain; feeds on leaves, stems and spikes, puncturing them and sucking the sap. Adults are most abundant from July to August, sometimes being found as late as October. Eggs overwinter. In some countries it is a pest of grain. Distribution: the Palearctic and Nearctic regions.

**6.** *Pilophorus clavatus* L. 3.9 — 5 mm. Found on deciduous trees and shrubs. Adults live from July to September. Eggs overwinter. Distribution: all Europe, North America. Rare in Britain.

**7.** Black-kneed Capsid — *Blepharidopterus angulatus* Fall. 5.1 — 5.9 mm. Occurs abundantly, mainly on apple, elm, birch and lime, where it feeds on spider-mites. Adults may be found as early as the end of June and sometimes as late as October. Eggs are deposited in young twigs, and nymphs begin to emerge in May. Distribution: practically the whole of Europe, Siberia, Turkestan, north Africa.

**8.** *Deraeocoris ruber* L. 6.5 — 7.5 mm. A beneficial species, for both adults and nymphs feed on aphids and other small insects. Very variable in colour; many colour forms have been described. Occurs on various deciduous trees as well as on herbs, chiefly nettle. Adults are found from July to September. Eggs overwinter. Distribution: the whole of Europe, north Africa, North America.

**9.** *Salicarus roseri* H. Sch. 3.7 — 4.3 mm. Occurs abundantly from June to August mainly on willow bushes. Feeds primarily on aphids. Eggs overwinter and hatch the following spring. Distribution: Europe (not the south), Asia Minor, Siberia.

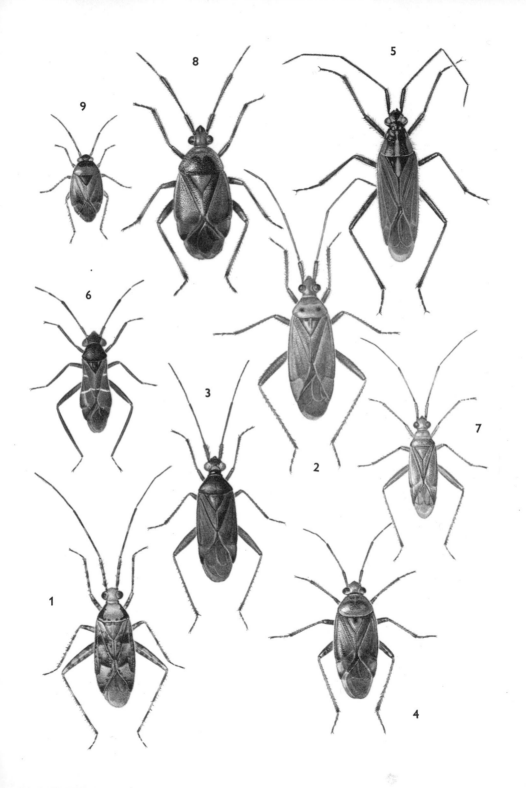

Family: **Water Measurers — Hydrometridae**

1. *Hydrometra stagnorum* L. 9—11 mm. Most common is the short-winged (brachypterous) form. Found on the surface of water near banks. Adults hibernate. Distribution: much of Europe (absent from the north), the Caucasus, Middle East, north Africa.

Family: **Water-striders** or **Pond-skaters — Gerridae**

2. *Gerris gibbifer* Schumm. 10—13 mm. Common on the surface of pools and puddles or the water of peat-bogs from lowland to mountain elevations. There are two generations a year. Adults hibernate and sometimes emerge already during the first warm days heralding spring. Distribution: Europe (rare or absent in the north), Middle East, north Africa.

Family: **Shore-bugs — Saldidae**

3. *Saldula saltatoria* L. 3.5—4.5 mm. One of the commonest of shore-bugs. Found in muddy water, around ponds and ditches and even on dry land. Jumping species. Two generations occur in a year. Adults hibernate in tufts of grass beside water or under bark. Distribution: the Palearctic and Nearctic regions.

Family: **Backswimmers — Notonectidae**

4. *Notonecta glauca* L. 14—16 mm. Several geographical races exist. Predatory bug, with a short but strong beak whose thrust is keenly felt. Found mostly in still water in ponds, pools and puddles amidst vegetation. Eggs are deposited in the stems of aquatic plants in late December and January. Nymph moults five times and changes into the adult in June, which is when the old backswimmers die. There is only one generation a year. Distribution: all Europe, the Caucasus, north Africa.

Family: **Water-boatmen — Corixidae**

5. *Corixa punctata* Ill. 13—15 mm. Inhabits streams, pools and river creeks where it occurs on vegetation. Males can produce sounds. Adults hibernate. Eggs are laid between the end of January and end of March. New generation appears in July. Distribution: Europe, and much of western and central Asia.

Family: **Water-Scorpions — Nepidae**

6. *Nepa cinerea* L. 18—22 mm. Lives in mud in shallow stagnant or slow-flowing water. Eggs are deposited in the stems and leaves of aquatic plants in April to May. Adults appear in August and hibernate. Feeds on small aquatic animals (mosquito larvae, small fish, etc.). Distribution: much of Europe. A rapidly declining species.

7. Water Stick Insect — *Ranatra linearis* L. 30—35 mm. Waits motionless amidst aquatic vegetation for prey. Adults hibernate. Eggs are deposited in the stems of aquatic plants. Lifespan of the adult is two years. Distribution: much of the Palearctic.

Family: **Creeping Water-bugs — Naucoridae**

8. Saucer Bug — *Ilyocoris cimicoides* L. 15 mm. Inhabits slow-flowing water, pools, marshes and puddles. Adults hibernate. Eggs are deposited in aquatic plants in April and May. Though the wings are well developed the weak muscles make flight impossible. Distribution: much of Europe, the Caucasus.

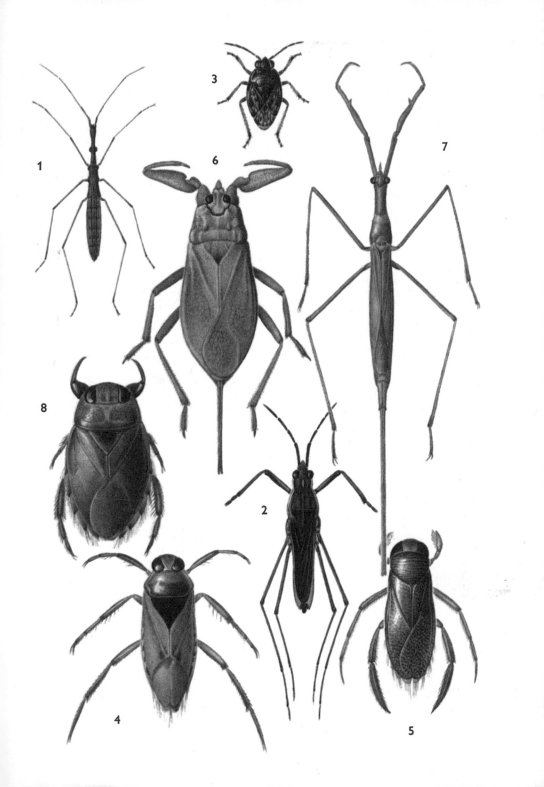

Order:    **Homoptera**

Sub-order: **Auchenorhyncha**

Family:    **Issidae**

**1.** *Issus coleoptratus* Geoffr. 6—7 mm. Occurs on the bark of various trees, primarily beech, oak, rowan, etc. Found even high up in the mountains. Distribution: practically all Europe, north Africa.

Family: **Cicadas — Cicadidae**

**2.** *Tibicen haematodes* Scop. 26—38 mm, wingspan 75—85 mm. One of the largest of European cicadas. Male cicadas have a special sound-producing organ, located on the underside of the first abdominal segments, which produces a shrill note. Most species of cicadas emit sounds but not all are equally loud or shrill. This species is thermophilous and especially fond of vineyards. Distribution: southern and central Europe, the Caucasus.

**3.** *Cicadetta montana* Scop. 16—27 mm, wingspan 45—52 mm. Fond of sun and in summer common on slopes overgrown with thickets and in clearings. Males also produce a 'song', a high continuous musical note, beginning about 8 or 9 o'clock in the morning and stopping only at sunset. Females lack the sound-producing organ. Eggs are deposited in plant tissues. Nymphs burrow in the ground, where they live on the roots of plants. When fully grown they surface and then change into adults. Distribution: practically all Europe, absent from northern Scandinavia. The only British cicada.

Family: **Spittle-bugs** or **Frog-hoppers — Cercopidae**

**4.** *Cercopis vulnerata* Rossi 9.5—11 mm. Found on grass and shrubs from May or early June to July, primarily in wooded country. Nymphs feed on plant roots. Distribution: most of Europe, apart from the far north.

**5.** *Aphrophora alni* L. 8—11 mm. Very common. Found from June to October on shrubs, deciduous trees and plants. Nymphs produce 'cuckoo spit' on plants. Distribution: the Palearctic.

Family: **Tree-Hoppers — Membracidae**

**6.** *Centrotus cornutus* L. 8—10 mm. Common on bushes in clearings and forest margins. Good distinguishing character is the backward-turned extension of·the prothorax, forming a sort of 'hood'. Distribution: Europe, except the north, Asia Minor and Siberia.

Family: **Leaf-Hoppers — Cicadellidae (or Jassidae)**

**7.** *Cicadella viridis* L. 5—9 mm. Common from July to August in marshes, peat-moors and damp meadows. Distribution: the Palearctic and Nearctic.

**8.** *Typhlocyba jucunda* H. Schaeff. 4—4.5 mm. Very plentiful from July to September wherever alders grow. Distribution: practically all Europe.

**9.** *Iassus lanio* L. 6.5—8.3 mm. Sometimes more brownish in colour. Found in summer on oak trees. Distribution: all Europe.

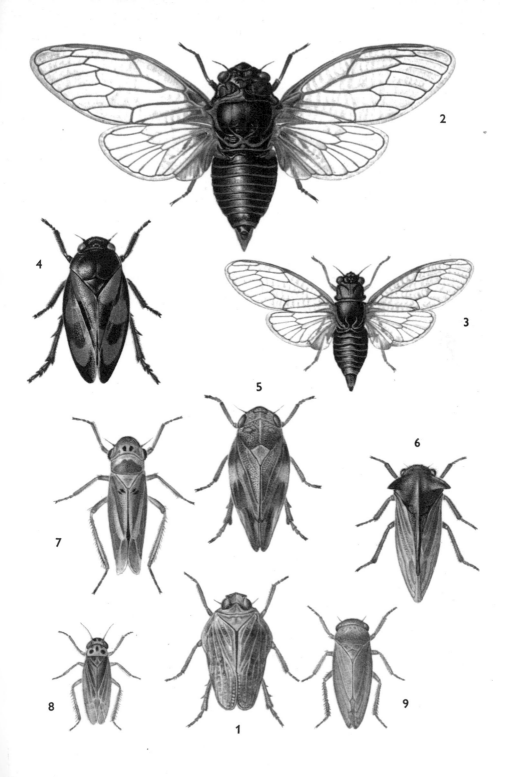

Sub-order: **Sternorhyncha**

Super-family: **Aphids — Aphidoidea**

Family: **Lachnidae**

**1.** *Lachnus roboris* L. 4—5 mm. One of the large aphids. Found on oaks. Eggs are black and laid one beside the other on slender oak twigs. Distribution: practically the whole Palearctic.

Family: **Callaphididae**

**2.** *Phyllaphis fagi* L. 2—3 mm. Found on the underside of leaves of beech *(Fagus)* and on young shoots. The wealth of white wax threads is very striking. Distribution: from northern Europe to the Caucasus, North America, Australia, New Zealand.

Family: **Typical Aphids — Aphididae**

**3.** Cabbage Aphid — *Brevicoryne brassicae* L. (wingless c. 2 mm, winged c. 1.9 mm long). Found on cabbages and other Cruciferae. It is covered with a coat of greyish wax that conceals its colouring. A widespread pest wherever cabbages are cultivated.

**4.** *Myzus cerasi* F. c. 2 mm. Found on the underside of cherry leaves which it often curls. Like many other aphids, it alternates host plants. Distribution: originally a Mediterranean species, it has been introduced to all parts of the world.

Family: **Pemphigidae**

**5.** Woolly Apple Aphid — *Eriosoma lanigerum* Hausm. 1.8—2.3 mm. Has a woolly white covering. As in most aphids, the development is very complex. Thermophilous but requires some moisture. It dies in dry years. Found on the trunks and branches of apple trees, where it causes swellings. A brownish-red stain appears if a colony of these aphids is crushed with the hand. Passes the winter on elm trees or else on apple roots. Distribution: originally a North American species, it is now found throughout the world.

**6.** *Pemphigus bursarius* L. 2—2.5 mm. Produces galls on the petioles of poplar leaves, inside which the winged individuals develop by the end of June, when they emerge and fly to lettuce or other herbaceous plants and attach themselves to the roots. Distribution: Europe, Asia Minor, north Africa, North America, Australia, etc.

Family: **Adelgidae**

**7.** *Sacchiphantes viridis* Ratz. 1.7—2 mm. Well known for the characteristic pineapple-shaped galls it produces on young spruce shoots. The gall is composed of a great many small chambers in which the development of the nymph takes place. Life-cycle of the species is very complex. Galls are ripe at the end of summer after which they turn woody and remain on the branch. Young nymph hibernates. Distribution: Europe, wherever spruce grows.

**8.** *Pineus strobi* Hart. 1 mm. Easily overlooked were it not for the abundant white waxy excretion which covers the body. Attaches itself to the young leaf-bearing shoots of Weymouth pine; if abundant it is also found on the trunk which then looks as if it were whitewashed, due to the layers of white excretion in which it hides. Distribution: native of North America, introduced to Europe.

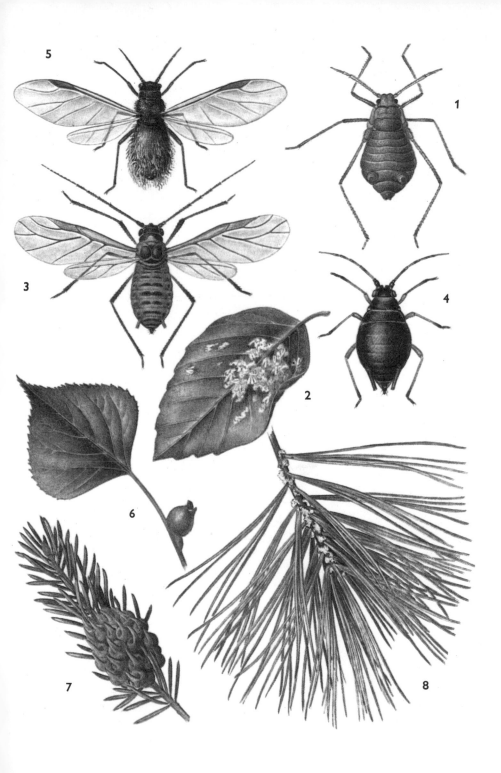

Super-family: **Scale Insects — Coccoidea**

Family: **Ensign Coccids — Ortheziidae**

**1.** *Orthezia urticae* L. ♀ with egg-sac 8—10 mm. Like all coccids characterized by marked sexual dimorphism. Male has one pair of wings, female always wingless. She is covered with symmetrically arranged waxy plates and during the egg-laying period forms a long egg-sac at the end of the abdomen for containing the eggs. She is most often found attached to the stems of nettles *(Urtica)*, where she feeds on the plant juices. Distribution: most of Europe, Asia Minor, central Asia, Siberia, Mongolia, north Africa.

Family: **Mealy Bugs — Pseudococcidae**

**2.** *Phenacoccus aceris* Sign. 3—5 mm. Found on various deciduous trees including fruit trees. During the egg-laying period the female produces a long egg-sac woven of white waxy threads in which she lays several hundred minute eggs. She favours crevices in the bark of tree trunks and branches. Nymphs hibernate. Distribution: Europe, Transcaucasia, Asia Minor, Middle East (Iran, Iraq), north Africa, North America.

Family: **Cryptococcidae**

**3.** *Cryptococcus fagi* Barensprung. 0.8—1 mm. Very common on trunks of beech trees where it forms large colonies. Female is yellow and covered with white waxy threads. Trees infested by a large colony of these insects are covered with bands of white wax visible from afar. Distribution: from Great Britain to Armenia, Asia Minor, North America, etc.

Family: **Eriococcidae**

*Pseudochermes fraxini* Kalt. 0.7 mm. Very common on trunks and branches of ash. The red-coloured females and nymphs are covered with a coat of whitish wax. They rest close beside each other. Distribution: Europe, Crimea, northern Caucasus.

Family: **Coccidae**

**5.** *Parthenolecanium corni* Bouché 3—6 mm. Polyphagous; feeds on various deciduous trees including fruit trees. Adult female is brown. Her body is flat at first, later becoming markedly convex and resembling a minute tortoiseshell. Large numbers of eggs are deposited beneath her body. Usually occurs in colonies attached to the woody portion of plants. Distribution: Europe, Asia Minor, Middle East, Siberia, Korea, China, North and South America, Australia, etc.

Family: **Diaspididae**

**6.** *Lepidosaphes ulmi* L. 1.8—3.5 mm. One of the commonest species of this family. The tiny, whitish, blind and legless females, covered by a longish brown scale, occur on branches and trunks of various trees and shrubs. Distribution: cosmopolitan.

**7.** *Chionaspis salicis* L. 1.9—2.5 mm. Gregarious on the branches and stems of host plants. The red, flat females are covered by a white scale beneath which they lay their carmine red eggs. Eggs overwinter. A very common polyphagous species that regularly occurs on the stems of willows and on the fruits of the blueberry. Distribution: the whole Palearctic.

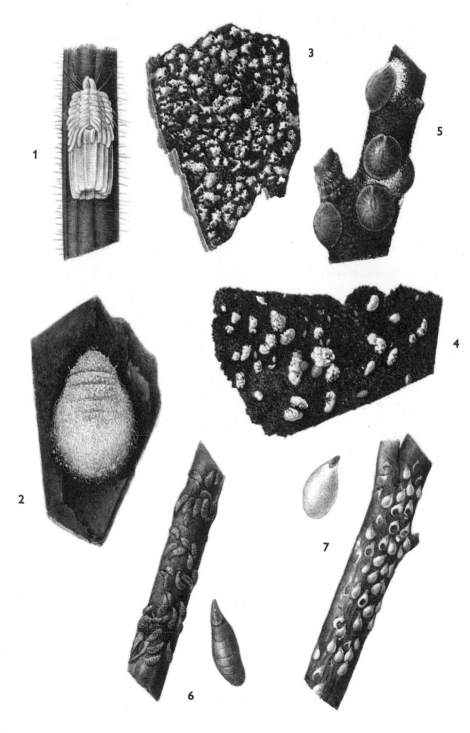

## Super-family: White Flies — Aleyrodoidea

**1.** *Aleurochiton complanatus* Baer. (puparium 1.5—1.9 mm). Two generations a year. Better known than the white-winged adults are the small, winter puparia covered with white wax attached to the underside of maple leaves. In autumn they fall to the ground with the leaves and overwinter. Adults emerge in spring. These establish a new generation with entirely different puparia. Unlike the winter puparia, the summer puparia occur on leaves only briefly and are not conspicuous. Distribution: all Europe wherever maple grows, but not the British Isles.

**2.** *Aleurolobus asari* Wünn (puparium 1—1.3 mm). The adult greatly resembles other white flies found in Europe, but the puparium is easily identified by the black colouring and abundant waxy secretion which forms long marginal fibres and dorsal plates. The puparium is the longest stage in the insect's development. It lasts from summer through winter until May, when the adults emerge. This white fly feeds mainly on *Asarum* and *Clematis,* also on certain shrubs. Distribution: practically the whole of Europe, but not the British Isles.

**3.** Greenhouse White Fly — *Trialeurodes vaporariorum* Westw. (puparium 0.7—1.1 mm). Conspicuous waxy processes on the back. Generally found on the underside of leaves of various plants; in temperate regions, in greenhouses; farther south also freely in the wild. Often classed as a pest of cultivated plants. Distribution: almost worldwide.

## Super-family: Jumping Plant Lice — Psylloidea

Family:     **Psyllidae**

**4.** Apple Sucker — *Psylla mali* Schmidb. 3.5 mm. Found from June to September on apple trees. In summer adults are coloured green; in autumn dark brown. Antennae are pale yellow, the two terminal segments black. Wing venation is pale yellow; in darker individuals it is darker. Female lays about 100 eggs in autumn, depositing them on young branches in crevices near buds. The egg-laying period may continue till late November, sometimes even till early December. Eggs are very frost-resistant (they tolerate temperatures of $-40°C$). The minute, flat nymphs emerge in spring, settling on young buds, the stems of flowers and buds and the petioles of young leaves. They excrete large amounts of sweet honeydew which causes buds and leaves to become sticky. The buds do not open, dry up and drop. If strongly infested even the tree as a whole may be damaged in that it has slower growth and the wood matures poorly. Nymphs also suck the juice of fruits, which results in deformed growth. Nymphs moult several times. Adults emerge from late May to June. At first they live on apple trees, but then they visit other trees in the neighbourhood, returning again at the end of summer. In some regions this species is a troublesome pest. Distribution: all Europe except the far north, Japan. Introduced also to North America and Australia.

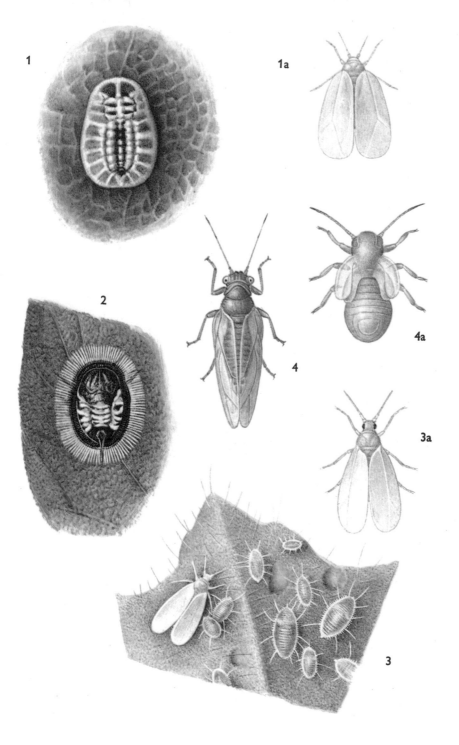

Order: **Alder Flies — Megaloptera**

Family: **Sialidae**

**1.** *Sialis lutaria* L. 25 mm. Flies in spring round aquatic plants. Wings folded roof-like over abdomen when at rest. Eggs are laid on aquatic vegetation or stones. On hatching, the larvae quickly make their way to water where their development takes place. They are predacious and feed on small aquatic animals. Young larvae are found amidst vegetation, older ones in mud at the bottom. When fully grown the larva climbs out of the water and pupates in the soil. Development usually takes two years. Distribution: Europe (except south-eastern part), Siberia.

Order: **Snake Flies — Raphidioptera**

Family: **Raphidiidae**

**2.** *Raphidia notata* F. Wingspan 25 — 29 mm. Common from May to July in coniferous and deciduous forests. Often found on shrubs. Female places her longish eggs in crevices in tree trunks. Very flat larvae live under bark and on leaves where they hunt small insects and their larvae. They can crawl backwards. Both adults and larvae are beneficial in forestry. Distribution: northern and central Europe, absent from the Balkan and Iberian peninsulas.

Order: **Lacewing Flies — Planipennia**

Family: **Hemerobiidae**

**3.** *Hemerobius humulinus* L. Wingspan 13 — 18 mm. Common in forest margins and clearings. Lives from May to September. Both adults and larvae are predacious; they feed chiefly on aphids and are therefore very beneficial. Distribution: Europe, Siberia, North America.

Family: **Chrysopidae**

**4.** *Chrysopa flava* Scop. Wingspan 35 — 45 mm. One of the largest members of the family. Lives from June to September on the leaves of trees in forests and gardens. Distribution: all Europe, north Africa, North America.

Family: **Osmylidae**

**5.** *Osmylus fulvicephalus* Scop. 25 mm, wingspan 37 — 52 mm. On the wing from May to August by flowing water. Nocturnal. Eggs are laid on the leaves of plants. Larva is amphibious and both adult and larva are predacious. Larvae hibernate near water. Distribution: almost all Europe, as far north as southern Sweden.

Family: **Ant-lions — Myrmeleonidae**

**6.** *Myrmeleon formicarius* L. Wingspan 65 — 75 mm. On the wing from June to August in sandy localities. Larva buries itself at the bottom of a funnel-shaped pit it excavates in the sand. Insects crawling past (chiefly ants) fall into the pit and are seized by the larva's strong jaws. Larva hibernates once or twice and pupates in a cocoon. Distribution: greater part of Europe, north to southern Sweden and Norway (absent from the British Isles).

Family: **Ascalaphidae**

**7.** *Ascalaphus libelluloides* Schaef. Wingspan 45 — 53 mm. On the wing from June to August in very warm localities. Now on the decline. Distribution: south-western Europe (northern and eastern limits pass through Bohemia), north-western Africa.

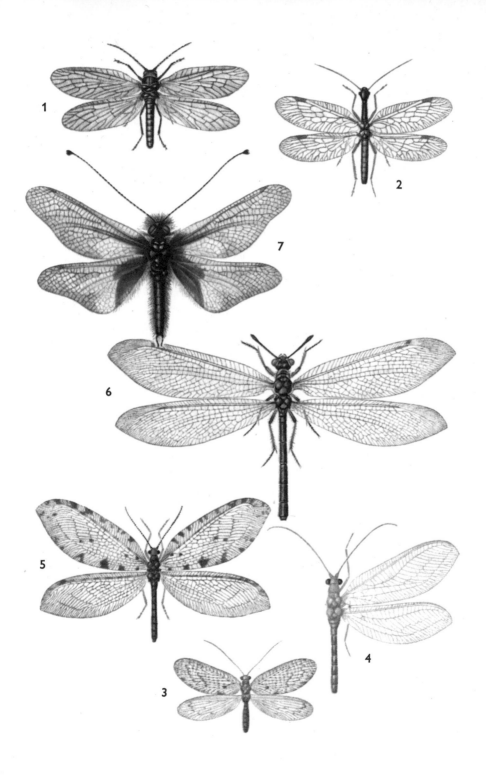

Order:  Beetles — Coleoptera

Family: **Tiger Beetles — Cicindelidae**

**1.** Green Tiger Beetle — *Cicindela campestris* L. 12—15 mm. Commonest of the European species. Occurs already in early spring. Flies short distances on field paths, in sandy localities and hedgerows. Hunts various insects and their larvae. Larva is also predacious; it lies in wait for insect prey in a little burrow made in a sandy bank. When it seizes its victim it drags it to the bottom of the burrow, which may be several decimetres long. Here the larva also pupates when fully grown. Distribution: all Europe, Siberia, north Africa.

Family: **Ground Beetles — Carabidae**

**2.** *Calosoma sycophanta* L. 25—35 mm. Good flier, predator found on tree trunks and in treetops in deciduous forests, where it hunts the larvae of injurious Lepidoptera, chiefly the gipsy moth and processionary moth; also hunts cockchafers. Occurs mostly in spring. At the beginning of summer it burrows deep in the ground, where it makes ready for hibernation. Larva is also predacious and feeds on caterpillars. Distribution: the Palearctic, North America (introduced). In Germany and Czechoslovakia it is protected by law. Only occasional visitor to Britain.

**3.** *Calosoma inquisitor* L. 16—21 mm. Found in treetops and on pathways where it hunts caterpillars — usually in stands of oak or beech, as well as on fruit trees. Larva is also predacious. Like the preceding species, it lives two to three years. Eggs are deposited in the ground in May. Development is rapid. Larva grows quickly and pupates in the ground. Young beetles emerge in June but remain in the ground until the following spring. Distribution: Europe, the Caucasus, north Africa. In Czechoslovakia protected by law.

**4.** *Cychrus rostratus* F. 15—18 mm. Found in mountain forests beneath decaying logs, under the bark of old tree stumps and under stones. Distinguished from common type of large ground beetle by the elongate front part of the body. Predacious. Distribution: most European mountain ranges — even at elevations above 2,000 metres.

**5.** *Carabus nemoralis* Müll. 20—28 mm. Found in groves and forest margins. Common also in country gardens where it settles permanently. Hides under stones, logs, beneath the bark on trunks of old felled trees and amidst moss. Mostly in lowlands but found also in foothills. Quite abundant locally. Distribution: most of Europe (from northern Spain to Norway, Sweden and Finland). Introduced also into North America, where it became widespread within several years.

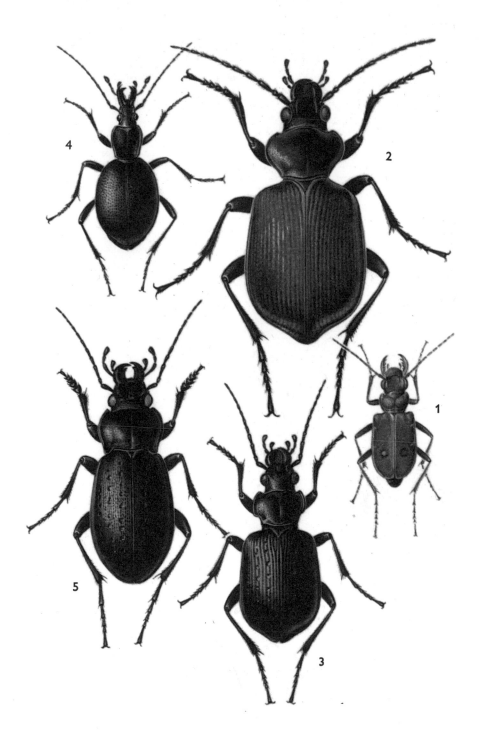

## Family: Ground Beetles — Carabidae

**1. *Carabus coriaceus*** L. 26—42 mm. One of the largest and stoutest of European ground beetles (only *Carabus gigas,* up to 60 mm long, is larger). Fierce predator. Hunts slugs, snails, various larvae and earthworms at night. During the day it hides under logs, the bark of old tree stumps, stones, etc. Does not fly. When disturbed it adopts a threatening pose with legs erect. In recent years its numbers have been declining and in many places it has disappeared altogether. Distribution: most of Europe (absent from Great Britain).

**2. Violet Ground Beetle — *Carabus violaceus*** L. 18—34 mm. Has a violet or greenish to blue-green, flattened rim round the edge of the elytra and scutum. Usually found in woodlands and fields, sometimes also in gardens, from lowland to mountain elevations. Quite plentiful in places, particularly damp woodlands. Distribution: practically all Europe to the Caucasus, western Siberia.

**3. *Carabus intricatus*** L. 24—35 mm. Found in damp woods under logs, under the bark of trees, in moss, under stones, etc. from lowland to mountain elevations. Like other large ground beetles, it cannot fly but is a good runner. Hunts various insect larvae, slugs and snails, but avoids dead animals. Fond of the sweet juices of fruits and wounded trees. Several beautiful colour forms exist. In France individuals have green elytra; in Greece blue elytra with golden-red rim. Distribution: most of Europe, but very rare in the British Isles.

**4. *Carabus nitens*** L. 13—18 mm. Found in fields and woodlands, mainly on sandy soil. Widespread in lowlands, hilly country and mountains up to 1,200 metres. Not common — in some regions has disappeared altogether. Distribution: Europe from northern Spain and northern Italy to Finland.

**5. *Carabus auronitens*** F. 17—28 mm. Inhabitant of foothill and mountain forests. Hunts in the evening; during the day hides under the bark of tree stumps, under logs and stones. Hibernates in rotting tree stumps and emerges in April. Like other large ground beetles it forms several geographical races that differ in the colouring of the scutum and elytra, the colour of the legs and antennae, and in size. Distribution: from western to central Europe, absent from the north and the British Isles.

**6. *Carabus hortensis*** L. 23—30 mm. Found in damp woods and groves, quite often also in country gardens as well as large city parks. Both adult and larva are nocturnal predators. Hunts various insect larvae, slugs and beetles and often attacks even relatively large creatures, such as cockchafers. During the day hides under the bark of tree stumps, logs and stones. A fairly common species even today. Distribution: mostly northern, eastern and central Europe, southward to Greece, east to the Urals. Absent from certain parts of Germany.

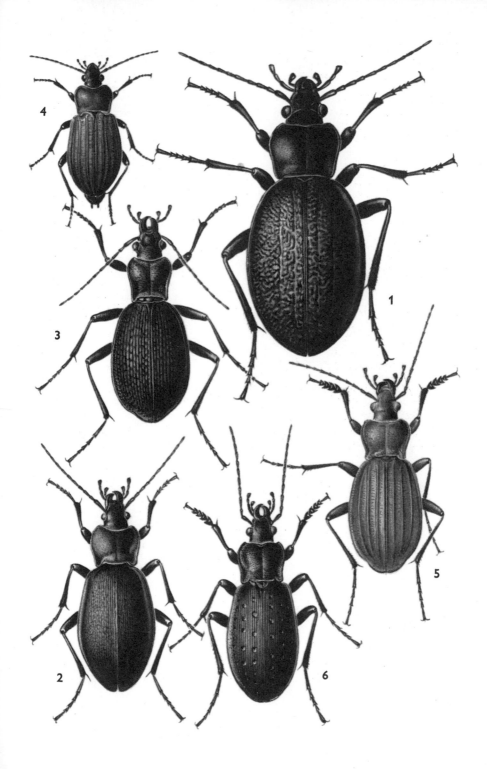

Family: **Carabidae**

**1.** *Carabus splendens* Ol. 25—35 mm. One of the loveliest of the large ground beetles. Distribution: mountain belt in France and Spain (Pyrenees).

**2.** *Carabus arvensis* Herbst. 13—18 mm. Exceedingly variable in colour, which may be predominantly brownish, greenish, violet, copper or black. Elytra slightly convex with three ridges. Found in mountain and foothill forests. Distribution: Europe (from northern Italy northwards to central and western Europe), Siberia and Japan.

**3.** *Carabus variolosus* F. 23—33 mm. Classed in the sub-genus *Hygrocarabus*, which indicates that it favours damp situations. Found in muddy places primarily in mountain and foothill regions, also in the mud of puddles on forest rides. A rare species. Distribution: west, south and central Europe from France to Rumania and Bulgaria.

**4.** *Carabus silvestris* Panz. 16—25 mm. Greatly resembles the related *C. linnei*, both being classed in the sub-genus *Orinocarabus*. Quite variable in colour, ranging from metallic green to coppery to black. Like *C. linnei* it also inhabits forests in mountain belts. Distribution: central Europe.

**5.** *Carabus auratus* L. 20—27 mm. Easily mistaken for *C. auronitens*, from which it is distinguished by the larger and broader scutum and the smooth, broad, golden ridges on the elytra (in *C. auronitens* they are narrow and dark). Adult hibernates. Female lays eggs in spring and summer and then dies. Offspring emerge in late summer. Found in cultivated fields and gardens. Very beneficial; preys on various slugs, cockchafers and larvae of the Colorado beetle. Its daily consumption of food equals 1.3 times its body weight. Distribution: Europe from northern Spain to central Europe (Poland marks its eastern limit). Rare in the British Isles.

**6.** *Carabus cancellatus* Illig. 18—27 mm. One of the large ground beetles with ridges on the elytra. Resembles several other species, for which it might easily be mistaken. Ground colour copper, sometimes with greenish tinge. Legs reddish-brown or black. A fast and good runner, found both in field and forest. Adult hibernates. Eggs, 4.5 mm long on average, are laid in late spring and summer. Development is the same as in other large ground beetles. Adults of the new generation appear in late summer. Both adult and larva predacious. Feeds on various molluscs, earthworms and the larvae of various insects, including the Colorado beetle. Several geographic races exist. Distribution: Europe from northern Italy to Finland and Norway; rare in Great Britain; Siberia.

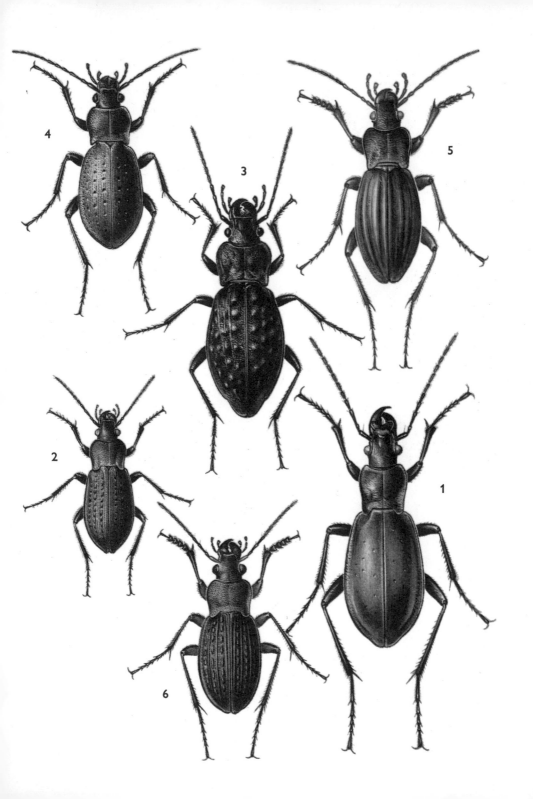

Family: **Carabidae**

**1.** *Carabus granulatus* L. 16—23 mm. Generally coloured bronze with greenish tinge, rarely black. Found mostly in fields. The beetle hibernates in a 'cradle' in the ground at a depth of c. 50 cm. Some 40 eggs, about 4 mm long, are laid in spring. Larva always burrows in the ground before moulting; when fully grown, it burrows even deeper and makes a cradle in which it pupates. Adult beetle usually remains in the ground until the following spring. Both adult and larva are predators that rid fields of the Colorado beetle. Distribution: vast parts of the Palearctic (in Europe from northern Spain and central Italy to central Scandinavia and Finland).

**2.** *Carabus glabratus* Payk. 22—32 mm. Found from lowland to mountain elevations (2,000 metres). Lives in forests and hunts also during the day. Fond of damp situations and abundant on forest rides and by forest streams, particularly after a rainfall. Distribution: Europe, the Urals.

**3.** *Carabus irregularis* F. 19—30 mm. One of the mountain species of large ground beetles. Favours old rotting stumps of fir and beech. In places where it occurs one may find several dozen beetles in one spot. As a rule, however, it is quite rare. Occurs from May to August. Distribution: mountain and foothill regions of central and western Europe, Yugoslavia, Rumania.

**4.** *Nebria brevicollis* F. 9—14 mm. A smaller, dark-coloured ground beetle. Found on humus-rich soils in lowlands and foothills. Common. Distribution: Europe, the Caucasus, Asia Minor, north Africa (Algeria).

**5.** *Notiophilus biguttatus* F. 5 mm. Commonest European member of this genus, recognized by the conspicuously large eyes. Runs about on the ground with great agility and is plentiful throughout its range. Distribution: the Palearctic.

**6.** *Omophron limbatum* F. 6—7 mm. Lives buried in sandy riverbanks, where it may be found in spring and summer. Distribution: Europe, north Africa.

**7.** *Bembidion lampros* Herbst. 2.8—4 mm. Member of a genus comprising several dozen species of tiny beetles very similar in form. Like other ground beetles, it is also a predator. Generally found in fields and meadows. Distribution: most of Europe, Siberia and North America.

**8.** *Broscus cephalotes* L. 17—22 mm. Occurs primarily in lowlands and hilly country; favours situations with sandy soil. Digs corridors in the ground, where it lies in wait for passing prey. A predator, it kills a great number of various larvae and is thus beneficial, the same being true of practically all ground beetles. Distribution: primarily central and northern Europe, extends to France, central Italy and in the Balkan peninsula to Yugoslavia. Mainly coastal in Britain.

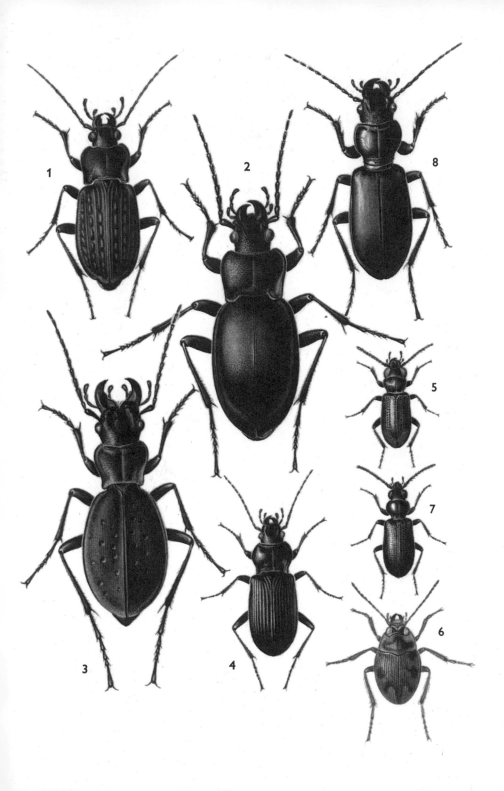

Family: **Carabidae**

**1.** *Calathus melanocephalus* L. 6—8 mm. A common, small ground beetle. Favours damp situations from lowland to mountain elevations. Distribution: all Europe, the Caucasus, Siberia.

**2.** *Agonum sexpunctatum* L. 7—9 mm. Notable for its beautiful metallic colour. Usually scutum is green and elytra golden-red; often, however, scutum is blue and elytra bronze, bluish, blue-violet, or entirely black. On each elytron is a row of six delicate pits, which are only visible through the lens — hence its scientific name. Found under stones in hedgerows and field paths. Occurs primarily in hilly country and mountains, less frequently in lowlands. Distribution: practically the whole of Europe, much of Asia.

**3.** *Agonum dorsale* Pontopp. 6—7.5 mm. Easily recognized by the green spots at the tips of the elytra. A common beetle often found together with other individuals under stones at the edges of dry fields or on dry field paths. Distribution: practically all Europe, including the Mediterranean, Siberia.

**4.** *Pterostichus niger* Schall. 16—21 mm. Easily mistaken in the wild for numerous other similar species. Common in field and forest, often found also in gardens. Distribution: Europe, the Caucasus, Siberia.

**5.** *Pterostichus metallicus* F. 12—15 mm. A fairly conspicuous and common inhabitant of foothill and mountain localities. Found under stones, old logs, etc.; may also be seen running along forest rides in search of prey. Distribution: abundant in the Alps, Carpathians and mountains of the northern Balkans.

**6.** *Abax ater* Villers. 18—22 mm. Resembles a great many other species. Identified by the absence of small pits on the elytra, usually present in related species. Found at lower elevations as well as in mountains, where it occurs in a different, smaller form. Distribution: primarily southern and central Europe; rare or absent in the north.

**7.** *Amara aenea* Deg. 6—8 mm. Very common. Oval in outline. Hind end of scutum is the same width as the elytra. Distribution: the whole Palearctic.

**8.** *Zabrus tenebrioides* Goeze 14—16 mm. An exception amongst the predacious ground beetles in that it is herbivorous. Adults appear in June. During the day they hide under stones; at night, they climb up the stems of grain to feed on the seeds in the spike. After a time, however, they emerge during the day and fly to new territory, later reverting again to their night-time habits. Female lays eggs in the autumn, after which she usually dies. Sometimes, however, she hibernates and lays eggs anew the following year. Larva soon emerges and feeds on the leaves of young autumn crops. After hibernating it continues feeding and ultimately pupates. In former times this beetle was regarded as a serious cereal crop pest but nowadays the damage it causes is local. Distribution: Europe (less frequent in the north and in Great Britain), Asia Minor.

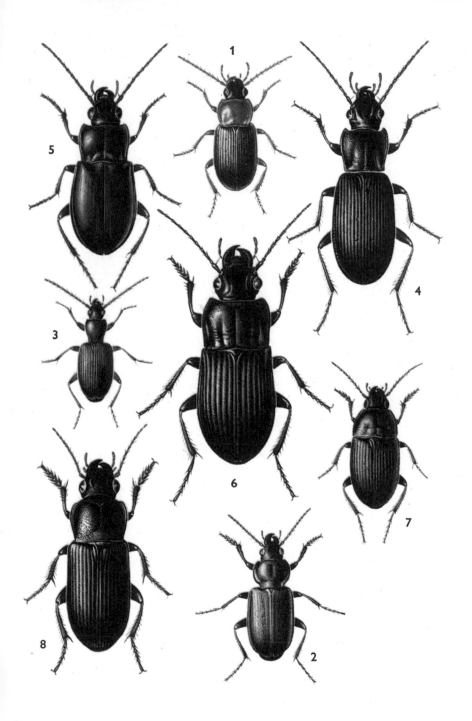

Family: **Carabidae**

**1.** *Harpalus aeneus* F. 9—12 mm. Usually metallic green or copper, but quite common also with a bluish tint or entirely black. Antennae and legs always brownish-orange. Very common in fields and on field paths, often under stones. Distribution: Europe, western Asia, North America.

**2.** *Harpalus rufipes* Dej. 14—16 mm. Elytra thickly covered with short, fine hairs. Found everywhere but mostly in fields and on field paths under stones. Distribution: the whole Palearctic.

**3.** *Badister bipustulatus* F. 4—6 mm. Occurs, often abundantly, under stones and old logs in damp situations. Pattern on the elytra is quite variable. Distribution: Europe, the Caucasus, Siberia, North America.

**4.** *Chlaenius nitidulus* Schr. 10—12 mm. Commonest of the several related green ground beetles in Europe. Favours damp situations, mainly near water, where it is locally abundant. Distribution: chiefly southern and central Europe (rare in Great Britain).

**5.** *Callistus lunatus* F. 6—7 mm. Thermophilous. Found on sunny slopes and steppes under stones, often in the company of other smaller ground beetles. Distribution: Europe (absent in the north and very rare in Britain, common in southern Germany, absent in the northerly parts), Asia Minor, Middle East.

**6.** *Lebia cyanocephala* L. 5—8 mm. Greatly resembles the closely related *Lebia chlorocephala*, from which it may be distinguished by the coarser spotting of the elytra and colour of the legs — the femur is darker where it joins the tibia. Distribution: practically all Europe (rare in Britain), western Asia, Siberia.

**7.** *Brachynus explodens* Dftsch. 4—6.5 mm. Found under stones at the edges of fields. This and other bombardier-beetles *(Brachynus)* have a peculiar method of defence against enemies. It has at the hind end of the body special glands secreting fluids which undergo a complex chemical reaction when mixed. They are ejected in the form of a bluish gaseous substance, the action being accompanied by a popping sound. This gas looks like a bluish puff of smoke which blinds the enemy, allowing the beetle to escape. Distribution: Europe (absent in the north, northern France, Holland, Great Britain), Siberia.

**8.** *Brachynus crepitans* L. 6.5—10 mm. Greatly resembles the preceding species but is much larger. Found also under stones, favouring a limestone substrate. Can also 'fire' at enemies; its 'pops' are much more intensive than those of *Brachynus explodens*. Distribution: Europe (more abundant in southern and central Europe, usually rare in the north), Siberia, north Africa.

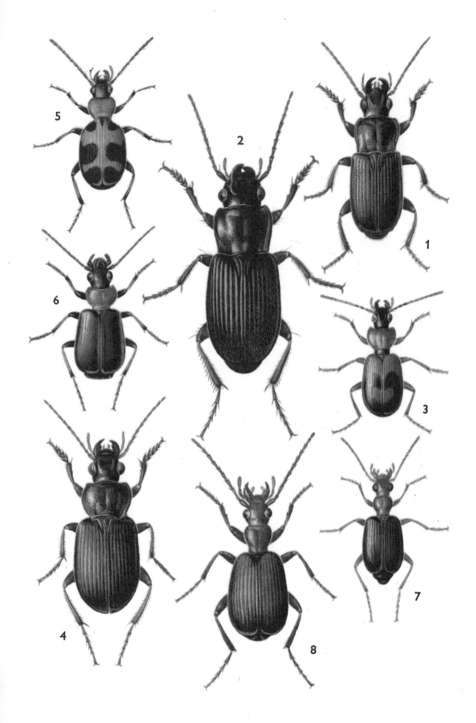

Family: **Crawling Water Beetles — Haliplidae**

1. *Haliplus flavicollis* Strm. 3.5 — 4 mm. Very similar to many other European beetles in form and colour. Best distinguished by the spots on the scutum (they are smaller at the front than at the base) and by the hind coxae which form broad plates. Found below the surface of clear water round vegetation. Distribution: Europe, Asia, Siberia, Turkestan, north Africa.

Family: **Predacious Diving Beetles — Dytiscidae**

2. *Hyphydrus ovatus* L. 4.5 — 5 mm. Marked sexual differences. Male is thickly patterned with double dots, female has the elytra almost smooth. Common. Distribution: Europe, Siberia.

3. *Hygrotus versicolor* Schall. 3.5 mm. Distinguished by the black longitudinal stripes on the elytra. Also visible with a strong lens are very fine dots interspersed with a few larger ones. Occurs abundantly in still water. Distribution: Europe (from Scandinavia to northern Balkans, Italy and Spain), Iran.

4. *Hydroporus palustris* L. 3.5 — 4 mm. Distinguished by the yellow pattern on the elytra. Sometimes the yellow colouring predominates. One of the commonest of aquatic beetles. Found from lowland to mountain elevations. Distribution: Europe, Siberia, Asia Minor, Transcaucasia.

5. *Graptodytes pictus* F. 2.3 mm. Pattern on the elytra resembles that of the preceding species. Formerly classed in the genus *Hydroporus*. Found in pools with vegetation. Becoming rarer in some places. Distribution: Europe (primarily central and northern Europe, southwards as far as northern Spain and northern Italy).

6. *Platambus maculatus* L. 7 — 8 mm. Found in overgrown streams and grassy ditches in lowlands, in mountain springs and streams. Easily recognized by the yellow pattern on the elytra. Distribution: Europe (to northern Scandinavia), the Caucasus, Transcaucasia (Armenia), western Siberia.

7. *Ilybius fenestratus* F. 11 — 12 mm. Found in backwaters of streams, pools and small forest springs. Distribution: chiefly central and northern Europe to Lapland, the northern parts of southern Europe, Siberia, North America.

8. *Acilius sulcatus* L. 16 — 18 mm. Marked sexual differences. Female has three longitudinal ridges on the elytra with fine hairs in between. Male has smooth elytra. Another distinguishing feature is the circular suction discs on the male's front legs. Found in various types of water but mostly in the calm waters of rivers, springs or ponds. It also visits puddles on forest rides after a heavy rainfall, settling there for a brief period. Both adult and larva are predacious, hunting small aquatic larvae, crustaceans, etc. Distribution: Europe (from central Italy and northern Spain across central Europe north to Lapland), Transcaucasia, Siberia, north Africa.

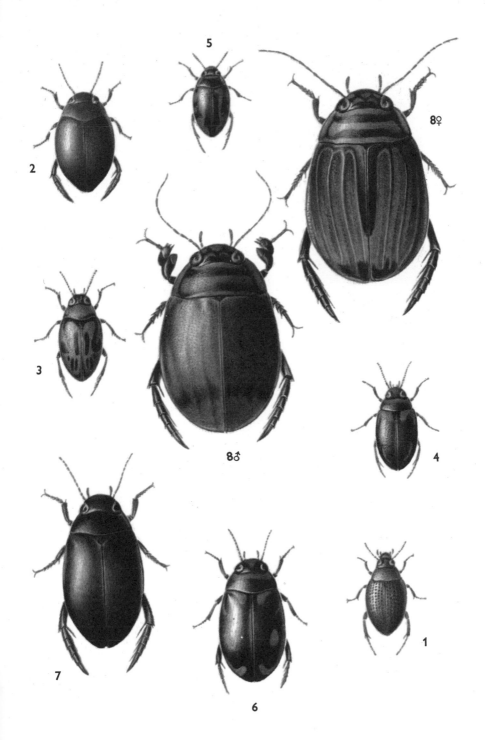

Family: **Dytiscidae**

**1. Great Diving Beetle** — *Dytiscus marginalis* L. 35 mm. Form of body and legs excellently adapted to life in water. Beetle comes to the surface about 4—7 times an hour to take a fresh supply of air into its air reservoir. Male distinguished from female by the smooth elytra, but this is not always a reliable distinguishing character for some females also have the elytra smooth instead of furrowed. A definite means of identifying the male are the circular discs on the fore legs, on the underside of which are two large cup-like suckers in the centre encircled by some 150 smaller ones similar to those on the middle tarsi. Predacious beetle that hunts various small animals, feeding also on carrion. It can go without food for 1—2 months. Males live 1 year, females 6 months longer. Eggs are deposited in aquatic plants. Larva is predacious and feeds by thrusting the mandibles, which contain a narrow canal, into its prey and sucking it dry. When fully grown, the larva climbs out of the water and pupates in an earthen cocoon on the shore. Beetle is not a pest of fish-fry as stated in literature. Generally hunts only diseased and weakened fish. Distribution: Europe from the Iberian peninsula to Scandinavia (generally absent from the Balkans), the Caucasus, Siberia, Japan, North America.

**2.** *Dytiscus latissimus* L. 35—44 mm. Largest member of the whole family. Much rarer than the preceding species; during the past decade has disappeared entirely in many places or else is on the verge of extinction. Distribution: Europe (western limit in France, in the north extends to central Sweden and Finland; absent from Lapland and Great Britain; extends southwards to northern Italy), western Siberia.

**3.** *Cybister lateralimarginalis* Deg. 30—32 mm. Occurs in stagnant and running water where the adults may be found from spring until midsummer. Distribution: Europe (from southern and western Europe to Denmark and southern Sweden), the Caucasus, Asia Minor, Iraq, Iran, southern Siberia and elsewhere. Rarely seen in the British Isles.

Family: **Whirligig Beetles — Gyrinidae**

**4.** *Gyrinus natator* L. 5—7 mm. Occurs abundantly throughout its range. Skims round and round gracefully on the surface of water. Exceedingly well adapted to life on the surface. Body spindle-shaped and flat, antennae short and thick. Best developed of the limbs are the forelegs, the remaining legs are short. The eye also is remarkable, being divided into two parts — an upper part for seeing over the surface and lower for seeing down into the water. Distribution: much of Europe, Siberia, Mongolia, north Africa.

**5.** *Gyrinus minutus* F. 3.5—4.5 mm. A smaller and rarer species. Distribution: all Europe (chiefly in the north as far as Lapland), Siberia, northern China, North America.

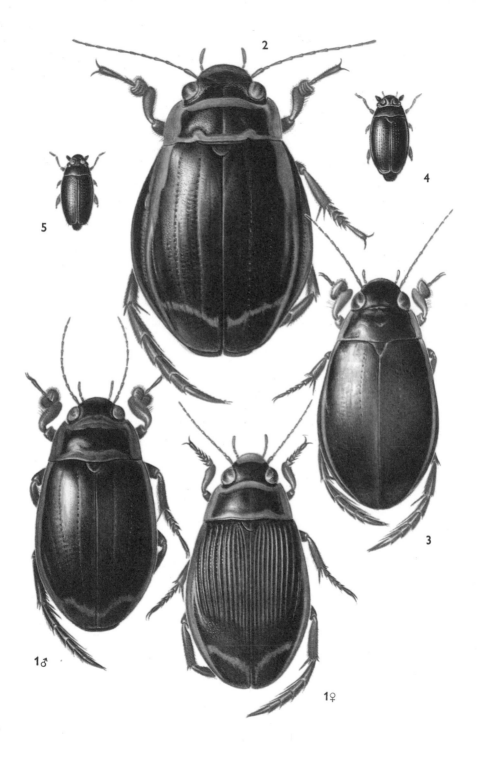

## Family: **Rove Beetles — Staphylinidae**

**1.** *Eusphalerum florale* Panz. 2.7 — 3 mm. This and the other related species are found on flowers. Elytra are fairly long for a rove beetle. Usually abundant. Distribution: central Europe (absent in the north).

**2.** *Anthophagus caraboides* L. 4.4 — 5.5 mm. Found on flowers, often together with other species of rove beetles. Fairly abundant in foothill and mountain areas, absent in lowlands. Distribution: central Europe.

**3.** *Oxyporus rufus* L. 7 — 12 mm. Distinguished by its large mandibles as well as bright colouring. In summer occurs abundantly on old mushrooms and toadstools, in which the larva also lives. The closely related *O. maxillosus* (not British) also occurs on mushrooms but favours the *Boletus* type. It, too, has large mandibles but the scutum is black and the elytra yellowish with a dark patch at the anal angle. One cannot be mistaken for the other if carefully examined. Distribution: much of the Palearctic.

**4.** *Stenus biguttatus* L. 4.5 — 5 mm. Very common in damp places, for example, on the banks of watercourses. Distinguished by the form of the body, unusually large eyes and two orange-yellow dots on the elytra (several similar species, however, also have dots!). Adult hibernates. Distribution: Europe, Siberia, northern China.

**5.** *Xantholinus tricolor* F. 7.5 — 11 mm. Commonest of the closely related European species. Scutum is not uniformly coloured — hind end is darker. Usually found in forests amidst fallen leaves and moss; fond of hiding under stones, old logs and tree stumps. Occurs from lowland to mountain elevations. Distribution: much of Europe, the Caucasus, Siberia.

**6.** *Othius punctulatus* Goeze 10 — 14 mm. In general appearance resembles many other species. Elytra and tip of abdomen are brown, scutum usually black with lighter brownish margin on the sides. Very common forest beetle. Like many other rove beetles it occurs in humus, fallen leaves, moss and similar habitats. Found from lowlands to high in the mountains. Distribution: much of Europe, Siberia, north Africa.

**7.** *Philonthus politus* L. 10.5 — 13 mm. One of several dozen related and similar species found in Europe. They are very difficult to identify and as with most rove beetles, this can be done only by an experienced entomologist. This species is found in widely varied localities, but always in places with sufficient decaying animal and vegetable matter, where it seeks the larvae of the various insects it feeds on. It is generally found on small dead animals, amidst decaying leaves, in old mushrooms, on mammal faeces, etc. It also visits injured trees with oozing sap. Distribution: much of the Palearctic, Nearctic (North America), Australian region (Tasmania, New Zealand).

## Family: **Staphylinidae**

**1.** *Staphylinus caesareus* Ced. 17 — 25 mm. Form of body and colouring similar to that of several related large rove beetles. Found under stones and in other hiding places; may be seen running swiftly on paths early in spring. Seeks dead animals and decaying vegetable matter, where its hunts various larvae. Common in foothills, rare or absent in lowlands. Distribution: all Europe, North America. Not common in the British Isles.

**2.** *Ocypus tenebricosus* Grav. 20 — 32 mm. One of the largest of rove beetles. Distinguished from other, similar, large black rove beetles of Europe by several minor characteristics. Found under logs and stones from lowland to mountain elevations: less numerous, as a rule, in lowlands than higher up. Distribution: central Europe, the Balkans, Italy.

**3.** *Ontholestes tessellatus* Geoffr. 14 — 19 mm. Common on decaying matter and in dung as well as on juices oozing from injured trunks. Distribution: central and northern Europe, Siberia.

**4.** *Creophilus maxillosus* L. 15 — 25 mm. A predator that hunts its prey in dung, piles of rubbish and decaying animal matter. Locally very abundant. Distribution: the Palearctic, North America, Oriental region.

**5.** *Quedius cinctus* Payk. 7.5 — 8.5 mm. Found on decaying matter, also in the soil and amidst moss. Common. Distribution: Europe, north Africa.

**6.** *Bolitobius lunulatus* L. 5 — 7 mm. Found on forest mushrooms, where it preys on various insect larvae. Its development also takes place in mushrooms. Distribution: most of Europe (mainly central and northern), the Caucasus, northern Asia.

**7.** *Tachyporus obtusus* 3.3 — 4 mm. Distinguished by its broad, light-coloured scutum. Found mostly in moss and in forest litter. Distribution: much of Europe.

**8.** *Aleochara curtula* Goeze 5.5 — 8 mm. One of the largest members of the genus which includes some 40 species of small beetles that are difficult to identify. Occurs abundantly on dead animals, in mushrooms, detritus, on old skins etc. Distribution: much of Europe.

## Family: **Pselaphidae**

**9.** *Pselaphus heisei* Herbst 1.6 — 1.8 mm. Found in damp places, under stones, among moss and decaying leaves. Locally abundant. Distribution: most of Europe.

## Family: **Clavigeridae**

**10.** *Claviger testaceus* Preyssl. 2 — 2.5 mm. Lives together with the ant *Lasius flavus,* providing it with a sweet fluid exuded by special glands. The beetle itself is very dependent on ants. It is blind and unable to procure food for itself and is fed by the ants and carried off to safety in their mandibles when danger threatens. Found mostly on warm, sunny slopes in lowlands; occurs at elevations up to 1,000 metres. Distribution: in various places throughout most of Europe.

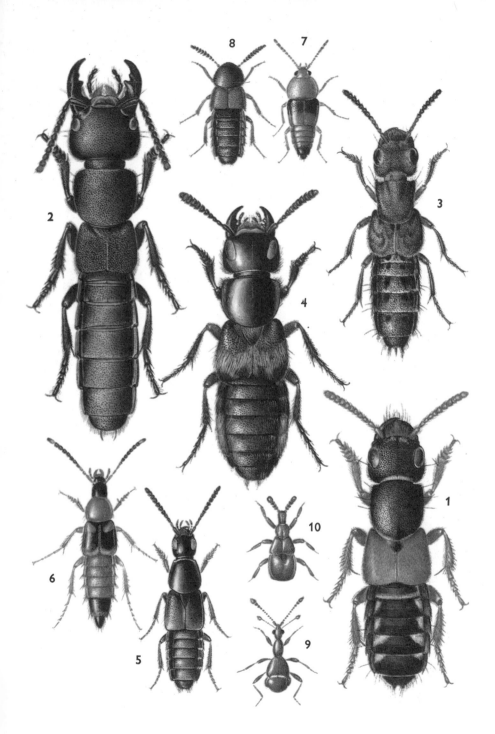

## Family: Carrion Beetles — Silphidae

**1.** *Necrophorus vespilloides* Herbst 10 — 18 mm. One of several species of burying beetles with yellow-orange patches on the dark elytra. Abundant in forests. Like its relatives, seeks out small dead animals such as mice and birds and buries them. Several individuals usually converge on a single carcass, fighting amongst themselves until only one pair remains. The male and female generally bury the carcass together, but in related species the female chases off the male. The buried carcass serves as a food store for the female and her offspring. Eggs are laid in a special passage near the carcass. The larvae, which emerge shortly, crawl to the carcass where they are fed by the female, sometimes also by the male, during the first hours as well as subsequently after every moult. When fully grown the larvae pupate in the carcass. Distribution: the Palearctic.

**2.** *Necrophorus humator* F. 18 — 28 mm. Elytra black, the same as in *N. germanicus,* from which it is distinguished by its size as well as the red-clubbed antennae. Distribution: all Europe, the Caucasus, Middle East (Syria), north Africa.

**3.** *Necrophorus germanicus* L. 20 — 30 mm. Largest of the European burying beetles. Antennae terminated by a black club. Attracted to carrion at night, but also found on excrement in which it hunts earth-boring dung-beetles and aphodian dung-beetles. Distribution: Europe (absent from Great Britain, the north and the Iberian Peninsula), the Caucasus, Middle East (Syria).

**4.** *Oeceoptoma thoracica* L. 12 — 16 mm. Found on dead organisms, in excrement and in old mushrooms. Common on the stinkhorn *(Phallus impudicus)*. Abundant throughout its entire range. Distribution: Europe, Siberia, Japan.

**5.** *Blitophaga opaca* L. 9 — 12 mm. Feeds on various, mostly economically unimportant, plants such as grasses and various wild Cruciferae. Sometimes, however, eats sugar-beet and is thus regarded as a pest in certain parts of Europe. In central Europe and in Britain it is nowadays a rare species. Hibernates at forest edges under stones and amidst litter; emerges in early spring. Distribution: all Europe, northern and central Asia, North America.

**6.** *Thanatophilus sinuatus* F. 9 — 12 mm. A common black species. Found on carrion. Distribution: all Europe, Middle East (Iran), north Africa.

**7.** *Xylodrepa quadripunctata* L. 12 — 14 mm. Distinguished from related species chiefly by its colouring and habits. Unlike other carrion-beetles that generally visit carrion or decaying plants, this species hunts live prey. Found chiefly in oak as well as in other hardwood stands, where it pursues primarily caterpillars of various injurious Lepidoptera. It is therefore also an important beneficial beetle. Distribution: Europe (unknown in the Iberian Peninsula and in Greece).

## Family: **Colonidae**

**1.** *Colon brunneum* Latr. 1.4—2.7 mm. Most widely distributed member of this small and as yet little investigated family. Distribution: practically all Europe, the Caucasus.

## Family: **Catopidae**

**2.** *Catops chrysomeloides* Panz. 3.5—5.5 mm. Favours decaying matter, including carrion, and sometimes also found in the burrows of mammals. Locally abundant. May be seen as late as December, for the adults hibernate. Distribution: from the northern parts of southern Europe to southern Scandinavia, the Caucasus.

## Family: **Shining Fungus-Beetles — Scaphidiidae**

**3.** *Scaphidium quadrimaculatum* Oliv. 5.5—6.5 mm. Hides under the bark of stumps and felled trees where moulds abound, or else in tree fungi. When disturbed runs very swiftly. Occurs mainly in foothills and mountain regions and tolerates even very dry situations. Distribution: most of Europe (in the north to central Sweden and Karelia, in the south to Italy and the Balkans), Asia Minor.

## Family: **Histeridae**

**4.** *Hister illigeri* Duftschm., 4—5 mm. Found mostly on carrion. Distinguished by red spots on each elytron. Distribution: central and southern Europe, the Caucasus, Afghanistan.

**5.** *Hister impressus* F. 4—7 mm, better known by its earlier name *H. cadaverinus.* Very common. Found mostly on carrion but also common on decaying vegetable matter and decomposing mushrooms. May likewise occur on juices oozing from injured tree trunks. Distribution: all Europe, Siberia, Japan.

## Family: **Lycidae**

**6.** *Dictyopterus nigroruber* Deg. 7—10 mm. Found resting on various white-flowering Umbelliferae which set off its red and black colouring. Also occurs on decaying stumps in which its larvae develop. Found mostly in foothill and mountain regions. Not very plentiful. Distribution: Europe, Siberia, Korea, Japan.

## Family: **Fireflies and Glowworms — Lampyridae**

**7.** *Phausis splendidula* L. 8—10 mm. Distinguished by marked differences between the sexes. Male is winged and flies; female has only wing stumps and is incapable of flight. Both sexes (as well as the larvae) emit a bright light. The light organs are located on the underside of the body. The male's differ from those of the female. Light is produced by a very complex chemical process. The beetle is able to convert all energy into light without loss. Males fly on summer nights in meadows and around water. This species is locally abundant. Adults do not feed but subsist on the food stored in their bodies. Larvae are carnivorous. Distribution: Europe (absent from Great Britain and the north), the Caucasus.

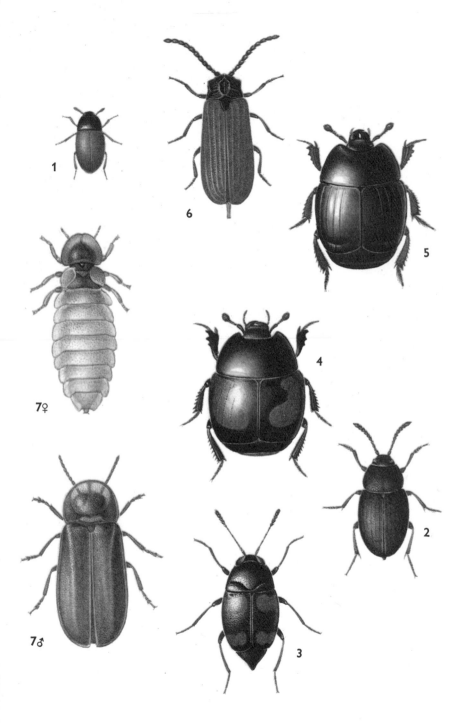

Family: Soldier-Beetles — Cantharidae

**1.** *Cantharis fusca* L. 11 — 15 mm. Found in flowers, where it hunts chiefly aphids. Both adults and the black larvae are beneficial. Larvae may sometimes be found on snow, where they are washed up or blown by the wind from their winter shelters. Occurs abundantly from lowlands to elevations of about 1,000 metres. Distribution: Europe, from Italy and northern Spain as far as southern Scandinavia.

**2.** *Rhagonycha fulva* Scop. 7 — 10 mm. One of the commonest members of the family. Occurs in late summer. Regularly found on Umbelliferae from lowland to mountain elevations of about 1,000 metres. Distribution: Europe (from the south to southern Scandinavia), the Caucasus, Middle East.

Family: **Melyridae**

**3.** *Malachius bipustulatus* L. 5 — 6 mm. Generally common on flowers and grasses. When danger threatens it protrudes reddish vesicles from the sides of the body to frighten off the enemy. Found from lowlands to elevations of about 1,000 metres. Distribution: most of Europe, Siberia.

**4.** *Anthocomus bipunctatus* Har. 3 mm. Often seen in the vicinity of human habitations — settles on walls and in rooms on window panes. Distribution: Europe (absent from the north, from Britain and Spain), the Caucasus.

Family: **Checkered Beetles — Cleridae**

**5.** *Thanasimus formicarius* L. 7 — 10 mm. Very beneficial. From spring until autumn runs swiftly over felled logs and stacked wood, where it hunts bark-beetles. The rose-coloured larvae, living under bark, are also predacious. Distribution: Europe, Asia, north Africa. Introduced into North America.

**6.** *Trichodes apiarius* L. 10 — 16 mm. Still locally abundant on flowering Umbelliferae where it hunts small insects and licks the pollen. The carnivorous larvae develop in the nests of wild bees and sometimes even in the hives of honey-bees, but usually only in neglected hives. It is pointless to include this now-declining species among the pests of bee colonies. Distribution: Europe (mostly southern and central), Asia Minor, north Africa.

**7.** *Korynetes coeruleus* Deg. 3.5 — 6.5 mm. Development takes place in wood. Both adults and larvae hunt death-watch beetles and bark beetles. Adults occur on flowers near human habitations; often found climbing out of beams and thick boards in attics. Distribution: practically worldwide, in Europe mostly in the central and southern parts.

Family: **Lymexylidae**

**8.** *Hylecoetus dermestoides* L. 6 — 18 mm. Flies as early as April. Lifespan very short — only 2 — 4 days. Larvae develop in the wood of oak and beech, chiefly in stumps and diseased trees, where they bore long, narrow tunnels. They do not feed on wood but on ambrosia fungi. Female dusts the eggs with the spores of the fungus which the larvae carry with them into the wood where the spores germinate and produce new fungus. Beetle is locally abundant. Distribution: Europe (central and northern), Siberia.

Family: **Helodidae**

**9.** *Helodes minuta* L. 4.5 — 6 mm. Common on flowers around water. Larvae develop in water. Distribution: almost all Europe.

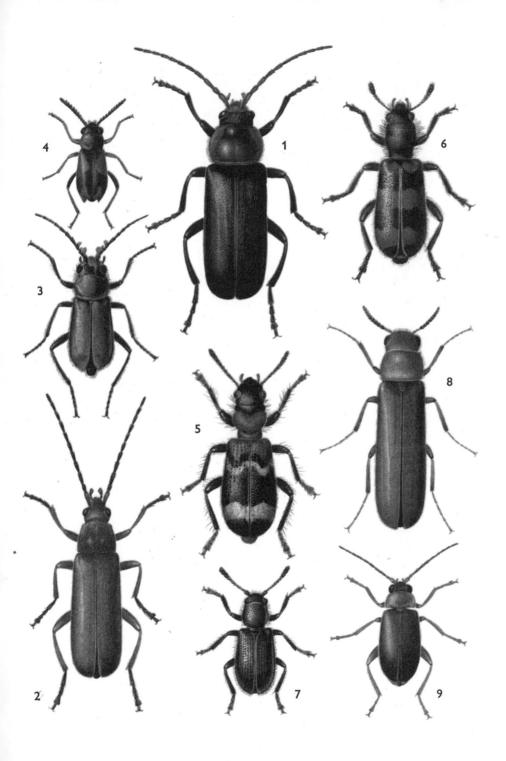

Family: **Click Beetles — Elateridae**

**1.** *Adelocera murina* L. 11 — 17 mm. Occurs abundantly from lowland to mountain elevations. Found practically throughout the growing period in forests, fields and gardens. Elytra and scutum covered with tiny whitish scales. Their quantity determines the beetle's colouring. Some specimens are almost whitish. Larva feeds on the roots of various plants and may be injurious in tree nurseries. Distribution: all Europe, the Caucasus, Siberia, North America.

**2.** *Elater sanguineus* L. 13 — 18 mm. One of several click beetles with red elytra and black scutum. Found mostly in coniferous woods in hilly country; locally abundant but very rare in Britain. Distribution: Europe, Siberia.

**3.** *Athous niger* L. 10 — 14 mm. Found on flowers and in thickets in hardwood forests and forest margins. On the wing from lowland to foothill elevations. Larvae, coloured brownish or reddish-yellow (as in most click beetles), live on the roots of grasses and other plants. Distribution: mainly central and northern Europe, eastern Asia.

**4.** *Athous vittatus* F. 8 — 10 mm. So variable in colouring that the band on the elytra is sometimes entirely wanting and the elytra are then a uniform yellowish-brown to dark brown, which explains the great number of described colour forms. Common in deciduous forests from lowlands to foothills and sometimes even in mountains, especially on young trees. Distribution: all Europe, the Caucasus, Asia Minor.

**5.** *Corymbites cupreus* F. 11 — 16 mm. An upland species. Quite variable in colour, which may be green, violet, bronzy-green or blue. Male and female differ in the arrangement of the antennae — the male's are pectinate; the female's serrate. Found on flowers and grasses. Locally abundant. Eggs are laid in batches in the soil. Fully grown larva is about 25 mm long. Distribution: Europe, the Caucasus.

**6.** *Corymbites aeneus* L. 10 — 17 mm. Very common. Always has a metallic sheen but variable in colour — usually greenish, but often blue-violet, coppery, blue or black. Adult beetles found on various flowers and herbs; very common on shrubs, in meadows and on field paths from lowland to mountain elevations. May be seen from the first days of spring until late autumn. Female lays some 300 eggs in the soil. Larvae live in the ground, are long and narrow with a very hard cuticle. Commonly known as 'wireworms'. This term, however, is applied also to the larvae of other species, for the larvae of click beetles are all very similar. Wireworms may be injurious to cultivated plants. Distribution: Europe, Siberia.

**7.** *Corymbites purpureus* Poda. 8 — 14 mm. Found early in spring on tender leaves of shrubs and trees, mainly in hilly country and in foothills. Locally common. Distribution: central and southern Europe, Asia (Iran, the Himalayas, etc.).

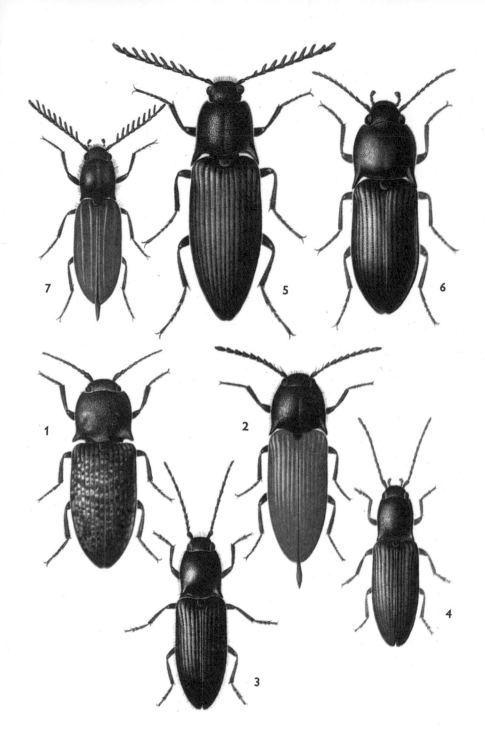

## Family: Metallic Wood-Borers — Buprestidae

**1.** *Capnodis tenebrionis* L. 22—25 mm. Found in spring on various woody plants. Eggs are laid in the ground. Larva bores into the root of the host plant. Larval state lasts 2 years. When fully grown (up to c. 7 cm long) it pupates. In Europe this beetle is very rare nowadays and in many places has disappeared altogether. However, in the south, in the Caucasus and Transcaucasia, it is a pest of fruit trees. Distribution: Europe (southern and central), the Caucasus, Transcaucasia, Asia Minor, Middle East, north Africa.

**2.** *Scintilatrix rutilans* F. 12—15 mm. Lives on lime trees, flying rapidly round them from May to July. Eggs are laid in cracks in the bark of the tree trunk and thicker branches. Larvae bore tunnels beneath the bark. Development takes one year in southern Europe and two to three years in central Europe. Distribution: southern and central Europe, the Caucasus and Transcaucasia.

**3.** *Ancylocheira octoguttata* L. 9—15 mm. Has several colour forms. Flies in sunny spots in pine woods. Settles on trunks, tree stumps and protruding roots. Larval stage is passed not only in pine-tree stumps but also in the roots and bottom parts of pine trunks. Distribution: most of Europe, Transcaucasia, western Siberia, Middle East (Syria). Absent from Britain.

**4.** *Anthaxia fulgurans* Schr. L. 5—5.5 mm. One of the loveliest members of the genus. Male is a metallic green. Female has red elytra with green stripes down the sutures and at the base. As in related species, the adults visit flowers on sunny days from spring till late summer. Distribution: central and southern Europe, the Caucasus, Syria, north Africa.

**5.** *Chrysobothris affinis* F. 12—14 mm. In June and July settles on felled tree trunks, generally beech or oak. Very agile and wary. Larvae live in diseased or felled hardwood trees, including fruit trees, boring tunnels beneath the bark. If they are held responsible for damage, it should be pointed out that they usually only attack trees already weakened by some other pest. Distribution: Europe (from the south to southern Scandinavia), Siberia, Asia Minor, Transcaucasia, Iran, north Africa.

**6.** *Agrilus biguttatus* F. 10 mm. Flies from May to July, settling on felled oak trunks, tree stumps and young thickets. Larvae live under the bark of dying trunks or thick branches. Distribution: Europe (less plentiful in the north), the Caucasus, Asia Minor, Iran, north Africa.

**7.** *Trachys minuta* L. 3—3.5 mm. Occurs abundantly from onset of spring, on the leaves of willow and on various flowers. Eggs are cemented with a dark putty-like substance to the upper side of leaves of various trees. Larvae are leaf-miners. Distribution: practically all Europe (not very far north), the Caucasus, Asia Minor, Siberia.

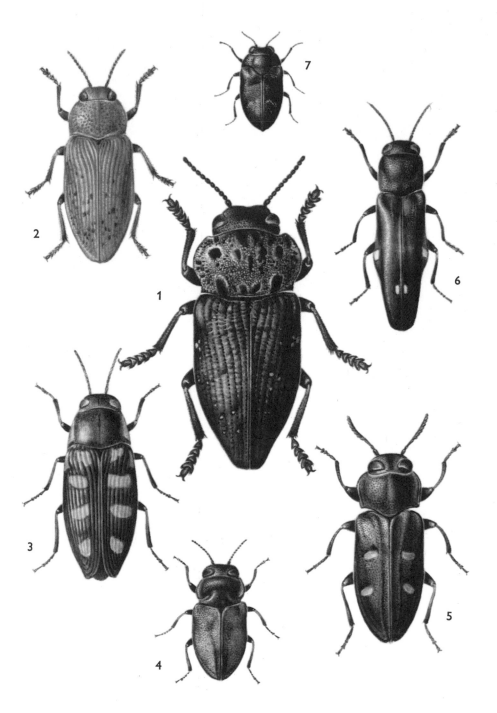

Family: **Dryopidae**

1. *Dryops auriculatus* Geoffr. 4.5—5.2 mm. Lives in stagnant water where it crawls on aquatic vegetation. Distribution: most of Europe, from the western Balkans north to Scandinavia; absent from Greece and Ireland.

Family: **Heteroceridae**

2. *Heterocerus parallelus* Kryn. 5—7.5 mm. Largest member of the whole family. Resembles several other species in shape and general colour and the beetles are very difficult to tell apart. Lives in moist banks of streams and rivers. Distribution: central and southern Europe, Siberia.

Family: **Water-Scavenger Beetles — Hydrophilidae**

3. *Helophorus minutus* Rey. 2.5—3.8 mm. Lives in stagnant water — ponds, springs, and transient puddles — where it is generally plentiful. Distribution: much of Europe, Siberia, north Africa.

4. Great Silver Beetle — *Hydrous piceus* L. 34—47 mm. Largest member of the family. On the underside the metathorax is prolonged into a needle-sharp spine with which it was thought to kill young fish, being mistakenly regarded as a predator. In reality it is quite harmless. It inhabits still water, ponds, forest pools or the dead-end branches of rivers where it feeds on aquatic vegetation. Like other aquatic beetles, it must come up for air. Unlike the predacious diving-beetles it obtains air by coming up head-first and using its short, club-shaped antennae to lead air down to the spiracles. Female is known for her care of the eggs, for which she makes a silk-like case. First of all she seeks out a leaf floating on the water's surface. Then she spins a spacious case of fine fibres round the leaf and her abdomen. In this she deposits about 50 eggs, closes the case and makes in it a small upright chimney. Larvae live in water and, unlike the adults, are predacious. They feed chiefly on small molluscs and Ostracoda. When fully grown they climb out of the water and bury themselves in the ground where they pupate. This beetle was still plentiful several decades ago, but it was persecuted as a 'pest' and exterminated so that now it is rare or even extinct in many regions. In some countries it is protected by law. Distribution: practically the entire Palearctic — extends to northern India and Pakistan.

5. *Hydrophilus caraboides* L. 14—18 mm. A faithful, smaller copy of the great silver beetle. Common in stagnant water, including small ponds with abundant vegetation. Distribution: the entire Palearctic.

6. *Sphaeridium scarabaeoides* L. 5.7 mm. Habits entirely different from those of many other water-scavenger beetles in that it is terrestrial. It seeks fresh cow dung in which it is sometimes found in large numbers. Easily recognized by the red-yellow spots on the elytra. Distribution: the entire Palearctic, Nearctic.

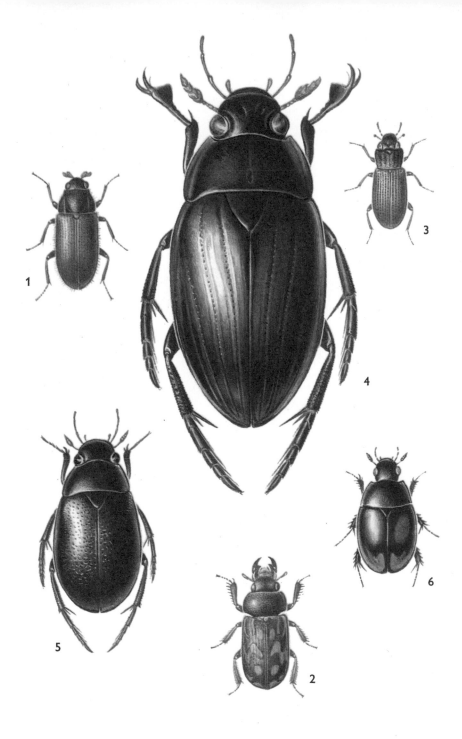

## Family: **Dermestidae**

**1.** Larder Beetle — *Dermestes lardarius* L. 7—9.5 mm. Cannot be mistaken for any other member of this family. Over the years it has become man's associate and lives in his dwellings. Larvae damage all kinds of material, ranging from fabrics to specimens in zoological and entomological collections, but especially fond of hides and dried meat. Occasionally found also in dove-cotes, the nests of other birds and in beehives. Otherwise it tends to be rare in the wild. Distribution: cosmopolitan. Introduced by man to regions where it was previously non-existent.

**2.** *Dermestes murinus* L. 7—9 mm. Body covered with fine black and grey-blue hairs. Abundant throughout its range. Distribution: the Palearctic.

**3.** *Attagenus pellio* L. 4—5.5 mm. An associate of man, in whose dwellings it generally lives. Larva has a long tail at the tip of the abdomen. Damages furs, fabrics and zoological collections. Adult beetles often appear in houses early in spring, later common on flowering blackthorn, hawthorn, fruit trees, etc. Distribution: practically worldwide.

**4.** Carpet Beetle — *Anthrenus scrophulariae* L. 3—4.5 mm. Adult is harmless but the 'woolly' larva is a notorious household pest. It damages fabrics, furs, carpets, feathers and also nature collections. Beetles may be found in households practically the whole year round. Distribution: most of Europe, Middle East, North America, Australasia, etc.

**5.** *Anthrenus verbasci* L. 1.8—3.2 mm. Serious pest of nature collections and fabrics. The damage caused by the larvae to collections of Lepidoptera and Coleoptera may be such that all that remains of the specimens are mounds of dust and pins with only data labels left. Distribution: introduced to practically all parts of the world with insect collections and other commodities.

## Family: **Nosodendridae**

**6.** *Nosodendron fasciculare* Oliv. 4—4.5 mm. Sole representative of this family. Found on the injured parts of hardwood trees where the sap oozes. Favours oaks and elms. Distribution: central Europe.

## Family: **Pill Beetles — Byrrhidae**

**7.** *Byrrhus pilula* L. 7.5—11 mm. A common and striking beetle found on forest and field paths. As soon as danger threatens, it withdraws the legs and antennae and feigns death. Distribution: the Palearctic.

## Family: **Byturidae**

**8.** Raspberry Beetle — *Byturus tomentosus* F. 3.2—4 mm. Found on blossoms of Rosaceae, chiefly raspberry and blackberry. Better known than the inconspicuous beetle is the larva which lives in the fruit of the raspberry (less often in blackberries) and is commonly known as the raspberry fruit-worm. Distribution: much of the Palearctic, except the north.

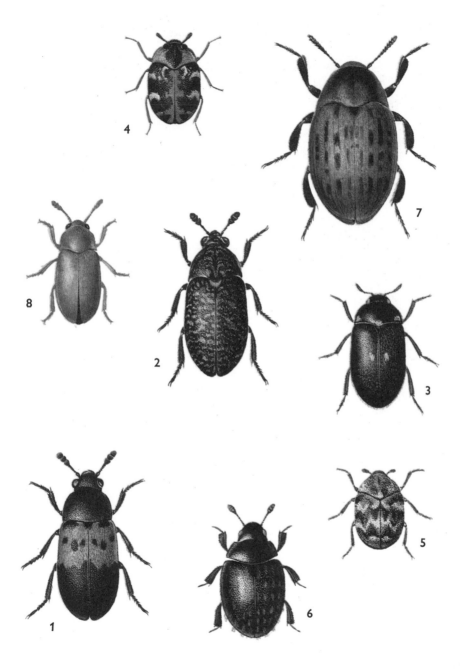

Family: **Nitidulidae**

**1.** *Meligethes aeneus* F. 1.5—2.7 mm. Emerges from its winter shelter in early spring and visits cinquefoil, colts-foot, marsh marigold and other spring flowers; later feeds on the tender leaves and buds of the rape. Eggs are laid in large buds. Larvae feed on pollen in flowers and in buds. When fully grown they drop to the ground and pupate just below the surface. Causes damage in some regions. Abundant from lowlands to mountains. Distribution: the entire Palearctic, North America.

**2.** *Pocadius ferrugineus* F. 2.8—4.5 mm. Generally found in puffballs of the genus *Lycoperdon, Bovista* and others, in which the larval stage is also passed. Sometimes inhabits also other toadstools and bracket fungi. Often occurs together with other related species. Distribution: Europe (far into the north), the Caucasus.

**3.** *Glischrochilus quadripustulatus* L. 3—6.5 mm. Usually occurs under the bark of coniferous trees, where it hunts bark beetles. Found also under the bark of certain deciduous trees, as well as on wounded spots oozing sweet juices. Distribution: Europe (from northern Balkans far to the north), Siberia.

**4.** *Pityophagus ferrugineus* L. 4—6.5 mm. Lives under the bark of coniferous trees. Hunts bark beetles and is therefore beneficial to forest management. Distribution: Europe (chiefly central and northern parts, in the south only in the northern Balkans, northern Spain and Italy), the Caucasus.

Family: **Rhizophagidae**

**5.** *Rhizophagus bipustulatus* F. 2.3—3.5 mm. Lives in large numbers under the bark of beech, oak, poplar and other deciduous trees, sometimes also conifers, often in spots covered with mould. Hunts bark beetles and other insects that live under bark. Distribution: Europe except northernmost parts, the Caucasus, Asia Minor, north Africa.

Family: **Cucujidae**

**6.** Merchant Grain Beetle — *Oryzaephilus mercator* Fauvel 2.5—3.5 mm. Introduced with merchandise. Lives in warehouses, where it is a pest of grain and other dried food materials. Often found in mills, shops and new buildings. Distribution: worldwide.

**7.** *Uleiota planata* L. 4.5—5.5 mm. Distinguished from other members of the family by the extremely long, filiform antennae and delicate sculpturing of the elytra and scutum. When danger threatens it feigns death, leaving the antennae pointing forward parallel to each other. Lives mostly under the bark of deciduous trees (oak, beech, elm, etc.), sometimes also of pine. Distribution: chiefly the southern part of the Palearctic.

**8.** *Cucujus cinnaberinus* Scop. 11—15 mm. An exception amongst the members of this family with its bright colouring and large size. Lives under the decaying bark of deciduous trees, mainly elm, oak, beech, sometimes also conifers. Generally a rare species found mostly in northern Europe and sporadically in central Europe (Bavaria, Slovakia and elsewhere).

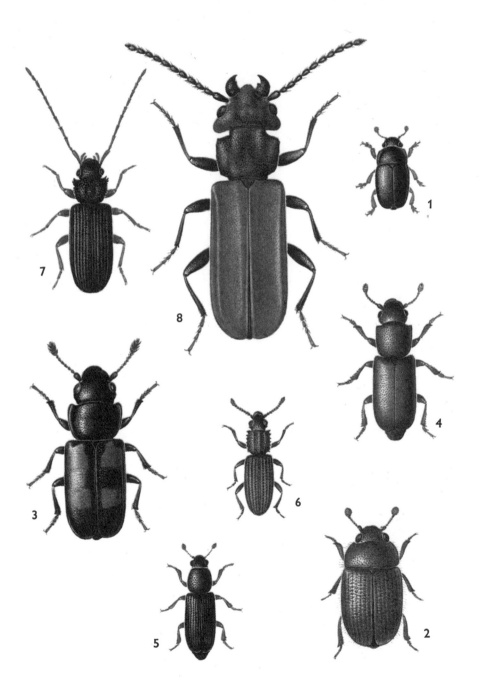

Family: **Erotylidae**

1. *Triplax aenea* Schall. 3.2 — 4.1 mm. Lives on tree fungi in which the larvae also develop. Often occurs in greater numbers. Hides under the old, mouldy bark of trees and stumps. Adults are abroad from June to July, after which they hide away to hibernate. Distribution: Europe (in the Mediterranean region mostly in the mountains), the Caucasus, Siberia, Japan.

Family: **Shining Flower Beetles — Phalacridae**

2. *Olibrus aeneus* F. 2.5 — 2.8 mm. Found in summer on flowering chamomile *(Matricaria chamomilla)*, in which the larval stage is also passed. Pupation, however, usually takes place in the ground. The beetle is locally very abundant. Distribution: Europe (chiefly central and northern, as far as Lapland), northern Italy, Siberia.

Family: **Lathridiidae**

3. *Cartodere filum* Aubé 1.3 — 1.4 mm. Occurs on mouldy vegetable matter, in old herbaria, in stables in mouldy straw, hay, in dried herbs and in insect collections. Generally lives in the neighbourhood of man. A harmless beetle; its presence in entomological boxes is a sign of mould! Distribution: Europe, north Africa, North and Central America.

Family: **Mycetophagidae**

4. *Mycetophagus atomarius* F. 4 — 4.5 mm. Favours tree fungi, especially those on beech, but found also in decaying vegetable material attacked by moulds. Distribution: All Europe, but only at higher elevations in the south.

5. *Typhaea stercorea* L. 2.5 — 3 mm. Found throughout the year on decaying vegetable material attacked by moulds, e. g. straw, wood, leaves, as well as in storehouses where it feeds on moulds. Not regarded as a pest. A synanthropic species. Distribution: the entire Palearctic.

Family: **Colydiidae**

6. *Bitoma crenata* F. 2.6 — 3.5 mm. Occurs under the bark of old stumps where it hunts mites and various larvae, chiefly of bark-beetles. Distribution: the entire Palearctic; both in lowlands and mountains.

7. *Colydium filiforme* F. 5 — 6 mm. Found under rotting bark, where it hunts bark-beetles. Not plentiful. Distribution: practically all Europe (absent in the north), the Caucasus, Asia Minor, north Africa.

Family: **Endomychidae**

8. *Endomychus coccineus* L. 4 — 6 mm. Found under mouldy bark and in tree fungi from spring till autumn, generally on beech or elm. Usually occurs in groups. Distribution: all Europe (in the south only at higher elevations).

9. *Mycetina cruciata* Schall. 3.8 — 4.5 mm. Found in damp places under the mouldy bark of old stumps and tree trunks or in tree fungi. Distribution: Europe (mainly central and southern parts, in the north only as far as southern Scandinavia), the Caucasus.

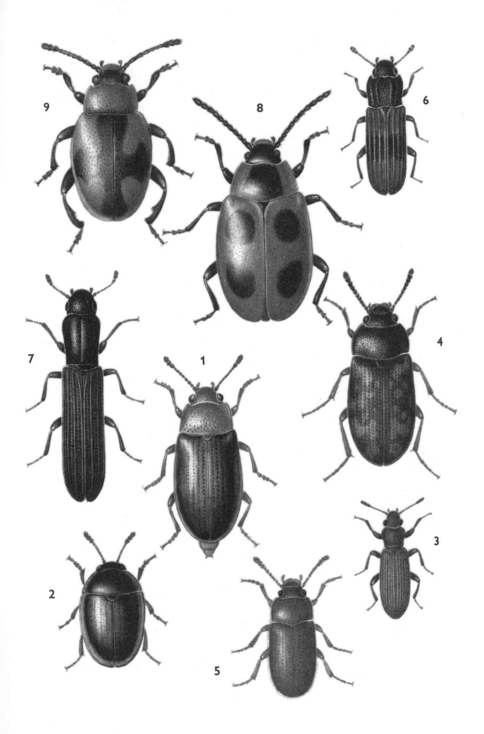

Family: **Ladybirds — Coccinellidae**

**1.** *Hyperaspis campestris* Herbst 2 — 3.5 mm. Thermophilous, favours thickets at the edges of woods and in forest stands. Feeds on aphids and scale-insects and their eggs. In the subtropical zone of the U.S.S.R. (Georgia etc.) it is used in the biological control of *Chloropulvinaria floccifera*. Distribution: Europe (except the northern part), the Caucasus, Transcaucasia, Asia Minor.

**2.** *Hippodamia tredecimpunctata* L. 4.5 — 7 mm. Found along water courses and on marsh plants. Adults hibernate. Abroad early in spring, but most plentiful in late summer. Feeds on aphids on aquatic and marsh plants. Distribution: much of the Palearctic.

**3, 3a.** Two-spotted Ladybird — *Adalia bipunctata* L. 3.5 — 5.5 mm. Very variable in colour. Typical individuals have orange elytra with a round or irregularly shaped black spot on each. In some, however, the black colour prevails. Adults hibernate, generally under the bark of trees, among mosses, under stones and often even in man's dwellings. The new generation is most plentiful in July. Because the beetles are very common in the wild and feed on various aphids, they are very important in the control of these pests. Distribution: most of the Palearctic; introduced to North America.

**4, 4a, 4b.** Seven-spotted Ladybird — *Coccinella septempunctata* L. 5.5 — 8 mm. Generally orange with seven black spots on the elytra. However, the spots are very variable in size and shape; often they merge to form bands or are absent altogether. Adults hibernate, usually in groups, under stones or bark, in tufts of grass, mosses etc. In early spring they appear in warm hedgerows from lowland to high mountain elevations. The yellow eggs are deposited on leaves. Larvae (4 b) are elongate, grey-blue with black and yellow spots and predacious — as are the adults. They feed on aphids and various species of coccids. When fully grown the larva attaches itself to a leaf by its abdomen and pupates. Pupa (4 a) is orange with black spots and stripes. Adult emerges after about a week. There is only one generation a year. Hibernating beetles are always a lighter and more yellow colour than the adults of the summer generation, which have bright red elytra. The seven-spotted ladybird is one of the best known of the beneficial species and is very important as a predator of aphids and coccids in fields, gardens and forests. Distribution: all Europe (far to the north), Asia, north Africa.

**5.** Fourteen-spotted Ladybird — *Coccinula quatuordecimpustulata* L. 3 — 4 mm. Sometimes variable to such a degree that there are no black spots and the yellow colour prevails. The spots may also merge. Beetle is found at the edges of forests, on heaths, fields and meadows. Distribution: almost all Europe except the far north, Asia Minor, Siberia, Japan. Absent from British Isles.

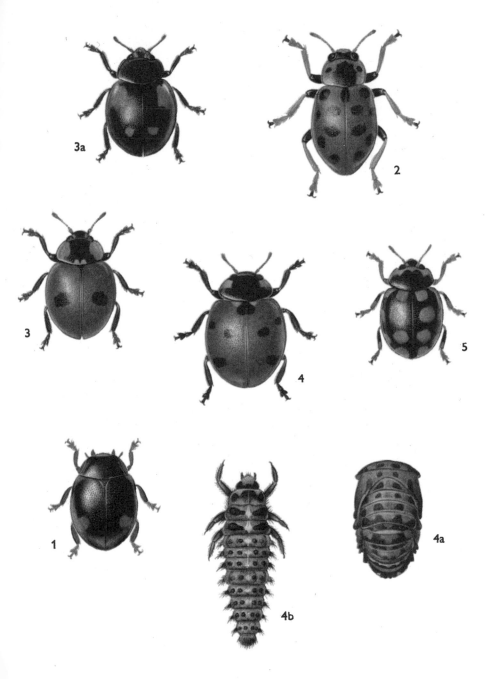

## Family: **Coccinellidae**

**1.** *Synharmonia conglobata* L. 3.5—5 mm. The black spots on the elytra are extremely variable in shape and number. Both adults and larvae hunt aphids, usually on poplars but also on fruit trees and certain conifers. Found in lowlands and foothills. Distribution: much of the Palearctic; in Europe more plentiful in warmer situations; its numbers decrease northwards and it is absent from Great Britain and Norway.

**2.** *Propylaea quatuordecimpunctata* L. 3.5—4.5 mm. Very common in varied localities — in fields, meadows and gardens — where it hunts aphids from spring till autumn. Adults hibernate in similar places to other species. Distribution: the Palearctic; in Europe its range extends from the south far to the north (Lapland, Norway).

**3.** Eyed Ladybird — *Anatis ocellata* L. 8—9 mm. One of the largest of the ladybirds. Just as variable as other species in size and colour of the spots. Spots sometimes merge. Very beneficial. Found mostly in coniferous forests. Appears early in spring. Hunts various species of aphids on spruce, pine and larch. Occurs from lowland to mountain elevations. The larva, greyish with black and yellow spots, is likewise predacious. Distribution: all Europe, the Caucasus, Siberia as far as Japan. Introduced to North America to control pests.

**4.** *Thea vigintiduopunctata* L. 3—4.5 mm. Very common in sunny situations from lowlands to mountains (elevation of c. 1,000 metres). Distribution: southern parts of the Palearctic. Common in England: absent from Scotland.

**5.** *Calvia decemguttata* L. 5—6.5 mm. Found chiefly in moist localities. Distribution: local; in some places plentiful, elsewhere rare. Central and southern Europe, southern Siberia, Japan.

**6.** *Calvia quatuordecimguttata* L. 4.5—6 mm. Often occurs abundantly in young thickets at the edges of forests. Distribution: Europe (in the south only in the mountains), Siberia, North America.

**7.** *Chilocorus renipustulatus* Scr. 3—4 mm. Well-known enemy of various coccids. Distinguished by two circular red spots on the black elytra. The related *Ch. bipustulatus* also has two spots of the same colour, but these are elongate. The head is black (that of *Ch. bipustulatus* is red or brown). Distribution: much of the Palearctic.

**8.** *Exochomus quadripustulatus* L. 3—5 mm. May be seen early in spring when it emerges from its winter shelters. Occurs on trees infested by various coccids on which it feeds. Commonly found amongst spring colonies of *Pseudochermes fraxini* on the trunks and branches of ash. A single beetle captures some 30 coccids a day; the larva consumes even more. Distribution: almost all Europe, but not the far north.

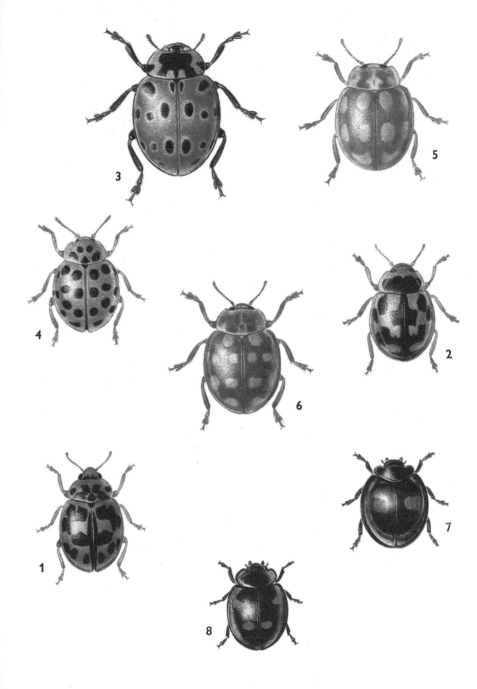

## Family: Cisidae

**1.** *Cis boleti* Scop. 2.8 — 3.5 mm. Common on bracket fungus (chiefly of the genus *Trametes*). Distribution: the entire Palearctic, in Europe far to the north.

## Family: Bostrychidae

**2.** *Bostrychus capucinus* L. 8 — 14 mm. In former times frequently classed as a pest of hard wood, nowadays it is a rarer species. Larvae found under the bark of stumps and decaying trunks of oak, beech and, in southern Europe, also other deciduous trees. Distribution: Europe (chiefly central and southern; in the north only in southern Scandinavia), the Caucasus, Asia Minor, Middle East, Siberia, China.

## Family: Anobiidae

**3.** *Hedobia imperialis* L. 3.5 — 5.5 mm. Distinguished from other dark species by its more striking coloration. Larvae live in branches and slender trunks of beech, hornbeam, oak and other deciduous trees, also in ivy. They excavate tunnels between the wood and bark. They pupate in autumn and the newly emerged adult hibernates. It is on the wing early in spring. Distribution: practically all Europe except the north.

**4.** Woodworm or Furniture Beetle — *Anobium punctatum* Deg. 3 — 5 mm. One of several species that occur in the vicinity of man. Infests chiefly timber and furniture, rafters, antiques, etc. Larvae bore tunnels in wood. Beetles which emerge from the pupae, likewise in wood, cast out mounds of fine wood shavings as they climb out. Development takes one year, sometimes more. A serious pest. Distribution: all Europe, the Caucasus, North America, Australia.

## Family: Spider Beetles — Ptinidae

**5.** *Ptinus fur* L. 2 — 4.3 mm. Quite variable in colour. Marked differences also between the male and female. Generally found in man's dwellings, mostly country privies, flats, stables; also in bird nests. If it occurs in large numbers in stored provisions it may be regarded a pest. Distribution: the entire Palearctic, North America.

## Family: Oedemeridae

**6.** *Oedemera podagrariae* L. 8 — 13 mm. Elytra diverge at the back to reveal the folded membranous wings underneath. Males have very stout femora. Adults are found on flowers from June to July. Distribution: most of Europe, Asia Minor, the Caucasus.

## Family: Cardinal Beetles — Pyrochroidae

**7.** *Pyrochroa coccinea* L. 14 — 15 mm. Commonest member of this small family. Notable for its magnificent colouring. Found from May onwards on trunks of felled trees and on flowers. The long and extremely flat larva lives under the bark of stumps. Distribution: western and central Europe, from the northern regions of southern Europe to southern Scandinavia.

## Family: Anthicidae

**8.** *Anthicus flavipes* Panz. 1.7 — 2.2 mm. Lives in decaying vegetable material but is not plentiful. Distribution: chiefly central and northern Europe.

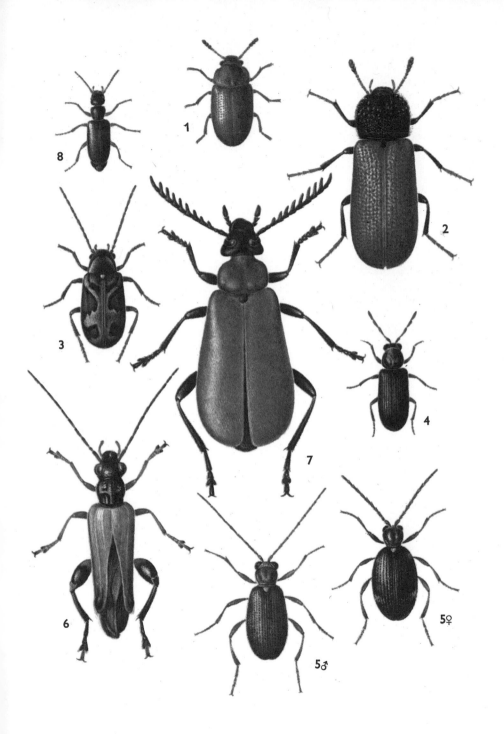

## Family: Oil Beetles — Meloidae

**1.** *Meloë violaceus* Marsh. 10—32 mm. Like other related species, undergoes an unusual and complicated development. Eggs, of which large numbers are laid, hatch into tiny larvae called triungulins. These crawl up on flowers and await the arrival of a solitary bee. If they are carried to the bee's nest they continue to develop, otherwise they die. Between the larval and pupal stage there are several other stages, mainly the pre-pupa followed by a further stage which changes into the pupa. For this reason the metamorphosis of oil beetles is called hypermetamorphosis. Distribution: throughout Europe, mostly in foothill and mountain regions, Siberia.

**2.** Spanish Fly — *Lytta vesicatoria* L. 12—21 mm. Found mostly from June to July, chiefly on ash, lilac, privet and other plants on the leaves of which it feeds. Has a penetrating, unpleasant smell. Eggs are deposited near the nests of solitary bees and the young larvae (triungulins) make their way into the nest where they undergo a complex metamorphosis. Of all Meloidae, the Spanish Fly contains the greatest quantity of the toxic substance cantharidin, used as a poison and as medicine by doctors in ancient times as well as during the Renaissance. Cantharidin is a complex chemical substance with an unpleasant effect on kidney function. Distribution: Europe (chiefly central and southern), Siberia, North America (introduced).

## Family: Rhipiphoridae

**3.** *Metoecus paradoxus* L. 8—12 mm. Development takes place in the nests of wasps *(Vespa vulgaris)*, where the young beetles devour the wasp grubs. Adults emerge in August to September. Rare in the wild. Distribution: central and western Europe.

## Family: Mordellidae

**4.** *Variimorda fasciata* F. 6—9 mm. Found on flowers where its prolonged abdomen is in continuous motion. Distribution: Europe, the Caucasus, Asia Minor, Iran, etc.

## Family: Lagriidae

**5.** *Lagria hirta* L. 7—10 mm. Occurs abundantly from June sometimes until September on flowers in damp meadows and along streams from lowland to mountain elevations. Larvae live under decaying leaves. Distribution: Europe, Siberia.

## Family: Darkling Beetles — Tenebrionidae

**6.** *Blaps mortisaga* L. 20—31 mm. Occurs in the neighbourhood of man, in cellars, sheds and stables. Feeds on vegetable matter. Distribution: Europe, the Caucasus, Transcaucasia, Asia Minor, Middle East (Iraq, Iran) and elsewhere.

**7.** *Diaperis boleti* L. 6—8 mm. Lives in soft tree fungi. Distribution: Europe, the Caucasus, Asia Minor, Siberia, north Africa.

**8.** *Tenebrio molitor* L. 15 mm. Lives in flour. Well-known is its larva, the 'mealworm', used as food for birds and pet animals. Distribution: cosmopolitan.

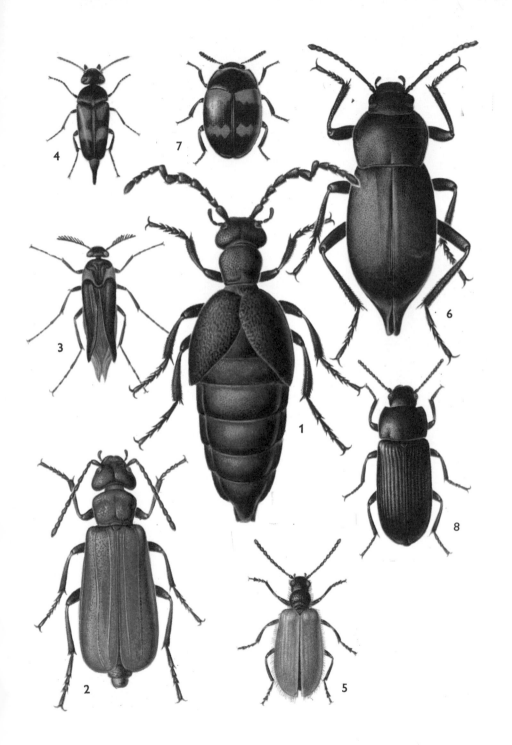

## Family: **Stag-beetles — Lucanidae**

**1.** Stag Beetle — *Lucanus cervus* L. Distinguished by marked differences between male and female. Male, reaching 75 mm in length with its mandibles, is one of the largest beetles in Europe. The mandibles, however, are not used for biting but as weapons in jousts for the female. In some individuals they are not so developed (the form *capreolus*). Beetles feed on sweet fermenting juices oozing from wounded oaks. One may often find several beetles at one such spot. Beetles fly in the late afternoon and evening. Female is smaller, measuring 30 — 45 mm in length. Development takes at least three, but frequently as much as five years. Eggs are laid in stumps and trunks of old oaks, sometimes also beeches, elms and others. Larvae have huge mandibles with which they chew up the wood. They reach 10 cm in length and make a hard cradle about themselves before changing into the pupa. The sex of the future adult can be determined by the general apperance of the pupa. The adult emerges in the autumn but it hibernates and does not appear in the wild until June or the first days of July. Distribution: most of Europe. In some countries it is protected by law.

**2.** *Sinodendron cylindricum* L. 12 — 16 mm. Likewise marked sexual dimorphism. Male has a distinct recurved 'horn' on the head, whereas the female has only a small bump at this spot. Body is cylindrical. Lives in hardwood forests, most commonly in foothills and mountains. Larvae generally found in decaying beech stumps and old logs, sometimes also in other deciduous trees. Adults occur from June to July, being generally found under bark and beneath logs. Distribution: from western Europe to Siberia.

**3.** *Systenocerus caraboides* L. 10 — 14 mm. Differs in colouring from other European stag-beetles, which are predominantly brown to black whereas this one may be green or blue, often even blue-green, blue-violet to blue-black. Legs are generally black but in some specimens may be reddish-brown. Beetles are on the wing on sunny days in early spring. Found in hardwood forests from lowland to mountain elevations and quite abundant in some regions. Feed on tender leaves and buds. Larvae live mostly in oak and beech, sometimes also in other deciduous trees. Distribution: western and central Europe. Absent from British Isles.

**4.** *Dorcus parallelopipedus* L. 18 — 32 mm. Found on deciduous trees, mostly oak and beech. Larvae develop in decaying stumps, logs and trunks of old diseased oak, beech, ash, elm, willow, lime, sometimes also fruit, pine and larch trees. When fully grown they measure about 20 mm and are a glossy yellow. Beetles are on the wing in the late afternoon, sometimes as early as late April but mostly from late May to June. Several geographical races exist. Common in places, but extinct in some. Distribution: much of Europe, Asia Minor, Middle East.

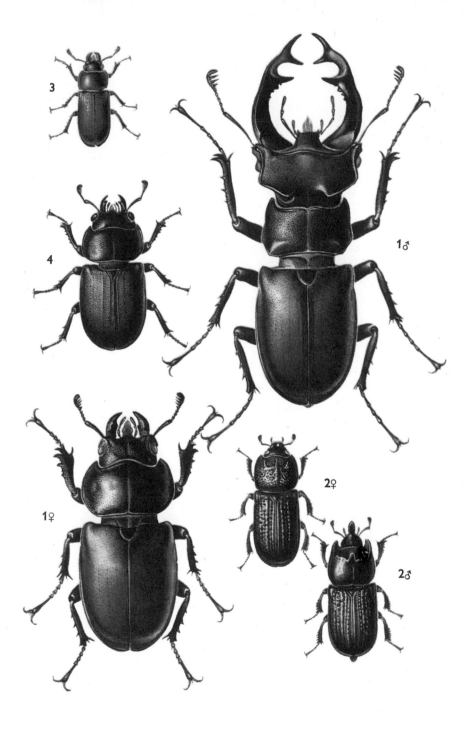

Family: **Scarabaeidae**

**1.** *Oryctes nasicornis* L. 25 — 40 mm. Marked sexual dimorphism. Male has a recurved 'horn on the head and on the scutum a hollow topped by a high comb. The female has only a triangular plate instead of a horn on the head. Originally an inhabitant of old oak stands, the beetle is gradually making its way into the neighbourhood of man's dwellings and the larvae may be found in compost heaps and frames. In forests, development takes place in old stumps of deciduous trees (beech, oak, etc.) and lasts two to three years. Fully grown larva measures up to 120 mm. It pupates in a large oval chamber. Beetles are on the wing at dusk in spring and summer, remaining hidden during the day. Distribution: almost all Europe (absent from British Isles), Asia Minor, Middle East, part of central Asia, north Africa.

**2.** *Trichius fasciatus* L. 9 — 12 mm. Patterning on the elytra shows marked variability. Found in foothill regions on blossoms of rose, hawthorn, spiraea, chrysanthemum and other plants, favouring ones with white blossoms. Larvae live in the rotting wood of old deciduous tree stumps. Development takes two years. Distribution: almost all Europe (in southern regions higher up in the mountains), the Caucasus.

**3.** Rose Chafer — *Cetonia aurata* L. 14 — 20 mm. Found on sunny days from mid-May on flowering rose, hawthorn, elder, etc. It flies with the elytra folded. Larvae favour rotting wood of beech stumps and garden compost heaps, occasionally also ants' nests (the latter are regularly inhabited by the larvae of the closely related *Potosia cuprea*). Development takes one year. Distribution: Europe, Asia Minor, Middle East, Siberia.

**4.** *Epicometis hirta* Poda 8 — 11 mm. Visits spring blossoms from as early as April. Common on the flower heads of wild chrysanthemum (ox-eye daisy) and hawkweed. Larva lives underground and feeds on old roots. Distribution: Europe, Asia Minor, Middle East, North America (introduced).

**5.** *Polyphylla fullo* F. 25 — 36 mm. Largest and most interestingly coloured of the European chafers. Fan on the male's antenna is composed of seven long lamellae, the female's of only five short ones. Beetles are on the wing in July from dusk until late at night in pine woods and their vicinity. Eggs are laid in sandy soil at the edges of forests and in vineyards. Larvae feed on the roots of various grasses, also those of the grapevine. Development generally takes four, but sometimes as much as five, years. This chafer is still locally abundant in Europe. Distribution: most of Europe (absent from British Isles), in the east as far as the lower Volga.

**6.** Cockchafer or Maybug — *Melolontha melolontha* L. 20 — 30 mm. Commonest of the European chafers; very destructive to trees in places. Male best distinguished from female by the antennae which have large fans composed of seven lamellae whereas those of the female are small with only six lamellae. Larvae (grubs) live underground and feed on plant roots. In periods of drought and before onset of winter they burrow deeper in the ground. Development takes two to three years, depending on local conditions. Adult hatches in autumn but remains in the ground and hibernates. Distribution: most of Europe (absent from Spain, southern Italy and elsewhere).

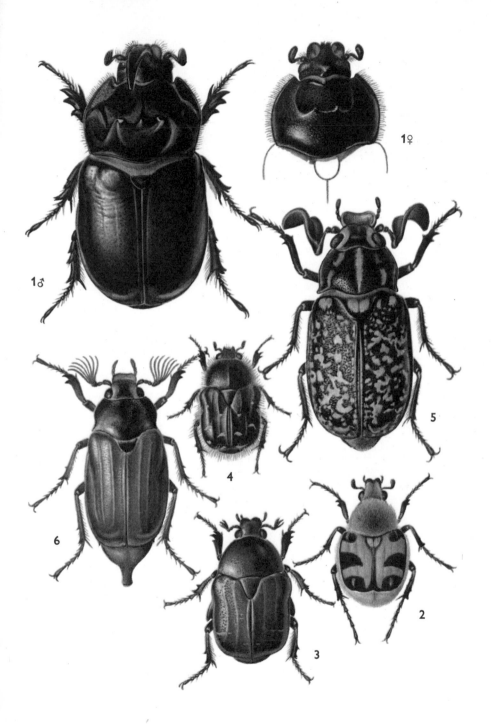

Family: **Scarabaeidae**

**1.** Summer Chafer — *Amphimallon solstitialis* L. 14—18 mm. On the wing on July evenings, often in large numbers. Flies around treetops, in meadows, at the edges of forests and in parks from lowland to mountain elevations. Eggs are laid in the ground. Development takes three years. Distribution: the Palearctic.

**2.** Garden Chafer — *Phyllopertha horticola* L. 8—11 mm. Most plentiful in June when it visits rose blossoms, rests on foliage and flies around mounds of hay in meadows and gardens. Larva develops underground. Development takes two to three years. Distribution: from Europe to Mongolia.

**3.** *Aphodius fimetarius* L. 5—8 mm. Plentiful from March on. In April the female lays about 30 eggs in partly dried horse or cattle dung. Fully grown larva burrows in the ground where it pupates. Distribution: Eurasia, north Africa, North America.

**4.** *Aphodius rufipes* L. 10—13 mm. One of the largest and commonest members of the whole group, breeding in the dung of various herbivores. Common from spring till autumn. Distribution: Europe, eastern Asia, south Africa, North and South America.

**5.** Lousy Watchman — *Geotrupes stercorarius* L. 16—25 mm. Like related species it is noted for its care of the offspring. The adult pair prepares a nest in the autumn, first of all excavating a shaft about 50 cm long to which the female adds several side shafts about 20 cm long and broadened at the end to form a chamber. The entire side-shaft is filled with excrement, with only a small space at the end for the egg. Then the opening is plugged with soil. The larva is thus supplied with ample food. It takes about two years to mature, but the adult beetle does not emerge from the ground until about three years after the egg was laid. Distribution: all Europe, Siberia, Japan.

**6.** *Geotrupes vernalis* L. 12—20 mm. Prepares a nest for its offspring, but of quite a different kind from that of previous species. First it excavates a funnel-shaped pit about 5 cm deep and at the bottom several horizontal tunnels about 20 cm long which are then filled with excrement. These serve as food stores. Only then do the beetles copulate, after which they prepare the chamber for the egg about 50 cm below the edge of the pit. A single egg is deposited in the chamber. The entrance is then plugged with excrement. Distribution: Europe, Asia Minor.

**7.** *Onthophagus fracticornis* Preyssl. 5—9 mm. Lives in excrement of any kind. Also makes preparations for the offspring, excavating several branched tunnels at a depth of 15—20 cm, each of which ends in an egg-shaped chamber. This the female fills with fine bits of excrement before depositing the egg, which hatches after about a week into a white larva. Distribution: all Europe, north Africa.

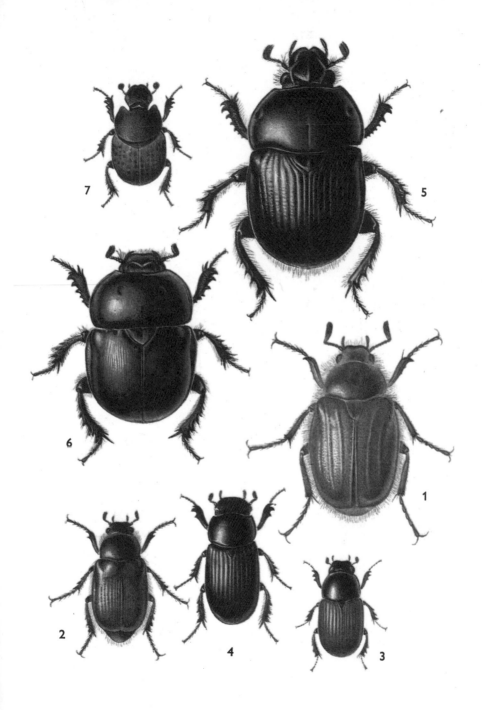

Family: **Long-horned Beetles** — **Cerambycidae**

1. *Ergates faber* L. 25 — 60 mm. One of the largest of the European cerambycids. Male and female differ in several respects: besides the length of the antennae, which in the male are longer than the body, there are differences in the colour, form and sculpturing of the scutum. Beetles are on the wing mainly in the evening and night from late summer till early autumn. Found in damp woods, where they also pass the larval stage. Female lays some 150 — 300 eggs on pine and other coniferous stumps, as well as in rotting and fresh wood. Larvae bore wide, irregular and crooked tunnels in sapwood. Larval stage lasts about four years. Fully grown larva is flat and measures about 80 mm. It burrows deep into the wood before changing into a pupa. Nowadays the larvae cause insignificant damage in forests for the species is becoming increasingly rarer, with the rapid disappearance of suitable situations where it can undergo its several-year development undisturbed. Distribution: Europe, Asia Minor, Middle East, north Africa.

2. *Megopis scabricornis* Scop. 29 — 50 mm. Distinguished by the long and sculptured third antennal segment. Male's antennae are slightly longer than the body, the female's extend only beyond the halfway mark. Characteristic, also, are the three to four ridges on the elytra. Beetles are on the wing at dusk, remaining concealed under bark during the day. They occur from July to August, sometimes even in September, depending on the locality. Larvae develop in deciduous trees, chiefly oak and beech, poplar, mulberry, lime, pear, walnut, willow etc. Distribution: southern and central Europe, the Caucasus, Asia Minor, Middle East, Iran. In some areas it is still a common species; in others, however, it has already become a rarity.

3. *Tragosoma depsarium* L. 15 — 31 mm. Differences in the length of the male's and female's antennae are much less marked than in the preceding species. The male's are about two-thirds as long as the elytra, the female's about half their length. Beetles fly at dusk from July to August in coniferous forests in mountains. During the day they hide under bark or fallen trunks, in stacked timber, etc. Eggs are deposited in the broken or uprooted and diseased trunks of spruce, pine and fir. This longhorn was never listed as a common, or more plentiful, species by older books, and nowadays it is a real rarity. It is one of the beetles that are becoming extinct in central Europe and may be seen generally only as an exhibit in large museum collections. Distribution: northern, central and southern Europe, the European part of the U.S.S.R., Siberia, North America. Absent from the British Isles.

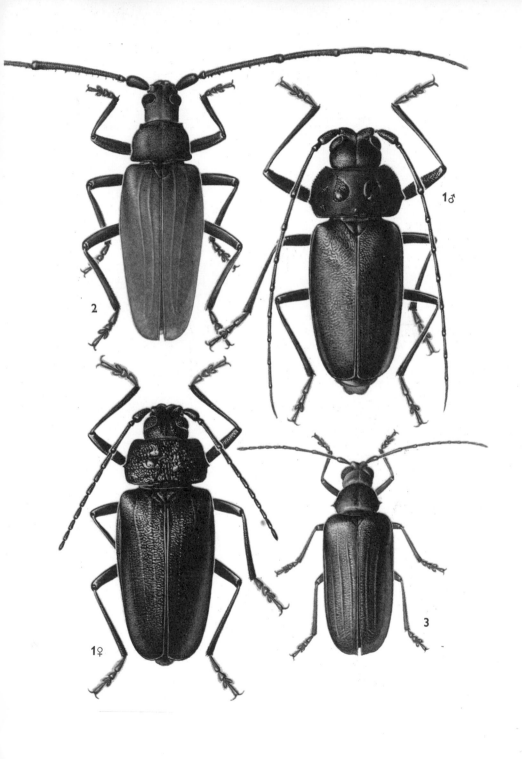

Family: **Cerambycidae**

1. *Prionus coriarius* L. 18—45 mm. Marked differences in the shape of the male and female antennae. Female's are eleven-jointed, comparatively slender and slightly serrate; male's are twelve-segmented, stouter and strongly serrate. Adults are on the wing in August at dusk in deciduous and coniferous forests. During the day they hide under bark and in stumps. They are a favoured food of various animals. Beetles emit piercing sounds by rubbing the margins of the elytra against the hind legs. Eggs are laid in the old stumps of deciduous and coniferous trees, where the larval stage is passed. Fully grown larva measures about 50 mm. Distribution: nearly all Europe, the Caucasus, Syria, Iran, western Siberia, north Africa.

2. *Rhagium inquisitor* L. 10—21 mm. Found mainly in coniferous forests from lowlands to mountains. Occurs chiefly from April to July on flowers and logs. Adults may be found as early as autumn in pupal cells under bark, where they remain for the winter. Distribution: Europe, western Siberia, North America.

3. *Gaurotes virginea* L. 9—12.5 mm. Several colour forms exist. Generally scutum is black and elytra blue or green, but these may also be violet or black and the scutum red, besides other combinations. Beetles found from May to July on flowering Umbelliferae from lowlands to mountains; more plentiful in mountains. Distribution: from western Europe across Siberia to Korea.

4. *Leptura rubra* L. 10—19 mm. Sexes markedly different. Male is more slender and pale yellow; female is stouter and orange. Antennae also differ in form. On the wing in midsummer, settling on flowers, felled tree trunks or stacked wood. Eggs are laid in the stumps of coniferous trees. Larvae bore long, zig-zag tunnels and aid in the decomposition of old wood. Development probably takes two years. Distribution: from western Europe to Siberia, north Africa.

5. *Strangalia maculata* Poda 14—20 mm. Elytra are yellow with black blotches and bands arranged in varying patterns. Common from May to August on various flowers. Larval stage is passed chiefly in deciduous but also in coniferous trees. Distribution: from Europe to Transcaucasia and the Middle East (Iran).

6. *Spondylis buprestoides* L. 12—24 mm. Quite different from the more typical cerambycids, the body being stout and cylindrical and the antennae short. Beetles fly in the evening from June to September in pine forests, hiding under logs or bark during the day. Larvae develop in old pine stumps, boring deep into the roots. They aid in the decomposition of old wood and may thus be regarded beneficial. Distribution: Europe, Asia Minor, Siberia, China, Japan.

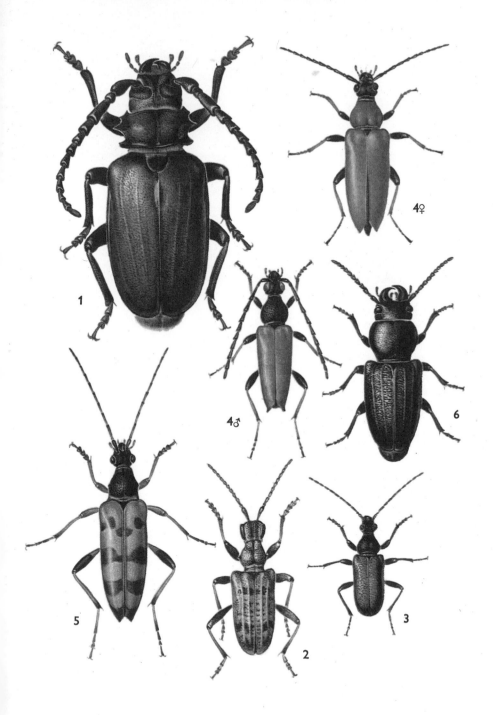

Family: **Cerambycidae**

**1.** *Criocephalus rusticus* L. 10—30 mm. Found in coniferous, chiefly pine, woods, where it flies in the evening and at night from July to August, occasionally even earlier. Larva lives under bark at first but later bores deeper into the wood. Distribution: Europe, Transcaucasia, across Siberia to Japan.

**3.** *Asemum striatum* L. 8—23 mm. Found chiefly in pine woods. On the wing from May to August. Larvae develop in the old stumps of pine, sometimes also larch or fir, trees. Adult bites its way out through an oval hole. Distribution: Europe, the Caucasus, Siberia, Japan.

**3.** *Tetropium castaneum* L. 9—18.5 mm. Commonest in spruce woods. Adults found from May to July. Eggs are laid under scales of bark. Larva lives in bark at first, later bores into the wood. When fully grown it excavates a chamber at a depth of 2—4 cm. Usually infests diseased trees often visited by woodpeckers which peck out the larvae. Distribution: all Europe, Siberia to Japan.

**4.** *Cerambyx cerdo* L. 24—53 mm. One of the largest European beetles. Occurs in old oak forests where it flies at dusk and at night. Beetles are fond of the sweet juices oozing from damaged trees. Larva lives in bark at first, later in the sapwood and phloem, and finally in the wood of old oaks, where it bores oval tunnels thick as a finger. When fully grown it measures 70—90 mm. It pupates in wood in a hook-shaped tunnel about 8 cm long. Beetle emerges in autumn but remains in the wood for the winter, flying out in June or July. Development takes three to five years. Distribution: most of Europe, but absent from British Isles; with the rapid disappearance of its original habitats, its numbers are also rapidly declining. It is protected by law in Czechoslovakia.

**5.** Musk Beetle — *Aromia moschata* L. 13—34 mm. Variable in colour. Elytra and scutum are usually green with a faint blue tint; sometimes the blue colour prevails, and some individuals are known with the elytra and scutum coloured purplish-red. Beetles fly from June to August, resting on flowers and felled wood. They have a strong musky smell. Locally abundant. Larvae prefer the living wood of willows, but sometimes may also be found in other deciduous trees, such as poplar and alder. Distribution: nearly all Europe, Siberia, Japan.

**6.** *Rosalia alpina* L. 15—38 mm. The grey-blue elytra have an extremely variable dark pattern. Found in foothill and mountain beech woods where they fly on sunny days; most numerous from June to August, sometimes still seen in September. Larva lives in old beech trees. Distribution: mostly central Europe, southern Scandinavia and southern Europe, Transcaucasia, Middle East. Protected by law in West Germany and Czechoslovakia.

**7.** House Longhorn — *Hylotrupes bajulus* L. 7—21 mm. Flies from mid-June to September at noon and in the afternoon in coniferous forests. Larva lives in the wood of conifers, often also in house timbers and furniture. Beetle is common in wooden constructions and in attics. Development takes an average of three to five years, but often much longer. Distribution: almost worldwide.

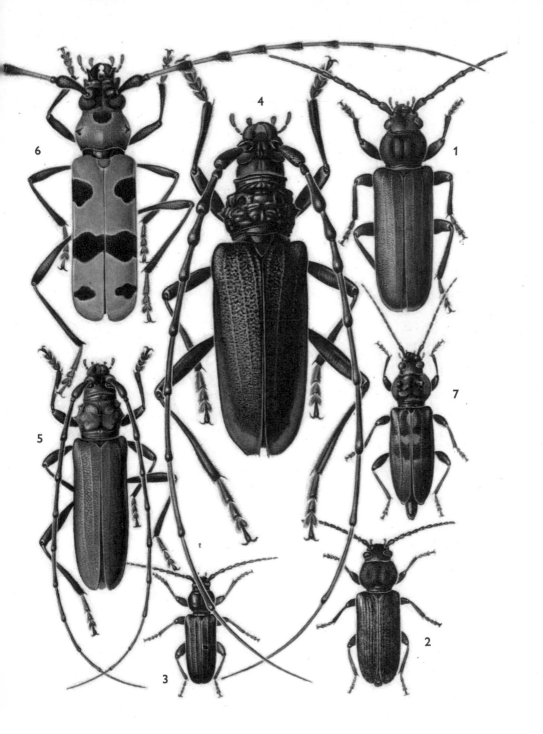

Family: **Cerambycidae**

**1.** *Callidium aeneum* Deg. 9 — 15 mm. Generally coloured bronze-green, but in some specimens the head and scutum may be green and the elytra yellow-red, or else blackish-brown and the elytra black. Found from May to July in deciduous and coniferous woods. Most plentiful at mountain elevations. Larva lives in dry wood of deciduous and coniferous trees, under the bark at first but later boring deeper into the wood prior to pupation. Distribution: most of Europe, Transcaucasia, Asia Minor, Middle East, Siberia.

**2.** *Pyrrhidium sanguineum* L. 8 — 12 mm. Body clothed with velvety-red hairs both above and below. A spring beetle, it may be found on felled logs, stacked wood and in sawmills from April to June. Larva lives and pupates in the wood of deciduous trees, mainly oak, beech and hornbeam. Distribution: central and southern Europe, the Caucasus, Asia Minor, Middle East (Syria, Iran), north Africa. Rare in British Isles.

**3.** *Phymatodes testaceus* L. 6 — 17 mm. Extremely variable in colour. Elytra may be yellowish, yellowish with a violet or blue shade, or entirely blue, violet or with a greenish tint. Scutum exhibits similar variability. Common in oak woods where it flies in June to July in the evening. Development lasts one year and takes place chiefly in oak trees, sometimes also in conifers. Beetles often hatch in warehouses where wood is stored. Distribution: Europe, the Caucasus, Transcaucasia, Asia Minor, Middle East, north Africa, North America.

**4.** *Plagionotus arcuatus* L. 6 — 20 mm. Colouring black-yellow but rather variable. It flies busily on sunny days in oak woods from May to June. Eggs are deposited in felled oak logs and in stacked wood with the bark still on. Larvae may feed also on other deciduous trees. They bore wide tunnels in the phloem, later into the wood where they pupate in spring. Distribution: Europe, Transcaucasia, Asia Minor, north Africa.

**5.** *Anaglyptus mysticus* L. 6 — 13 mm. As in other cerambycids, there is marked variability in the patterning of the elytra. Found from May to July in hardwood forests on various flowering plants, often on hawthorn. Distribution: central and southern Europe, including British Isles.

**6.** *Purpuricenus kaehleri* L. 9 — 21 mm. A rare species found in warm, sheltered localities where it flies mostly in June to July. Larva develops in deciduous trees, chiefly oak, but also in fruit trees. This beetle is continually declining in numbers and deserves to be protected. Distribution: southern Europe, southern part of central Europe, Transcaucasia, Iran.

**7.** *Dorcadion pedestre* Poda 11 — 17 mm. Differs from most European cerambycids both in the shape of the body and in habits, for the larva does not live in wood but in the roots of grasses. Beetles are very common in some regions, mainly in April to May. Of Eastern origin. Distribution: eastern part of central Europe, Balkans.

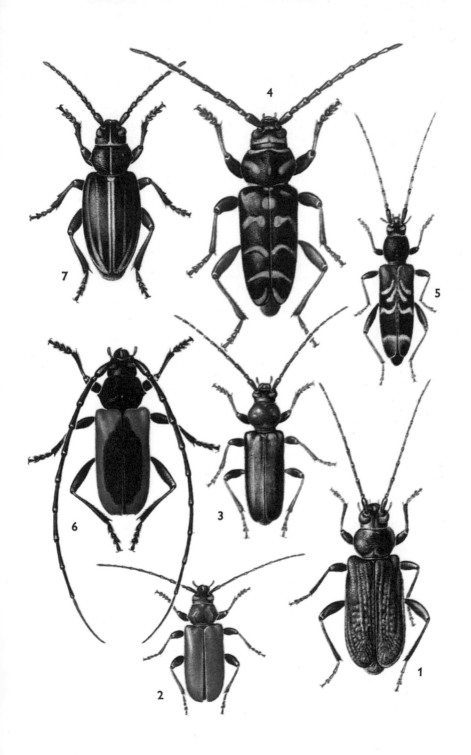

Family: **Cerambycidae**

**1.** *Lamia textor* L. 15—30 mm. Flies at dusk. During the day hides on branches and roots. Larva develops mainly in willows and aspens where it bores very wide tunnels. Distribution: variously throughout Europe, across Siberia to Japan.

**2.** *Monochamus sartor* F. 21—35 mm. Inhabits spruce forests where it flies agilely from July to mid-August. Larva lives mainly in felled spruce trunks, boring first under the bark, later into the wood, where it pupates about 10 cm below the surface. Beetles emerge through circular holes. Development lasts one year. Distribution: Europe; in some regions it is disappearing. Very rare in British Isles (introduced).

**3.** *Acanthocinus aedilis* L. 12—20 mm. A striking European cerambycid. Male's antennae are five times as long as the body; female's, however, are much shorter, about one-and-a-half times the length of the body. Female has a flat ovipositor with which she deposits her eggs deep into the bark of the stumps and felled trunks of pine and spruce. Larva bores broad, winding tunnels under the bark and pupates either in the bark or in the wood. Beetles emerge in autumn, but remain in the pupal cell during the winter, appearing in the open from late March to April. Distribution: Europe, Siberia, eastern Asia.

**4.** *Leiopus nebulosus* L. 6—10 mm. Occurs abundantly in deciduous forests as early as April. Larva develops in dry, slender trunks and branches of oak, beech, hornbeam and other deciduous trees. Bores winding tunnels filled with dust under the bark, where it also pupates. Beetles emerge in spring. Distribution: mostly central and northern Europe, including British Isles.

**5.** *Saperda populnea* L. 9—15 mm. Found from May to June around aspen, poplar and sometimes also birch and willow, on which the larvae feed. Female lays her eggs singly in holes she bites in the bark of young branches. Larva feeds on the plant tissues, penetrating inside the branch either in the first or second year. An elongate swelling appears at the spot where the larva settles. It pupates inside the branch and the adult emerges through a circular hole. Distribution: almost all Europe, Transcaucasia, Asia Minor, Siberia, Korea, north Africa, North America.

**6.** *Saperda scalaris* L. 12—18 mm. Pattern on the elytra, consisting of bands and blotches, is quite variable. Beetles first appear in the warm days of April, their favourite resting places being logs and stacked wood in hardwood forests. Female deposits the eggs singly in crevices which she bites in the bark of dry trunks or felled logs of oak, beech, elm, sallow and many other deciduous trees, including fruit trees. Distribution: from south-western Europe across central Europe to Siberia, Transcaucasia, Iran, north Africa. Rare in British Isles.

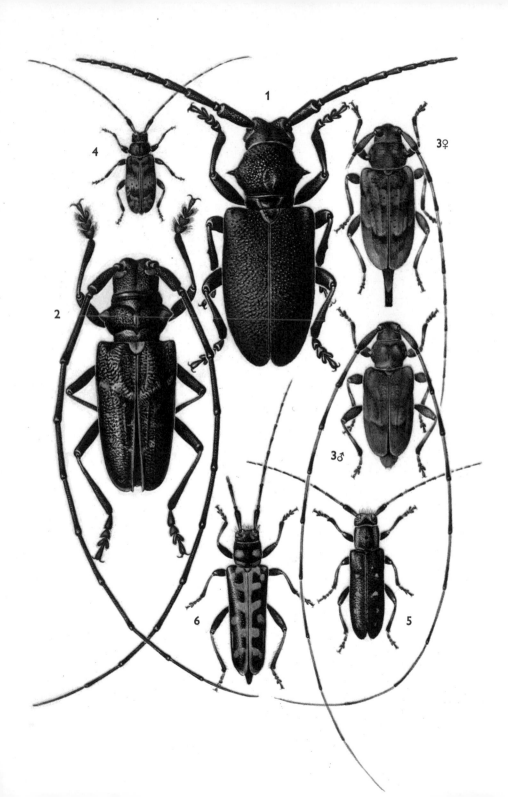

## Family: **Cerambycidae**

**1.** *Oberea oculata* L. 15—21 mm. Found from June to September on willow or sallow from lowland to mountain elevations. Eggs are laid singly on young branches, in hollows excavated by the female. Larva bores a narrow 3-cm-long tunnel in the twig. Development lasts one year. Distribution: Europe, Siberia.

**2.** *Phytoecia coerulescens* Scop. 8—14 mm. Abundant in warm situations — in pastures, hedgerows, semi-steppes and on railway embankments. In summer the beetles fly about here, resting on rough-leaved herbaceous plants such as *Echium vulgare, Lithospermum, Cynoglossum,* host plants of the larvae which live in the roots. Distribution: chiefly central and southern Europe, the Caucasus, Asia Minor, Middle East, north Africa.

**3.** *Tetrops praeusta* L. 3—5 mm. One of the smallest of cerambycids. Found from April to July on various blossoms; common in gardens. Larva develops in the twigs of rose, hawthorn, hazel and fruit trees. Infested trees are easily recognized by the drying branches tunnelled through by the larvae. Distribution: Europe, Transcaucasia, Asia Minor, north Africa.

## Family: **Leaf Beetles — Chrysomelidae**

**4.** *Donacia semicuprea* Panz. 5—9 mm. One of the commonest species of this genus. Its elongate body makes it resemble rather a cerambycid than a leaf beetle. Found on *Glyceria aquatica* (reed sweet-grass) by the water's edge. Distribution: Europe, excepting northern Scandinavia and Iceland.

**5.** *Oulema melanopus* L. 4—4.8 mm. Occurs abundantly from early spring in grain fields, chiefly on oats and barley whose leaves are eaten by the beetles and later by the larvae. Eggs are laid on the leaves either singly or in batches of two to seven along the length of the primary vein. In some regions the beetle is a pest of cereal crops. Distribution: all Europe, Siberia, north Africa, North America (introduced).

**6.** *Lilioceris lilii* Scop. 6—8 mm. Occurs in favourable weather as early as March, when it emerges from its winter shelter. Found on Liliaceae and therefore also in gardens, where one of its favourite foodplants is *Lilium album.* Generally two to three generations a year. Distribution: Europe, Asia, north Africa.

**7.** *Clytra laeviuscula* Ratz. 7—11 mm. Found from May to August on willow. The large dark blotches on the elytra may sometimes merge to form a transverse band; also, though less frequently, each may split to form two blotches. Distribution: central and southern Europe.

**8.** *Cryptocephalus sericeus* L. 7—8 mm. Common in summer on flowering hawkweed, wild thyme, yarrow and other herbs on slopes and in hedgerows and meadows. Distribution: Europe (from northern Italy to Scandinavia), Siberia, Asia Minor.

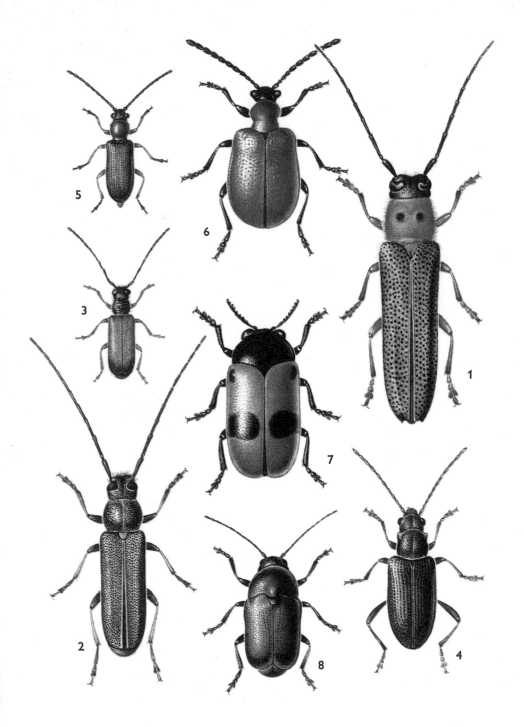

Family: **Chrysomelidae**

1. *Adoxus obscurus* L. 5—6 mm. Two sub-species exist: *A. obscurus obscurus,* found on various forest plants (willow-herb, hawkweed, etc.), and *A. obscurus villosus,* found on grapevines. The beetles, which live from May to October, bite out narrow bands of plant tissue 1—1.5 cm long in leaves and fruits. Eggs are laid on the underside of leaves. Larvae hatch within a few days and burrow in the ground. At first they feed on delicate plant roots; later they bite out bands of tissue in stronger roots. They hibernate and then pupate in spring. Beetles emerge in May. Distribution: Europe, north Africa, North and Central America.

2. *Chrysomela coerulans* Scriba 6.5—9 mm. Found on mint *(Mentha aquatica)* along streams or in damp meadows in foothills and mountains. Less common in lowlands. Several geographic races exist. Distribution: southern and central Europe, Asia Minor, southern China.

3. *Chrysomela staphylea* L. 6.5—9 mm. Found from spring till autumn. Favours plants of the family Labiatae around watersides, hedgerows, etc. Often found crawling on field paths. Distribution: almost the entire Palearctic, North America.

4. *Chrysomela sanguinolenta* L. 6—9 mm. Distinguished by the narrow red margin on the elytra. Found from March to October in sandy areas on toadflax *(Linaria).* Though quite common in some places, it is generally not an abundant species. Distribution: Europe (absent from the Mediterranean region), much of Asia.

5. *Dlochrysa fastuosa* Scop. 5—6.5 mm. Often occurs in large numbers from April to August on the leaves of stinging nettles, deadnettles, etc. Distribution: all Europe, Siberia, Japan.

6. *Chrysochloa cacaliae* Schr. 7.5—10.5 mm. One of the largest of European leaf-beetles. Though quite variable in colour, metallic green (6 a) or metallic blue (6 b) specimens are the most common. Favours groundsel *(Senecio)* but found also on other Compositae, e. g. *Adenostylis alliariae.* Occurs from midsummer till autumn in mountain areas, only occasionally in foothills. Several geographic races exist. Distribution: central and southern Europe.

7. *Plagiodera versicolora* Laich. 2.5—4.5 mm. Usually blue but sometimes blue-green or less frequently coppery. Very common from spring until autumn on willow and poplar. Economically unimportant. Distribution: most of the Palearctic, North America, part of the Oriental region.

Family: **Chrysomelidae**

1. *Melasoma vigintipunctata* Scop. 6.5—8.5 mm. Name derived from the twenty black spots on the yellow elytra. Unlike other species, the pattern exhibits little variability. Found from April to July on the leaves of willow. Distribution: most of Europe, Siberia, northern China, Japan.

2. *Melasoma aenea* L. 6.5—8.5 mm. Usually green, sometimes blue or golden-red. Found on alder and sallow. Distribution: Europe (except the Mediterranean region), Siberia, Mongolia, northern China, Japan.

3. *Melasoma populi* L. 10—12 mm. There are two other very similar central European species but these lack the dark patch at the end of the elytra. Found on various species of poplar from early spring, for the adult hibernates. Eggs are laid on the underside of leaves in batches of 20—30. Larvae feed on leaves. Neither the larval nor the pupal stage lasts very long, so that there are usually two or more generations. Distribution: the Palearctic, northern part of the Oriental region (India).

4. *Phytodecta viminalis* L. 5.5—7 mm. Common in summer on willows and sallows (*Salix* spp.). Coloured yellow-red with extremely variable black spots. Distribution: the Palearctic, North America.

5. *Phyllodecta vulgatissima* L. 4—5 mm. Emerges from its winter shelter very early in spring. Very abundant until autumn on the leaves of willow, where the larval stage is also passed. Distribution: chiefly central and northern Europe, Siberia, Korea, North America.

6, 6a. Colorado Beetle — *Leptinotarsa decemlineata* Say 6—11 mm. Cannot be mistaken for any other species. Emerges from its winter shelter in spring. Found chiefly on potato but also on other Solanaceae, e. g. deadly nightshade or belladona *(Atropa belladona)*, thorn-apple or Jimson Weed *(Datura stramonium)*, tobacco *(Nicotiana tabacum)*. It is increasingly being found far from potato fields. The yellowish eggs are deposited in batches and cemented to the leaves of the potato. The larvae, which emerge shortly after, are bright pink with two rows of black spots on the sides and grow very rapidly. They moult three times and finally change to orange. When fully grown they burrow in the ground to pupate. Adult beetles emerge after two weeks. In central Europe two generations occur. Distribution: originally native to the Nearctic region, where it fed on wild Solanaceae, the beetle has since spread throughout the world both by itself and through the medium of man.

7. *Galeruca tanaceti* L. 6.5—11 mm. Very abundant from spring till autumn on field and forest paths and other grassy places. Distribution: western part of the Palearctic, Asia Minor, north Africa.

8. *Agelastica alni* L. 6—7 mm. Often found in large numbers on the leaves of alder, where the larvae are also seen. The latter feed on the leaf tissues. Adults hibernate and therefore appear very early in spring. Distribution: entire Palearctic, Asia Minor, north Africa.

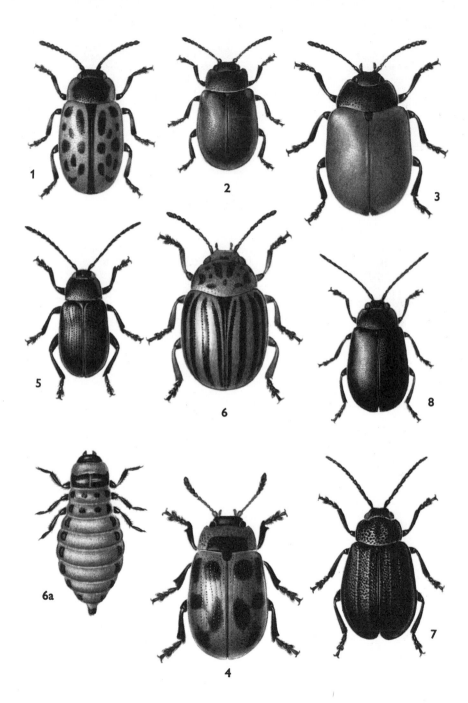

1

2

3

5

6

8

6a

4

7

Family: **Chrysomelidae**

1. *Phyllotreta undulata* Kutsch. 1.8 — 2.5 mm. One of the commonest as well as the most injurious of flea-beetles. Found on various wild as well as cultivated Cruciferae, chiefly mustard, radish and cabbage. In spring it often occurs in large numbers, causing great damage to young plants. Eggs are laid on the ground. Larvae burrow into the soil, where they feed on plant roots. Fully grown larvae pupate in the ground in earthen cells. The new generation occurs in July to August. Adults hibernate. Distribution: Europe, Siberia, Asia Minor, North America (introduced).

2. *Longitarsus exoletus* L. 2.3 — 3.2 mm. Abundant from June onwards, on viper's bugloss *(Echium vulgare)* and other Boraginaceae. Distribution: the Palearctic.

3. *Haltica oleracea* L. 3 — 4 mm. Like other flea-beetles, it has the hind legs adapted for leaping. Generally found in groups on various shrubs and herbs, such as willowherb and evening primrose, in meadows and forest margins. Often said to occur on vegetables but this is not true. Distribution: all Europe.

4. *Chalcoides aurea* Geoffr. 2.5 — 3.5 mm. Found chiefly on willows by running water and in forests. Adult hibernates. Beetles occur from spring till autumn. Distribution: Europe and Siberia.

5. *Chaetocnema concinna* Marsh. 1.8 — 2.4 mm. Visits various species of sorrel, *Polygonum,* and other plants. Sometimes also sugar-beet. Eggs are laid in soil just below the surface. The new generation of beetles appears in August. Distribution: Europe, Siberia.

6. *Hispella atra* L. 3 — 4 mm. The numerous spiny processes on the body make it look like the small fruits of plants. Found only in dry grassy localities. Larvae bore mines in grass. Distribution: Europe, Asia Minor, Middle East, north Africa.

7. *Cassida viridis* L. 7 — 10 mm. Bright green; in mounted specimens the green colour fades after a time. Beetles occur abundantly. They hibernate and emerge in April to May. Found on Labiatae (deadnettle family) and Compositae. Bite holes in leaves. Eggs are laid in batches on plants. Larvae are broadly oval, the margin of the body is fringed with spines and at the caudal end there is a forked appendage. Pupates on leaves. Distribution: the entire Palearctic.

Family: **Bruchidae**

8. *Bruchus pisorum* L. 4 — 5 mm. Common on peas. Adults hibernate in seeds stored in households and warehouses, less frequently in fields. Eggs are laid on young pods; larvae bore inside and into the seed. Distribution: cosmopolitan.

Family: **Anthribidae**

9. *Brachytarsus nebulosus* Forst. 2 — 4 mm. Important in forestry for the larvae feed on the eggs of the scale insect *Physokermes piceae.* Distribution: Europe.

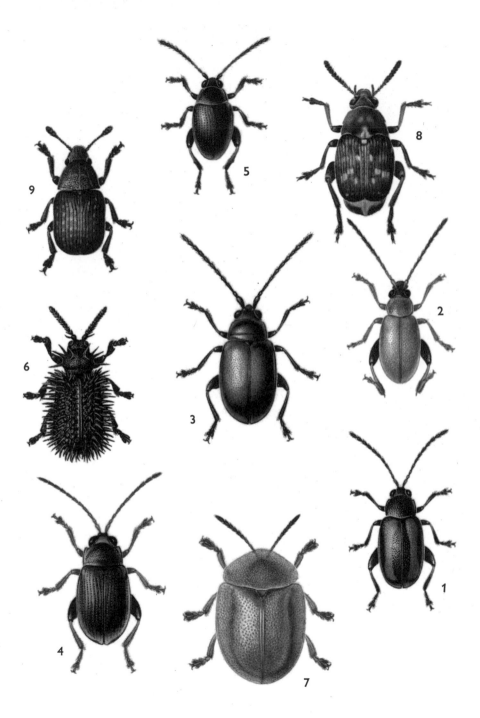

## Family: Weevils — Curculionidae

**1.** *Otiorrhynchus niger* F. 6.5—10 mm. Found in spruce woods mostly in foothills and mountains (in central Europe it is most abundant at elevations up to 800 metres). Eggs are laid in spring in the ground, where the larvae feed on small roots. Beetles feed on spruce needles and the leaves of birch or alder, but its consumption of plant tissue is stated to be quite negligible — only about 1—2 grams during its lifetime. Distribution: central and southern Europe.

**2.** *Polydrusus sericeus* Schall. 6—8 mm. Body covered with magnificent metallic scales. Usually abundant from May to June on various deciduous trees, very often on birch. Distribution: from southern Europe to southern Scandinavia, Siberia.

**3.** *Polydrusus mollis* Ström. 6—8.5 mm. Body scales are a coppery colour. Occurs abundantly chiefly on oak, beech and poplar. In central Europe it increases by parthenogenetic reproduction, males being unknown there. Distribution: Europe, from Balkans across central Europe to the north, Siberia. Rare in British Isles.

**4.** *Polydrusus picus* F. 2.7—4.4 mm. There are only a few patches of scales on the elytra. Common chiefly on birch, beech and oak. Distribution: central and south-eastern Europe.

**5.** *Bothynoderes punctiventris* Germ. 11.5—13.5 mm. Probably a native of the steppes of central Asia. In Europe the sugar beet became its foodplant and in some areas it is known as a pest of this crop. Feeds on the leaves of young plants. Favours light, sandy and warm soil. Eggs are laid in the ground near the surface beside young sugar-beet plants. Larvae eat the roots. They pupate in the ground. Beetles, which emerge in the autumn, remain in the ground until the following spring. Nowadays it occurs only occasionally in western Europe, being more plentiful towards the east (Balkans), in the Caucasus and in Transcaucasia.

**6.** *Lixus paraplecticus* L. 10.5—18 mm. Body narrow, elongate. Larva lives in the main stems of various kinds of water-dropwort and water parsnip. Distribution: Europe, Asia Minor, western Asia.

**7.** Pine Weevil — *Hylobius abietis* L. 7.3—13.5 mm. Found in spring in forest clearings, where it feeds on young pine trees, biting off the bark in spirals. In summer it moves to old pines where it bites the bark of young twigs in a similar manner. Eggs are laid in the stumps of newly felled trees. Larvae, yellow-white with brown head, hatch after two to three weeks. They bore tunnels in the phloem and later in the sapwood. They hibernate and pupate the following year in a pupal cell in the wood. Beetles hibernate under felled trees, amidst fallen leaves etc. They live to an age of three years. Distribution: Europe, Siberia, Japan.

**8.** *Hylobius piceus* Deg. 12—16.5 mm. One of the most robust of the European weevils. Found mostly on larch. Distribution: central and northern Europe, Siberia, North America.

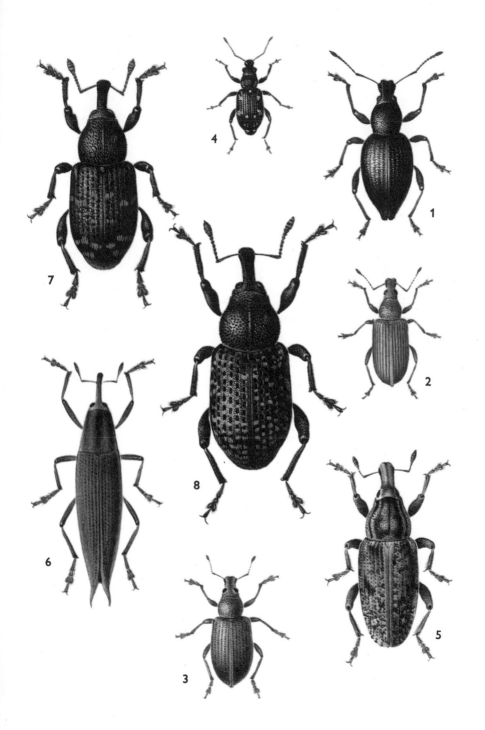

Family: **Curculionidae**

**1.** *Liparus glabrirostris* Küst. 14—21 mm. Distinguished from the related and similar *L. germanus* by the delicate sculpturing on the scutum and the rounded base of the elytra. Found in foothill and mountain regions generally on the leaves of various species of *Petasites* (butterburs). Locally abundant. Distribution: central and south-western Europe, northern Italy.

**2.** *Rhyncolus elongatus* Gyll. 3.7—4.1 mm. Very delicate and rich sculpturing visible under strong magnification. Resembles bark-beetles with head prolonged into a beak. Found under the bark of coniferous trees. Distribution: Europe (southern, central, southern Scandinavia), the Caucasus, north Africa (Algeria, Morocco). Very rare in British Isles.

**3.** Apple Blossom Weevil — *Anthonomus pomorum* L. 3.4—4.3 mm. Its presence is revealed by the rusty-brown colouring of apple buds which will not develop into flowers. Such buds are infested by the larvae, pupae and finally the young beetle. It bites its way out and settles in the foliage, where it devours leaf tissues. Adults hibernate in various places, generally under the bark of trees, amongst moss, and in fallen leaves. Distribution: much of Europe, Asia, north Africa (Algeria), North America (introduced).

**4.** *Curculio venosus* Grav. 5—7.5 mm. Resembles several other species in shape and general colouring. Snout is somewhat broader where the antennae arise. Found on various kinds of oak. Distribution: Europe, from southern Sweden to the Mediterranean, the Caucasus, Asia Minor.

**5.** *Pissodes pini* L. 5.1—8.7 mm. Lives on various species of pine. Eggs are laid in batches of about twenty under the bark of dead or dying tree trunks. Distribution: Europe (from Spain and northern Italy to Scandinavia), Siberia.

**6.** Grain Weevil — *Sitophilus granarius* L. 3—4 mm. In older literature it is classed in the genus *Calandra*. A serious pest of stored grain. Because its development is determined by temperature, the number of generations a year varies. All developmental stages may hibernate. Distribution: cosmopolitan.

**7.** *Cionus scrophulariae* L. 4—5 mm. Recognized from all other related species by the pale-coloured scutum and black spot in the centre of elytra. Common on figwort in summer. Distribution: Europe, the Caucasus, Asia Minor, Middle East (Syria), Turkestan.

**8.** *Apion pomonae* Fabr. 2.3—3.3 mm. One of many dozens of species. Only under a strong lens can one see the extremely delicate and remarkably complex sculpturing on the entire body. Occurs chiefly on various vetches. Distribution: the Palearctic.

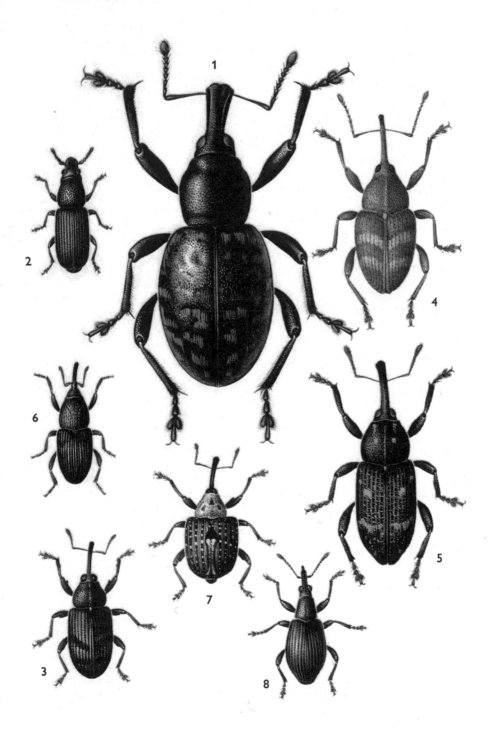

Family: **Attelabidae**

1. *Coenorrhinus aequatus* L. 2.5 — 5 mm. Occurs on the buds, flowers and leaves of apple, pear, cherry, rowan, hawthorn and other trees. Larva develops in the fruit and pupates in the ground. Distribution: Europe to the Caucasus, Asia Minor, Turkestan.

2. *Rhynchites auratus* Scop. 5 — 10 mm. One of the largest European members of this family. Male distinguished from female by the pointed spine on the scutum. Beetles live on cherry, blackthorn, bird-cherry, plum, etc. Larva develops inside the fruit, which is stunted in growth and usually falls. Not very abundant. Distribution: much of Europe, central Asia, Asia Minor, Siberia. Rare in British Isles.

3. *Byctiscus populi* L. 3.8 — 6 mm. Generally metallic green but some individuals are blue, occasionally even black. Male has two sharp spines on the scutum. Most often found on aspen and poplar, less frequently on sallow and birch. Eggs are laid in compact rolls made of aspen leaves. The female makes several such rolls during her lifetime. The roll is always made of a young leaf and is only 1.5 — 3 mm thick. When rolling the leaf (upper side of the blade inward), the female cements the egg to the leaf so that it is protected by the roll. Larva feeds on the inner parts of the roll. On young annual shoots there may often be several such rolls. They soon wilt and fall to the ground. Larva pupates in the ground. Distribution: Europe, central Asia, Siberia, Mongolia, northern China.

4. *Deporaus betulae* L. 2.5 — 4 mm. Common chiefly on birch, sometimes also on alder, hazel and beech. Males have remarkably stout hind femora. Eggs are laid in a leaf case. When making it the female first bites her way from the left or right side of the leaf to the primary vein, after which she continues on to the opposite side. All that remains entire is the base of the leaf. From the tip the female makes a roll: this is loose at first but she gradually pulls it tighter and then lays the eggs inside. She makes an incision in the leaf cuticle and lays a single egg in the resulting cavity. Each roll contains two eggs. Larva feeds on the leaf tissues. After a time the rolls fall and the larvae leave them to enter the ground where they pupate. Distribution: most of Europe, Siberia, Mongolia, north Africa.

5. *Attelabus nitens* Scop. 4 — 6 mm. Occurs chiefly on oak. Female makes a leaf case for the eggs. She makes her way from the left as well as right side of the leaf to the primary vein which she bites partway through, whereupon she prepares the leaf blade for the next step, biting the primary and secondary veins as well as the blade at several points so that all is pliant. Last of all she places the two sides of the blade together and then rolls the leaf from the tip. Inside she deposits one to seven eggs. Larvae hibernate in the fallen rolls and in spring enter the ground to pupate. Distribution: Europe, the Caucasus, Asia Minor and central Asia.

6. *Apoderus coryli* L. 6 — 8 mm. Found on various deciduous trees, chiefly hazel and alder, less frequently on birch, oak, beech, etc. Female lays one to four eggs inside a leaf roll. Distribution: Europe, Siberia, Japan.

2

4a

6

4

5

3

1

Family: **Bark Beetles — Scolytidae**

**1.** Large Elm Bark Beetle — *Scolytus scolytus* F. 3—6 mm. There are two generations a year (May, July to August). Develops under the thick bark of old elm trunks. Locally very abundant and injurious. Female bores a 4—6-cm-long main gallery, laying eggs on either side. Larvae bore lateral tunnels and pupate in chambers at their ends. Adults bite their way out through the bark. Infested elms usually die. The cause of death, however, is not primarily the tunnelling of the beetles and larvae but infestation by the fungus *Ceratocystis ulmi*, whose spores are spread by the beetle. Fully grown larvae hibernate. Distribution: much of Europe, Transcaucasia, North America (introduced).

**2.** Large Pine Shoot Beetle — *Myelophilus piniperda* L. 3.5—4.8 mm. Very abundant under the bark of pine trees, where female bores a 10—12-cm-long main gallery. Because the adults hibernate they emerge very early in spring, sometimes by the beginning of March if the weather is favourable. Distribution: entire Palearctic.

**3.** Lineate Bark Beetle — *Xyloterus lineatus* Ol. 2.8—3.8 mm. Infests conifers, chiefly spruce and fir. Before laying the eggs the female first excavates a 1—3-cm-long tunnel towards the centre of the tree, and at the end of this a gallery to both right and left round the annual ring. On the top and bottom of each gallery she excavates small chambers, in each of which she deposits one egg. Larvae bore very short tunnels. They do not feed upon cellulose but on ambrosia fungi brought to the galleries by the female. They pupate at the ends of their tunnels. Adults make their exit through the main galleries. This beetle infests mostly weakened or uprooted, unbarked trees and stumps. Distribution: from western Europe to Siberia and Mongolia, North America.

**4.** *Pityogenes chalcographus* L. 1.6—2.5 mm. Development takes place chiefly on slender trunks and on the branches of stronger spruce trees. The insects excavate a rich labyrinth of tunnels beneath the bark. Each consists of a nuptial chamber from which radiate three to six main galleries about 2—6 cm long. Branching off on either side are the lateral tunnels (2—4 cm long) made by the larvae in the bark. There are usually two but sometimes three generations a year. The adult as well as other stages hibernate. In some regions this beetle is a serious pest. Distribution: all Europe, Siberia, Korea, Japan.

**5.** Spruce Bark Beetle — *Ips typographus* L. 4.2—5.5 mm. Best known of the Scolytidae. Usually infests spruce with stronger trunks at least 60 years old, occurring on younger trees only when the insect population is particularly high. Makes typical burrows, usually with two to three branches, depending on how many females arrive in the male's nuptial chamber. Usually there are two, with one excavating a tunnel upward and the other downward. Branching from these main galleries are the lateral tunnels made by the larvae; these are smaller where they branch off and broader at the end, where the larva pupates. The newly born beetle does not leave the wood but feeds on the phloem. It is usually the adult that hibernates. Distribution: Europe, Asia Minor, Siberia, Korea, northern China.

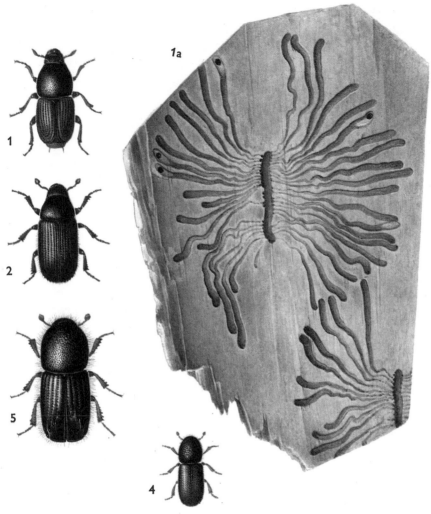

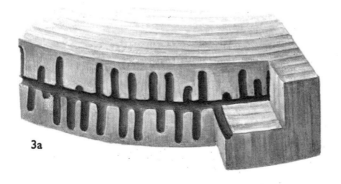

Order: **Hymenoptera**

Family: **Web-spinning and Leaf-rolling Sawflies — Pamphilidae**

**1.** *Acantholyda erythrocephala* L. 10 — 12 mm. Flies in late April and May. Eggs are laid on the previous year's needles of various pine species. Larvae live together in a nest, each in its own tube. In June, when fully grown, they enter the ground near the trunk where they pupate. In some regions the larvae are injurious. Distribution: chiefly central, western and northern Europe, North America (introduced).

**2.** *Cephalcia abietis* L. 11 — 16 mm. Flies on sunny days in April and June, chiefly in alder and old spruce stands in foothills and mountain regions. Female lays about 100 eggs in batches of four to twelve on the needles. Larvae live together in a nest on a branch. In August they burrow about 30 cm into the ground where they remain in earthen cells for two to three years before pupating. Development usually lasts three years. Adults, larvae and pupae have many enemies amongst insects and birds as well as mammals. Distribution: chiefly central and northern Europe, Belgium, Italy, Siberia. Absent from British Isles.

Family: **Argidae**

**3.** *Arge ochropus* Gm. 7 — 10 mm. There are usually two generations a year (April to May, July to August). Eggs are laid in the upper parts of young rose branches, always about sixteen to eighteen in a row. An infested branch may be recognized by characteristic scars. Young larvae first feed on the leaf epidermis, later on the leaf tissues. When feeding they always adopt a typical pose with abdomen coiled and hanging or held erect in the shape of an S. Fully grown larvae burrow in the ground where they pupate in a spherical cocoon. Sometimes injurious to roses. Distribution: all Europe, Asia Minor, Middle East, Siberia.

**4.** *Arge ustulata* L. 7 — 10 mm. Flies from May to July. Larvae common on willow and birch from July to September. Pupate in a cocoon amidst leaves or on the ground. Distribution: Europe, Siberia, Japan.

Family: **Cimbicidae**

**5.** *Cimbex lutea* L. 16 — 25 mm. Large sawfly with larvae found mainly on willows and poplars. They are plump and coiled when at rest. Distribution: all Europe, Siberia, Japan.

Family: **Diprionidae**

**6.** Pine Sawfly — *Diprion pini* L. 7 — 10 mm. Marked sexual dimorphism. Male is black with pectinate antennae; female more robust, more brightly coloured, with shortly serrate antennae. Found in pine woods with diseased trees. One to two generations a year. Males fly; females usually remain on branches. Female deposits up to 150 eggs, making an incision in the pine needle with her ovipositor and laying as many as twenty eggs in a row in the slit, which she covers with a protective layer. Young larvae are gregarious and feed on pine needles from the sides. First generation pupates in a sturdy cocoon in the branches, in crevices in the bark, etc. Larvae of the second generation usually burrow in the earth, hibernate once or twice and pupate in the soil. Distribution: central and northern Europe, Spain, north Africa.

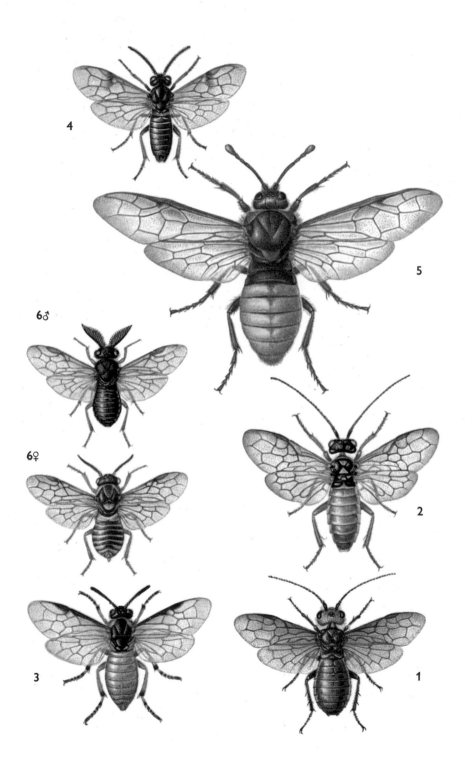

Family: **Typical Sawflies — Tenthredinidae**

1. *Tenthredo campestris* L. 12 — 14 mm. Flies from spring to August. Larva, up to 24 mm long, lives on ground elder *(Aegopodium podagraria)*. Distribution: all Europe, except British Isles.

2. *Rhogogaster viridis* L. 10 — 13 mm. Distinguished by its green abdomen which generally has a black stripe down the centre. Adult is carnivorous, fond of Colorado potato beetle larvae. Larva feeds on the leaves of various plants, often alder, willow, poplar and many smaller species — buttercup, etc. Distribution: all Europe, temperate regions of Asia as far as Japan, North America.

3. *Macrophya montana* L. 10 — 14 mm. Common on flowering umbels. Distribution: all Europe, Asia Minor, north Africa.

4. *Athalia rosae* auct. 6 — 8 mm. Two to three generations a year. Adults abundant from May on various blossoms and on the flowerheads of Compositae, Umbelliferae and Cruciferae, where they seek pollen and nectar. Eggs are laid singly between the epidermal layers at the leaf margins of Cruciferae. Larva, which hatches after about a week, first bores a tunnel in the leaf, then emerges and remains on the underside of the leaf where it bites holes. It pupates in the soil. In some regions the larvae are injurious. Distribution: all Europe, Asia Minor, India, Siberia, Japan, north and south Africa, South America.

5. *Allantus cinctus* L. 7 — 10 mm. Two generations a year. Eggs are usually laid on the leaves of the rose, less often also on strawberry. Larva reaches a length of c. 15 mm. It feeds on leaves, biting holes in them, and pupates in leaves and twigs. Distribution: all Europe, Siberia, North America.

6. *Caliroa cerasi* L. 5 mm. Two generations a year. Eggs are laid under the epidermis on the underside of cherry and pear leaves. Larva eats the upper surface of the leaves, leaving the skeleton of veins. It is black and smells of ink. It pupates in the ground. Male very rare, insect normally breeding parthenogenetically. Distribution: all Europe, Middle East, central Asia, Siberia, Japan, north and south Africa, Australia, North America (introduced).

7. *Hoplocampa flava* L. 3 — 4 mm. Found from April to May on fruit tree blossoms. Female, which lives only about two weeks, mates and then lays her eggs in the sepals of the opening blossoms of plum, sometimes also cherry and apricot. Larva first of all makes its way to the surface of the ovary and later bores inside. It devours the young fruit, then infests another, healthy one. When fully grown the larva falls to the ground with the fruit, burrows in the soil where it hibernates and then pupates in spring. Injurious. Distribution: all Europe to Turkestan.

8. *Trichiocampus viminalis* Fall. 7 — 9 mm. Eggs usually laid on the leaves of poplar. Larvae occur in groups of three or five on the underside of the leaves. They feed on leaf tissues. Distribution: central and northern Europe, Siberia, North America.

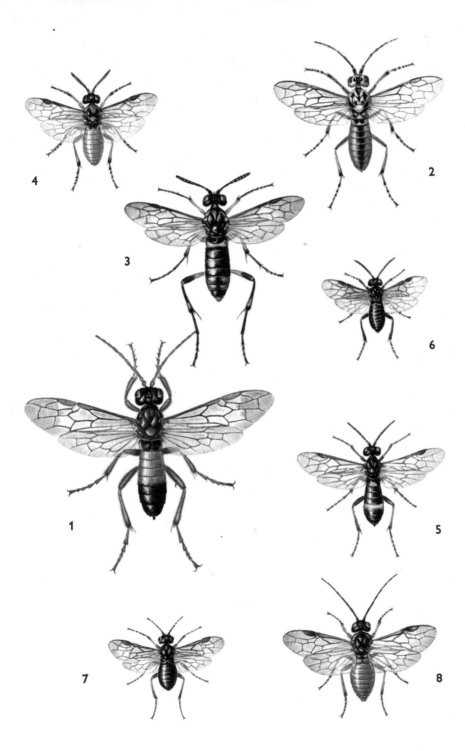

## Family: Xiphydriidae

1. *Xiphydria camelus* L. 10 — 21 mm. Head separated from the prothorax by a long, narrow neck. Larva found in alders, sometimes also in birch. Bores tunnels in the wood. Distribution: Europe, including southernmost parts, Siberia.

## Family: Horntails or Wood Wasps — Siricidae

2. *Xeris spectrum* L. 15 — 30 mm (without ovipositor). Abundant in coniferous forests. Ovipositor is the same length as the body and is used to deposit eggs in pine, spruce and fir trees, where the larval stage is passed. Distribution: Europe (not British Isles), Siberia, China, Japan, north Africa (Algeria), North America.

3. *Sirex juvencus* L. 14 — 30 mm. Distinguished from the closely related *S. noctilio* by its orange antennae. Larva usually lives in pine and spruce, sometimes also in fir. Occasionally the larva or pupa is brought with deliveries of logs to cities, where the adult then emerges. Distribution: all Europe, Japan, north Africa (Algeria), Nearctic region, Australian region.

4. *Urocerus gigas* L. 10 — 40 mm. A striking species both in its size and colouring. Sexes are markedly different. Males are smaller. On the wing in summer in sunny spots in forests. Not dangerous for it does not have a sting. When laying eggs the female pierces the wood with the ovipositor to a depth of about 1 cm. Larva found chiefly in conifers (pine, spruce, fir, larch), less often in deciduous trees. It bores a tunnel up to 40 cm long and pupates in a cradle in the wood. Adult makes its way out through a round exit hole. Larvae are parasitized by the larvae of *Rhyssa persuasoria,* which are common parasites also upon other Siricidae. Distribution: all Europe, temperate regions of Asia, north Africa.

## Family: Stem-sawflies — Cephidae

5. *Hartigia nigra* Harr. 11 — 15 mm. Common species. Larvae found in the stems of black-berry and raspberry. Distribution: most of Europe, Asia as far east as China.

6. Wheat Sawfly-borer — *Cephus pygmaeus* L. 5 — 10 mm. Greatest numbers on the wing in June. Found on flowers. Eggs are laid in various kinds of cereal, mostly wheat, rye and barley. Female slits the stem near the spike with her ovipositor. Eggs are laid singly, from 35 to 50, and hatch after about a week. Larva feeds on the cells inside the stem, proceeding slowly from top to bottom; the resulting hollow space is filled with a whitish debris. Before pupating it cuts the stem circularly on the inside close to the ground and waits out the winter in a delicate cocoon, changing to a pupa in spring. Adult emerges at the end of May. Larvae may be injurious in the grain-growing regions of some countries. Distribution: all Europe, Asia Minor, Middle East (Iran), north Africa, North America (introduced).

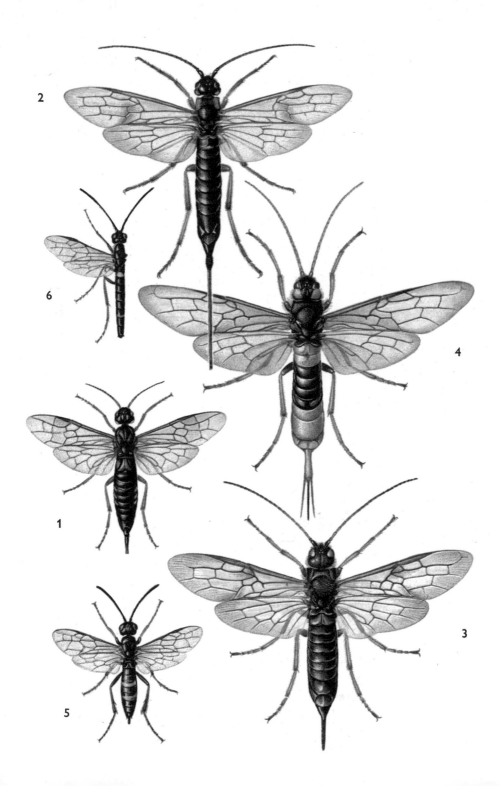

Family: **Ichneumon Flies — Ichneumonidae**

**1.** *Rhyssa persuasoria* L. 18—35 mm (ovipositor 30—35 mm). One of the largest and thus most striking members of this family. Its development takes place in the larvae of *Urocerus, Sirex, Xeris* and other horntails. The female must first find the host larva and when she detects it in a tree trunk she drills into the wood with her slender, needle-sharp ovipositor and deposits a single egg in each larva. While the ovipositor is being driven vertically into the wood the abdomen points upward. It is unbelievable that, despite the hardness of the wood, the whole process takes only a few minutes. Distribution: Europe, North America, New Zealand (introduced).

**2.** *Pimpla instigator* F. 10—24 mm. Commonest member of the whole family, which in Europe is roughly estimated to consist of more than 4,000 species. Ovipositor is half the length of the female's abdomen. Larvae are parasites of the caterpillars of various Lepidoptera. Distribution: Europe, north Africa.

**3.** *Ophion luteus* L. 15—20 mm. Greatly resembles several other rusty-brown European species. Body slender, abdomen laterally compressed. Often abundant in summer. In the country it is attracted to light and in the evening may often be found on lighted windows. Ovipositor is short. Larvae, like those of related species of this genus, parasitize caterpillars, including those of the black arches moth *(Lymantria monacha)*. Distribution: the Palearctic.

**4.** *Amblyteles armatorius* Först. 12—16 mm. Often visits flowering Umbelliferae (genus *Daucus, Heracleum, Chaerophyllum* and others). Larvae parasitize the caterpillars of various large Lepidoptera, such as large yellow underwing, cabbage moth, fox moth and emperor moth. Distribution: all Europe, Transcaucasia, Siberia, Sakhalin, Japan, north Africa (Algeria).

**5.** *Protichneumon pisorius* L. 22—28 mm. Flies from May on, visiting the flowers of hogweed and related plants. Larvae parasitize the caterpillars of Lepidoptera, generally noctuid moths, but also hawkmoths such as the eyed hawk. Distribution: all Europe.

**6.** *Ichneumon suspiciosus* Wesm. 14—18 mm. Like all other members of the family, it visits flowering Umbelliferae. Larvae parasitize the caterpillars of the injurious mottled umber *(Erannis defoliaria)*. Distribution: all Europe, Siberia, Sakhalin.

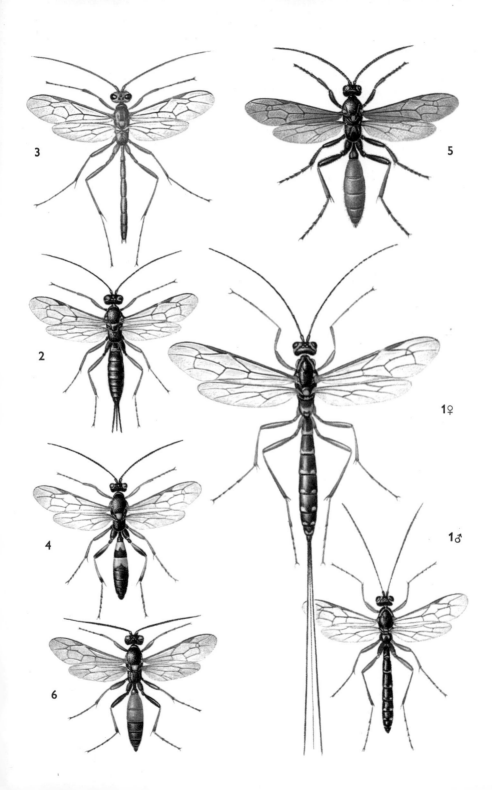

Family: **Braconidae**

**1.** *Spathius exarator* L. 4.5—5 mm. Very beneficial. Female has a long ovipositor (the same length as the body), with which she deposits the eggs in the larvae of death-watch and other beetles that bore in wood. Adults often found on windows of houses. Distribution: Europe.

**2.** *Apanteles glomeratus* L. 4 mm. A parasite of the large white butterfly *(Pieris brassicae)* and related species. Controls the numbers of caterpillars, which are often injurious in vegetable-growing regions. Female lays some 2,000 eggs in all, about 30 in a single caterpillar. Larvae feed upon the caterpillar's body. As soon as they are fully grown they bore to the outside where they pupate in tiny yellow elongate cocoons round the dead caterpillar. Pupae are often themselves attacked by small parasitic wasps so that the adult that emerges belongs to an entirely different species. This type of double parasitism in which a parasitic organism attacks another parasite is termed hyperparasitism. Distribution: Europe, North America (introduced).

Family: **Gall Wasps — Cynipidae**

**3.** *Biorrhiza pallida* Oliv. Sexual generation 1.7—2.8 mm, asexual generation 3.5—6 mm. Produces two types of galls: on the roots, and on the branches of oak. The wingless females, which emerge from the galls on the slender roots of oak, occur in winter. Without mating (there are no males in this generation), they climb to the tips of the branches and lay their eggs in the buds. Produced at the point of insertion is a many-chambered, roundish gall, up to 4 cm across, called an oak apple. Inside this gall the sexual generation develops and the adults emerge in June and July. The males and females of this generation are almost always fully winged. After pairing, the female burrows in the ground to lay eggs on slender oak roots. These eggs give rise to galls and to females which emerge in the winter of the following year (about 18 months later). The entire developmental cycle lasts two years. Distribution: Europe, Asia Minor, north Africa.

**4.** *Cynips quercusfolii* L. Sexual generation 2.3—2.5 mm, asexual generation 3.4—4 mm. Found on oak. Characteristic are the spherical, cherry-like galls on the leaves, from which females emerge in winter. They lay their eggs in dormant buds on the twigs, and these buds give rise to small inconspicuous galls only about 3 mm long. Adult males and females emerge in May or June. The females then lay eggs on the underside of oak leaves, and a new generation of cherry galls develops. Distribution: Europe, Asia Minor.

**5.** *Cynips longiventris* Hart. Sexual generation 2—2.7 mm; asexual generation 2.9—3.6 mm. Found on oak. Also produces two types of galls. Striking are the red-striped galls on the undersides of leaves inside which develop the agamic (asexual) females that may be seen from November to March. These lay eggs in buds which give rise to small, 2-mm-long galls in which the males and females of the sexual generation develop. Distribution: most of Europe, Middle East.

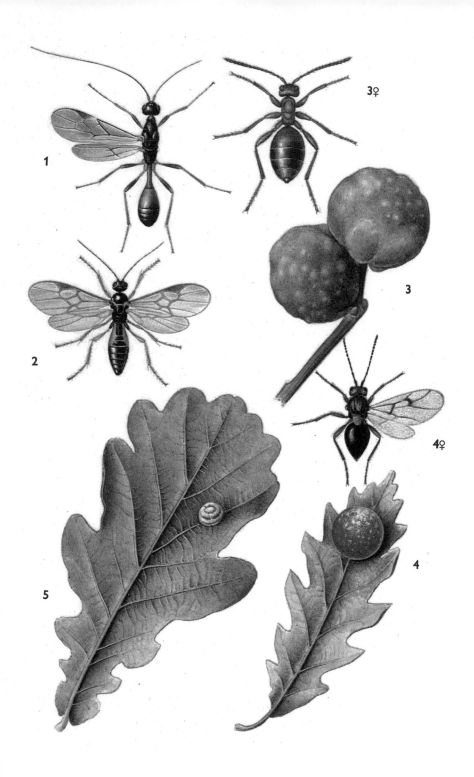

1

2

3♀

3

4♀

4

5

Family: **Cynipidae**

**1.** *Andricus kollari* Htg. Sexual generation 1.7 — 2 mm, asexual generation 4.8 — 6 mm. Found on oak. The galls in which agamic females develop are spherical and measure 1 — 2 cm or more across. Called marble galls, they are formed on the tips or along the length of young branches of common oak and are smooth and hard. They ripen in August and September but do not fall. The females emerge in September to October and lay eggs in the buds on young twigs of Turkey oak. Several tiny galls (only 2 — 3 mm long) are formed in a single bud. They mature in spring. The males and females appear in April to May. Distribution: much of Europe, including Great Britain; Asia Minor, north Africa.

**2.** *Andricus lignicolus* Htg. Asexual generation 4 — 4.5 mm. Found on oak. Agamic female grows in large, hard galls about 5 — 10 mm across. Adult emerges in the spring of the second year. Distribution: most of Europe, but absent from British Isles; Asia Minor.

**3.** *Andricus fecundator* Htg. Sexual generation 1.5 — 1.9 mm, asexual generation 4.3 — 4.8 mm. Produces galls on various species of oak. Galls in which agamic females develop are cone-shaped and up to 2 cm long. Concealed by the scales of the cone is the inner gall — brown, oval, about 6 — 10 mm long — in which the actual development takes place. Females appear in late autumn and early spring (March), depositing their eggs in male flower buds. The galls formed there are very inconspicuous, only 2 mm long; they mature during May and the males and females emerge in June. Distribution: most of Europe, Middle East.

**4.** *Neuroterus quercusbaccarum* L. Sexual generation 2.5 — 2.9 mm; asexual generation 2.5 — 2.8 mm. Also produces two types of galls on oaks. The flat spangle galls on the underside of leaves fall with the leaves in the autumn and females emerge from them only in spring. These females lay their eggs in male catkin buds, inducing the formation of little spherical galls about 5 mm across. Males and females emerge from these currant-like galls in June. The females of this generation lay eggs on the underside of leaves, inducing the growth of spangle galls. Development lasts one year. Distribution: Europe, Asia, Minor, north Africa.

**5.** *Diplolepis rosae* L. 3.7 — 4.3 mm. Produces bedeguar galls, or robin's pincushions, on roses in summer. These are not single but clustered and are found on both leaves and branches. As a rule only females emerge (males are extremely rare), and these lay eggs in buds in spring. The galls also yield large numbers of hymenopterous insects that parasitize the rightful inhabitants. Distribution: much of Europe.

Family: **Aphelinidae**

**6.** *Aphelinus mali* Hald. 2 mm. Very beneficial as the chief parasite of the woolly aphid *(Eriosoma lanigerum)*. The female lays an egg inside the body of the aphid where the larva develops and pupates. All that remains of the aphid is its skin through which the adult bites its way out. There are five to eight generations a year. In North America it was one of the most important agents in the control of the woolly aphid and was therefore introduced to all parts of the world, even becoming established in some regions. It is reared in insectaria and used in the biological control of the woolly aphid.

222

2 ♀

Family: **Scoliidae**

**1.** *Scolia maculata* Drury 20—40 mm. One of the largest hymenopterous species in Europe. Found on flowers from the warm days of May onward. Not aggressive and does not attack man. Female digs in the ground seeking the larva of *Oryctes nasicornis,* then paralyzes it with its sting and lays a single egg on the grub. The larva is carnivorous and feeds on the grub until it pupates. As *Oryctes* declines in number in the wild, so does this magnificent scoliid. Distribution: Europe (western and southern, but not British Isles; in central Europe the boundary of its range passes through Slovakia), Asia Minor, Middle East (Syria, Israel, Iran).

**2.** *Scolia quadripunctata* F. 10—18 mm. Usually has four yellow spots on the abdomen but sometimes only two, at other times six, eight or ten. Found from late June to August on flowers, where it feeds on nectar. Larvae are parasitic on the larvae of lamellicorn beetles *(Epicometis, Cetonia, Anisoplia* and others*).* Distribution: Europe (absent from Britain and the north), the Caucasus, Transcaucasia, Middle East, north Africa (Egypt, Algeria).

Family: **Velvet Ants — Mutillidae**

**3.** *Smicromyrme rufipes* F. 4—6 mm. Distinguished, as all related species, by marked sexual dimorphism. Female is always wingless and is usually found crawling on the ground in sandy terrain. Male has two pairs of membranous wings and is found on flowers. An abundant species whose larvae parasitize the larvae of various digger wasps (Sphecidae and Pompilidae). Distribution: the Palearctic.

**4.** *Mutilla europaea* L. 10—15 mm. One of the largest of the European mutillids. Recognized by the front abdominal segments which are bluish and unspotted. Larvae are parasites in the nests of bumblebees. Distribution: much of the Palearctic.

Family: **Cuckoo Wasps — Chrysididae**

**5.** *Chrysis cyanea* L. 3.5—8 mm. Very abundant. There are two generations a year. Found from May on the walls of buildings, fences etc. Larvae parasitize various solitary bees and wasps (Sphecidae, Eumenidae and others). Distribution: most of Europe as far north as Finland, the Caucasus, Asia Minor, Siberia.

**6.** *Chrysis nitidula* F. 7—13 mm. Occurs from June to August in warm as well as cooler localities up to mountain elevations. Often found on the warm walls of country buildings. Larvae are parasitic on the larvae of mason wasps *(Odynerus),* and bees *(Osmia).* Distribution: Europe (central Europe, southern Scandinavia, western Europe), central Asia, Siberia.

**7.** *Chrysis ignita* L. 7—10 mm. Exhibits marked variation in shape and colouring. Front part of the body is blue-green to blue, abdomen gold, reddish-gold or purple. Flies in summer. Fond of visiting the white flowers of Umbelliferae but found also on the walls of country buildings. Locally abundant. Larvae are parasitic on a great many bees and wasps (Eumenidae, Vespidae, Sphecidae, Apidae). Distribution: much of the Palearctic.

## Family: **Ants — Formicidae**

**1.** *Polyergus rufescens* Latr. 6—10 mm. Noted for the forays made by the female workers — 'amazons' — on the nests of other ants, e. g. *Formica fusca,* stealing their larvae and pupae to rear them as 'slaves'. There are several times as many slaves in the nest as amazons. The female cannot build her own nest but seeks out the nest of some other ant, kills the female and reigns in her stead. Amazons are so adapted for fighting that they cannot even feed themselves and are fed by the slaves. Found in dry, sunny situations. Distribution: central and southern Europe, southern Scandinavia; absent from the British Isles.

**2.** *Lasius fuliginosus* Latr. 3—5 mm. Black, very glossy. It builds its sponge-like nest in hollow trees (generally birch, lime, poplar or oak) and grows fungus there. Well-tended paths usually lead from the nests of these ants. Distribution: northern, central and southern Europe, Asia (India), North America.

**3.** *Lasius flavus* F. 2—9 mm. The nest is an earthen mound about 30 cm high. However, the ant also lives under stones and sometimes even in the company of other species. Favours slightly damp situations, abundant in meadows. Distribution: all Europe.

**4.** *Lasius niger* L. 4—10 mm. One of the most common European ants, often abundant in gardens. Nests under stones; if there is a lack of stones, it builds an earthen mound with a maze of tunnels above its underground nest. Distribution: all Europe, India.

**5.** Wood Ant — *Formica rufa* L. 6—11 mm. Occurs in forests where it makes large mounds, usually of pine needles, twigs, moss etc., above its underground nests. As in most ants, there are three castes: workers, males and females. The fertilized female does not build her own nest. She either joins a nest of her own species or else seeks out a nest of the related *Formica fusca.* If the *fusca* nest is without a female the newly-arrived queen is accepted without any fuss, but if the *fusca* nest has a queen there is usually a fight. If the *rufa* queen wins, she takes over as ruler. For a temporary period the nest then contains two types of inhabitants: the original inhabitants, and the offspring of the wood ant queen. The *fusca* ants gradually die out, for there is no queen to produce more *fusca* eggs, and the nest becomes a pure wood ant nest. *Formica rufa* is of great importance in forests in the extermination of larvae of various injurious insects, and it is thus protected by law in some countries. Nowadays it is rapidly declining in numbers. Distribution: Europe (except the south), the Caucasus, Siberia, North America.

**6.** *Camponotus ligniperda* Latr. 7—14 mm. Nests in old stumps and in the living wood of conifers, chiefly spruce. Excavates chambers along the annual rings. The nest is made by the female without the aid of another species of ant. Found generally in lowlands. Distribution: central and northern Europe (absent from the British Isles).

## Family: **Ants — Myrmicidae**

**7.** *Manica rubida* Latr. 5—9 mm (female worker). One of the largest members of the family. Occurs abundantly in foothill and mountain regions where it is found in the ground, often under stones. Adults may be seen from May to August. The sting of this ant is quite painful. Distribution: the Palearctic, absent from British Isles.

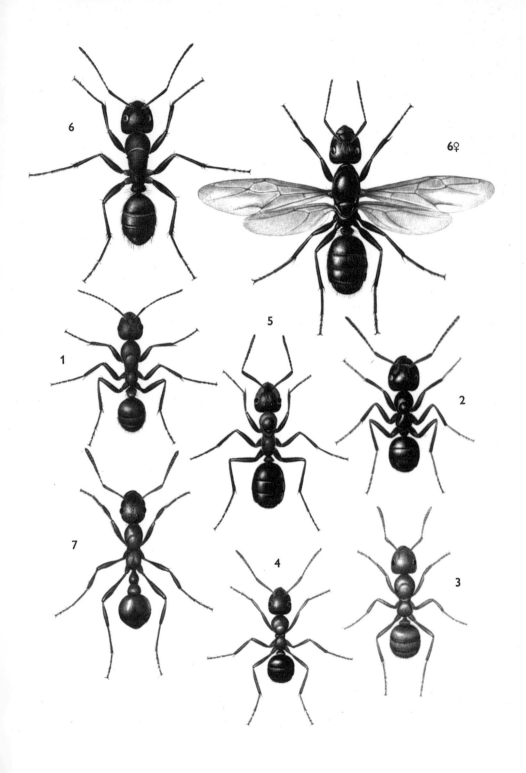

Family: **Spider Wasps — Pompilidae**

1. *Auplopus carbonarius* Scop. 5.5 — 10 mm. Found in June to July on the leaves of blackberry, grapevine, hornbeam and flowering Umbelliferae. The female makes an earthen cell for each egg, cementing together as many as five to seven in a row. Sometimes she attaches them to stones, at other times under bark or elsewhere. For the future larvae she stocks the nests with spiders which she has paralyzed and divested of their legs. Distribution: Europe, north Africa.

2. *Cryptocheilus affinis* Lind. 9 — 15 mm. Usually quite common on flowering Umbelliferae in June to July. Female captures various spiders of the family Lycosidae as food for the larvae. Distribution: Europe, but absent from the British Isles.

3. *Anoplius fuscus* L. 7 — 20 mm. Abundant, particularly in spring, on white-flowering Umbelliferae. On the ground it hunts spiders of the genus *Lycosa,* which it paralyzes and carries off to the nest. Distribution: all Europe.

Family: **Sapygidae**

4. *Sapyga clavicornis* L. 8 — 10 mm. Found in May to June on old beams or old fences, where solitary bees have their nests. Female lays her eggs in the bees' nests. The newly emerged larva devours the larva of the bee as well as the store of honey. Distribution: Europe, Asia Minor, north Africa.

Family: **Eumenidae**

5. *Eumenes pomiformis* F. 10 — 16 mm. Has a long-stalked abdomen and short spherical thorax. The yellow pattern on the black body shows considerable variation. Adults may be seen from spring till September, for there are several generations a year. Female makes a remarkable flask-like nest with a narrow neck for the larva. She attaches it to a stone, under bark, on a wall or on a shrubby plant and stocks it with several small caterpillars, which later serve as food for the larva. This wasp is attacked by various parasites and thus often a cuckoo-wasp *(Chrysis)* or other hymenopterous insect emerges from the flask instead of the rightful offspring. Distribution: much of the Palearctic (but not the British Isles), North America.

6. *Ancistrocerus antilope* Panz. 12 — 15 mm. Resembles many other species of this and related genera. Adults found from May to June on shrubs (e.g. snowberry). The nest is located in sandy banks. Hunts the larvae of Lepidoptera as food for its larvae. The nest of this wasp is often parasitized by various cuckoo-wasps (Chrysididae). Distribution: most of Europe.

7. *Odynerus spinipes* L. 9 — 12 mm. Found in May to June on soil banks in which the female makes the nest. She excavates a small chamber, carrying the bits of earth out and cementing them together to form a tube round the entrance to the nest. The egg is suspended by a slender thread from the ceiling of the chamber. She stocks the nest with several *Phytonomus* larvae. Like other species, this wasp is also attacked by parasites, chiefly cuckoo-wasps (Chrysididae). Distribution: all Europe, Asia Minor, Siberia, north Africa.

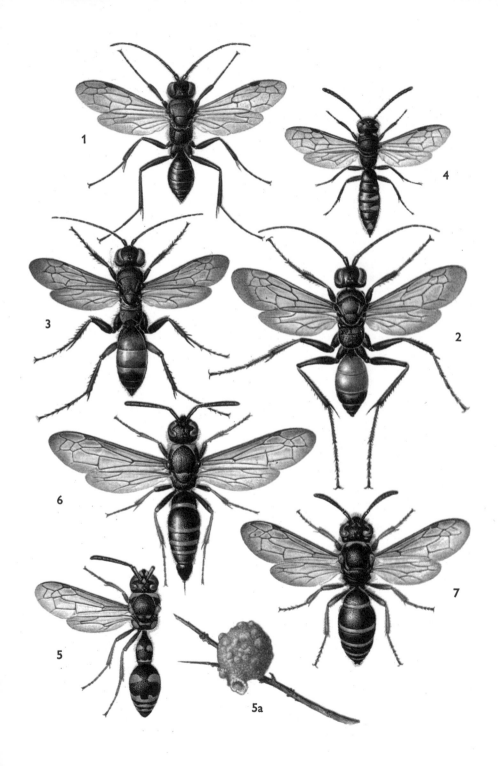

Family: **Vespidae**

1. Hornet — *Vespa crabro* L. 19—35 mm. Largest member of the family. Builds a large nest, usually in hollow trees, sometimes also in the ground. The nest is started by the queen in spring after hibernation. She makes the first cells of paper, lays eggs and begins making the paper envelope enclosing the nest. Five to seven weeks after the first eggs are laid, the nest already contains young workers which take over the queen's duties (apart from laying eggs). They build further tiers of paper cells, feed the larvae and clean the nest. There are usually five to eight tiers of cells in one nest, though larger nests may have as many as twelve. The cells are always on the underside and open downward and the individual tiers are joined by paper stalks. A moderately sized nest contains about 5,000 cells. Hornets are predators that attack even large insects (wasps, bees, etc.). At the end of summer the nest contains males and females that do not take part in building the nest. In the autumn the queen, workers and males all die. Only the young, fertilized females survive the winter, after which they start making a new nest. Distribution: all Europe, the Palearctic regions of Asia, north Africa, North America.

2. True Wasp — *Dolichovespula sylvestris* Scop. 11—18 mm. The nest is built in a variety of semi-dark situations such as caves and under rocky overhangs, but it is typically slung from the branch of a tree where it is clearly visible. In some instances, however, it is partly buried in the ground. It measures less than 10 cm across and contains only two to four tiers. Distribution: Europe (except the southernmost parts), the Palearctic regions of Asia, North America.

3. *Dolichovespula saxonica* F. 11—17 mm. The grey, spherical nest is built on branches and in forests, but more generally in man's dwellings in attics and under the eaves of wooden roofs. It measures 10—15 cm across and contains two to four tiers. The adult is not aggressive. Distribution: the Palearctic (not the British Isles) and Nearctic.

4. Red Wasp — *Vespula rufa* L. 10—20 mm. The nest is built underground. It is the size of a small ball and contains three to five tiers with several hundred cells. Distribution: most of Europe, western Siberia, North America.

5. German Wasp — *Paravespula germanica* F. 10—19 mm. Builds an underground nest, often taking over the abandoned nest of a mouse or some other mammal. The queen makes the first few cells, but the remainder of the nest is built by the workers. They enlarge the hole as needed, carrying grains of earth and stones out in their mandibles. The complete nest measures 20—30 cm across and in the autumn contains some 3,000 individuals. Like related species, these wasps are also predators that capture flies, caterpillars, etc., which they feed to their offspring. They themselves like sweet food, feeding on nectar and in the autumn on sweet fruits. Distribution: the Palearctic and Nearctic.

6. Common Wasp — *Paravespula vulgaris* L. 11—20 mm. Resembles the preceding species. Instead of the three black spots on the face, however, there is usually only a black line or an anchor-like mark. The nest is also built underground but is smaller than that of *P. germanica*. Distribution: the entire Palearctic (usually in the colder regions), North America.

7. *Polistes nimpha* Christ. 12—12.5 mm. The nest is a simple affair with only one tier of several cells. It is attached to a plant by a stalk and is not enclosed in a paper envelope. South of the Alps the nest is built in houses. Distribution: Europe (absent from the north), the Palearctic regions of Asia, north Africa.

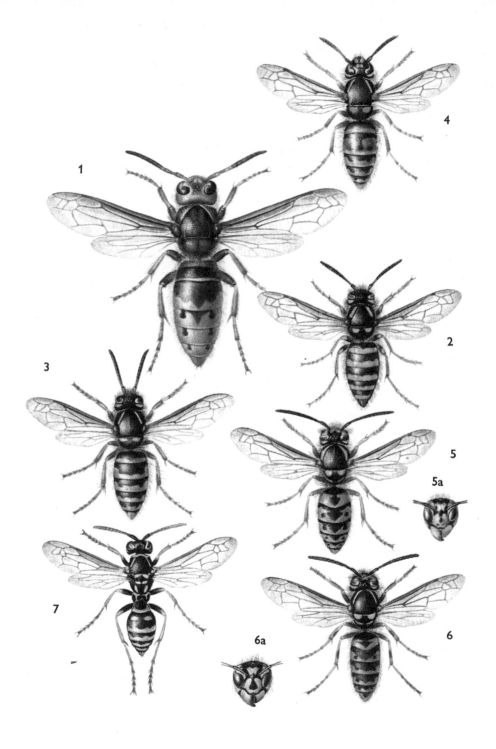

## Family: **Digger Wasps — Sphecidae**

**1.** *Ectemnius dives* Lep. et Brul. 7 — 11.5 mm. Common from June to July on flowering Umbelliferae. Also found on the leaves of young oaks. Nests in old beams. Female stocks the nest with small flies which she paralyzes and which serve as food for the larvae. Distribution: much of the Palearctic, North America.

**2.** *Crabro cribrarius* L. 11 — 17 mm. Common from July to August on flowering Umbelliferae. Nest is built in rotting wood and in soil and, as in the preceding species, is stocked with various flies for the future larvae to feed on. Distribution: much of the Palearctic.

**3.** *Trypoxylon figulus* L. 5.5 — 12.5 mm. Flies from May to July. Nests in straw stems, including thatch on the roofs of country buildings, or in blackberry stems. Nest consists of several cells separated by earthen partitions. For the future larvae, the female stocks the nest with various spiders which she paralyzes. The larvae are full grown in autumn and pupate in a delicate cocoon. Distribution: much of Europe, temperate Asia, north Africa.

**4.** *Larra anathema* Rossi 10 — 25 mm. A rare and extremely thermophilous species that flies from July to August. Nest is built in the ground and stocked chiefly with the larvae of mole-crickets and other Orthoptera. Distribution: southern Europe (extends to Slovakia in central Europe), Asia Minor, north Africa.

**5.** *Gorytes laevis* Latr. 7 — 9.5 mm. Found in summer on flowering Umbelliferae. Locally abundant. Nest is built in sandy soils. Food for the larvae consists of the adults and young of various frog-hoppers and leaf-hoppers. Distribution: Europe, Asia up to Turkestan.

**6.** *Bembicinus tridens* F. 7 — 11 mm. Extremely thermophilous and locally abundant. Found in dry and sandy situations with only sparse vegetation. Nest is built in the ground. The female feeds the larvae from day to day with fresh food — various species of Homoptera. Distribution: southern and central Europe, Asia Minor, central Asia, north Africa.

**7.** *Bembix rostrata* L. 17 — 24 mm. Has a large, robust body. Flies in July to August, mostly in sandy situations, with several individuals usually occurring in one place. Visits various flowers. Female digs a nest in sandy soil just below the surface. She captures various kinds of hover-flies and other two-winged flies for the larvae which are extremely voracious and consume great quantities of food, often several dozen flies a week. Distribution: Europe (in the north as far as southern Scandinavia but absent from the British Isles), Asia Minor, western part of central Asia, north Africa.

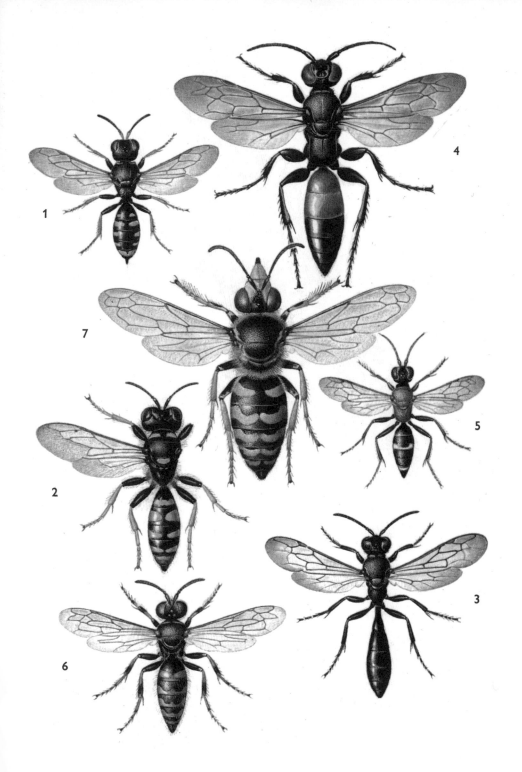

Family: **Sphecidae**

**1.** *Philanthus triangulum* F. 12—18 mm. A striking feature is the large head and short antennae thickened in the middle. Thermophilous, found mostly in steppe-like localities where the female builds the nest. She uses her fore legs and mandibles to carry out quite large grains of sand from her tunnels. She excavates a 20—100-cm-long main tunnel with several lateral tunnels each ending in a 'cell'. A single nest contains an average of five to seven such cells, in which the larvae develop. These feed solely on bees — mainly honey bees *(Apis mellifera)*. The wasp captures the bees on flowers, first paralyzing them and then carrying them off to the nest, grasped by all six legs. It sucks the honey from its prey and then abandons it if not nesting. Two bees suffice as food for the developing male larva, but female larvae require one more. The brood of a single mother requires about twenty bees. When fully grown, the larva spins a flask-like case of silken fibres round itself inside the cell. This is attached to the wall of the cell in horizontal position so that it does not touch the ground, thus protecting the larva from damp and mould. After a ten- to eleven-month period of inactivity, it pupates for a brief period. Distribution: much of the Palearctic, except the north. Very rare in the British Isles.

**2.** *Cerceris arenaria* L. 9—17 mm. Found in summer on sandy soil. Female hunts weevils (Curculionidae) as food for the larvae. Distribution: most of Europe.

**3.** *Sphex maxillosus* L. 16—27 mm. Found on flowering thyme. Nests in sandy soil at the edges of forests, the hole being dug by the female at a shallow depth. She captures various grasshoppers and crickets as food for the larvae. Distribution: southern and central Europe, Asia Minor, Middle East (Iran), Afghanistan, north Africa.

**4.** *Ammophila sabulosa* L. 16—28 mm. Found from June to October in sandy localities where it visits various flowers. Nest is a burrow in the sand excavated by the female. Before setting out to hunt a larva she carefully conceals the entrance hole. Paralyzing her prey she carries it back to the nest, places it inside and lays an egg on it, after which she closes the entrance, pounding down the earth with a small stone or some other object held in the mandibles. Distribution: much of the Palearctic.

**5.** *Podalonia hirsuta* Scop. 12—22 mm. Found from June to July in sandy situations. The female brings a paralyzed caterpillar into its nest and lays an egg on it. Distribution: much of the Palearctic, locally abundant.

**6.** *Sceliphron destillatorium* Ill. 15—30 mm. Occurs from July to August. The nest is made of mud and consists of several cells filled with paralyzed spiders. A single larva develops in each cell. Distribution: Europe (mostly in the south; absent from the British Isles), central Asia, Iran, etc.

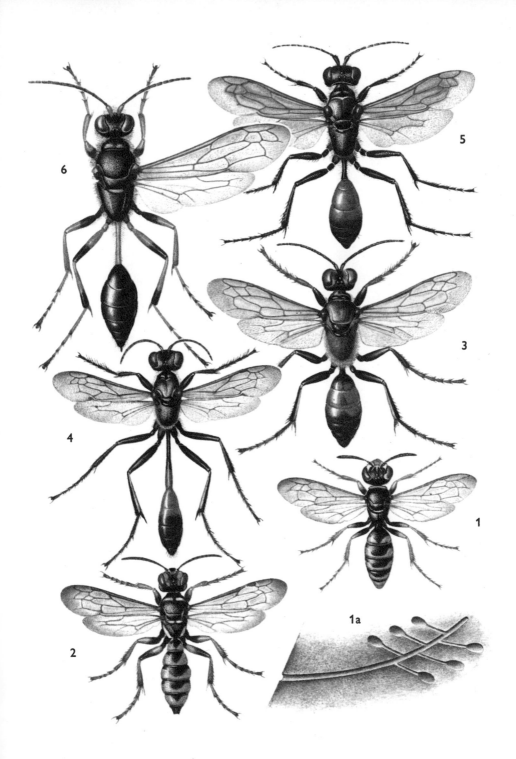

## Super-family: **Bees — Apoidea**

**1.** *Colletes daviesanus* Sm. 8 — 11 mm. Found in July to August on flower heads of Compositae; frequent on yarrow, tansy and other plants. Female digs the nest in soil banks, lining it with a sort of slime secreted by the mandibular glands. The substance quickly hardens, giving the walls a silky sheen. It is also used to close the entrance to the nest. Distribution: Europe, Siberia.

**2.** *Prosopis annulata* L. 6 — 7 mm. In Europe many related and very similar species occur that are extremely difficult to distinguish. Adults fly in June to July. Common on flowering Umbelliferae, yarrow etc. Nests in old beams. Distribution: central and northern Europe.

**3.** *Andrena tibialis* K. 13 — 15 mm. Member of a very large genus which in Europe numbers some 150 very similar species. Usually two generations a year. The first flies from April to May, visiting chiefly the flowers of currant and dandelion and the catkins of sallows. The second generation, which is somewhat smaller (12 — 13 mm), is common on bramble and Cruciferae. Female makes the nest in the ground — it is shaped like a grape cluster. Often parasitic bees of the genus *Nomada,* which do not have nests of their own, emerge instead of the rightful offspring. Distribution: all Europe.

**4.** *Panurgus calcaratus* Scop. 8 — 9 mm. Found from July to August, often very abundantly on various Compositae, chiefly on hawkweed, dandelion, etc. It crawls between the individual florets on its side so that it is covered with yellow pollen all over. Often nests gregariously. Distribution: all Europe.

**5.** *Halictus quadricinctus* F. 15 — 16 mm. Among the largest of the European *Halictus* species. Adults emerge in autumn and both sexes occur on flowers. After mating, the males die and the females hibernate in various hiding places, returning again to the flowers in spring. They make a fairly large nest in soil banks, consisting of a main corridor with cells opening on to it from either side. It already looks somewhat like the comb made by social Hymenoptera. Distribution: Europe.

**6.** *Sphecodes gibbus* L. 7 — 13 mm. Similar in shape and red colour of the abdomen to at least 50 other related European species. Adults emerge in the autumn. After mating, the males die, the females hibernate. In spring, as early as April or May, they visit flowering dandelions and the catkins of willow. Like other related species, this one is a parasite in the nests of *Halictus* bees. Distribution: Europe.

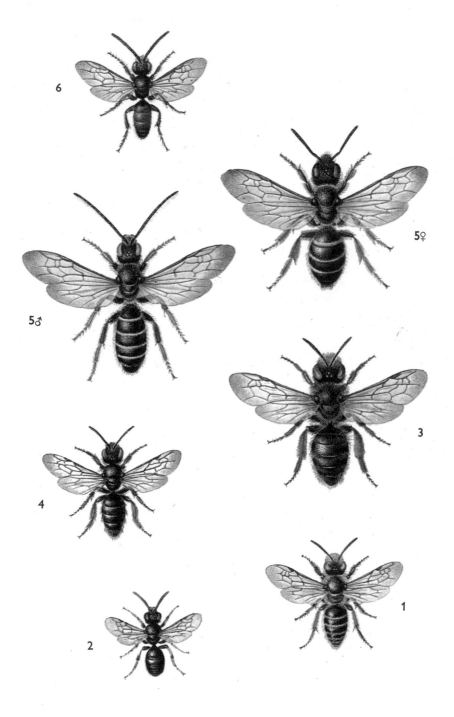

Super-family: **Apoidea**

**1.** *Melitta leporina* Panz. 11 — 13 mm. Commonest member of the genus. Flies from July to August, favouring the flowers of clover and lucerne. Nest consists of a small number of underground cells filled with a mass of pollen on which lies the egg. The full-grown larva spins a cocoon. Distribution: central and northern Europe.

**2.** *Dasypoda hirtipes* F. 13 — 15 mm. Flies from July to August, visiting hawkweed, wild thyme, etc. Female makes an underground nest reaching a depth of as much as 60 cm. Each cell contains a ball of pollen supported by three 'legs' so that it does not touch the ground and will not become mouldy. Egg is laid upon the pollen. Larva hibernates. Distribution: almost the entire Palearctic.

**3.** Leaf-cutter Bee — *Megachile centuncularis* L. 9 — 12 mm. Occurs from June to August. Nest is located in hollows in the ground or in plant stems. Cells are lined with fragments of rose leaves which the bee cuts with its mandibles and carries to the hollow. Larva feeds on the store of honey stored by the female. Distribution: central and northern Europe.

**4.** *Osmia rufa* L. 8 — 12 mm. Adults emerge in autumn, but do not leave their shelters until spring. In March to April they visit willow catkins, violets, lungworts and other spring flowers. Nest is located in various crevices and in roofs, and is made of a mixture of earth and saliva. Distribution: most of Europe, Transcaucasia.

**5.** *Anthidium punctatum* Latr. 8 — 9 mm. Flies in June to July. Nests in the ground. Distribution: central Europe, southern Scandinavia, Siberia. Absent from British Isles.

**6.** *Anthophora plagiata* Ill. 13 — 15 mm. Nests communally in soil banks. Leading to the nest is a down-curved entrance tube made of bits of earth cemented together. The species is rapidly declining. Distribution: central Europe.

**7.** *Eucera longicornis* L. 14 — 16 mm. Visits *Pilatus*, vetch and various orchids in April and May. Nests in the ground. Distribution: all Europe.

**8.** *Xylocopa violacea* L. 21 — 24 mm. One of Europe's largest bees. Adults emerge in autumn, hibernate, and in spring the female makes the nest in old trunks and branches. Making a short tunnel to enter the wood, she excavates a vertical tunnel some 15 — 30 cm long which she divides into about fifteen cells. She stocks each cell with a store of pollen upon which she lays the egg and then seals off the cell with a partition of wood chips. Larva feeds on the stored pollen and pupates in the cell. The adult cuts its way out through the side wall. If the wall is too thick, it waits until the bees in the upper part of the tunnel hatch and then the bees emerge one after the other through the opening made originally by the female. It is interesting to note that the female returns to her nest even from distances of several kilometres. Distribution: southern Europe, southern part of central Europe (Rhine valley, Lahn valley, southern Slovakia).

**9.** *Ceratina cyanea* Kirby 6 — 7 mm. Visits flowers. Adults hibernate in the stems of blackberry. The following spring the female excavates a tunnel in the dry stalks. This is made up of several cells which she stocks with pollen, laying an egg on top of each pile. Distribution: almost all Europe except the far north.

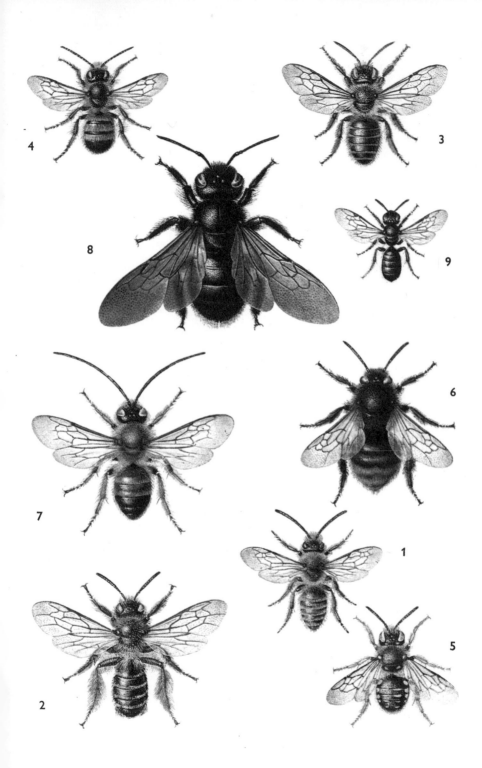

## Super-family: Apoidea

**1.** *Bombus pomorum* Panz. ♀ 20—24 mm. Nests in the ground. In May, after coming out of hibernation, the queen visits primroses, deadnettle, etc. Males are usually abundant in autumn, chiefly in fields of clover. Found at elevations of up to 1,900 metres. The colony is small, containing only several dozen individuals. Distribution: western Europe (rare), central Europe, Siberia.

**2.** *Bombus sylvarum* L. ♀ 18—20 mm. Flies mostly at lower and median elevations. Females are common in May on deadnettle, males in the autumn on Umbelliferae and scabious. Nest is located above ground, often in the deserted nest of a bird or mammal. Distribution: all Europe, absent in northern Scandinavia.

**3.** *Bombus muscorum* F. ♀ 20—24 mm. A rare species. Females occur in May on deadnettle and bugle; males in autumn in fields of clover. The colony is small and the nest is located above ground. Distribution: Europe, northern Asia.

**4.** *Bombus lapidarius* L. ♀ 20—25 mm. Most plentiful and best known of the European bumblebees. Females are on the wing early in April seeking a suitable spot for the nest. It is built underground, often amidst stones as well as in crevices and between bricks of country buildings. A single colony usually consists of 100—300 individuals. Like all other species of bumblebees, it is protected by law in Czechoslovakia for it is an important pollinator. The nest is often infested by the parasitic bumblebee *Psithyrus rupestris*. Distribution: Eurasia.

**5.** *Bombus terrestris* L. ♀ 24—28 mm. Has ochre-brownish-yellow bands on the thorax and abdomen. British race have buff tails. Females fly out of their winter shelters in April and are common on catkins. Nest is built deep in the ground, often in a deserted mousehole. The colony is quite large (200—300 individuals). Distribution: Europe, Asia Minor, northern Asia, north Africa.

**6.** *Bombus lucorum* L. ♀ 20—24 mm. Greatly resembles the preceding bee on the continent, the two being originally considered a single species. However, it is smaller and the bands are coloured lemon yellow. The two cannot be confused in Britain because of the buff tail of *B. terrestris*. Common. Females emerge in April. Distribution: Europe, northern Asia.

**7.** *Psithyrus rupestris* F. up to 25 mm. Resembles a large bumblebee but has much darker wings and female lacks the pollen baskets on the hind legs (besides other different characters). Unlike bumblebees it has no workers. Adults occur in late summer; males die after mating, females hibernate. In spring they lay their eggs in the nest of *Bombus lapidarius* or *Bombus sylvarum,* where the young are reared. Distribution: Europe, the Palearctic regions of Asia.

**8.** Honey Bee — *Apis mellifera* L. 12—20 mm. Best known of all insects. Lives in colonies ruled over by a queen which lays the eggs. The colony consist largely of workers which during their short lifetime perform various tasks (collecting pollen and nectar, feeding the grubs, cleaning the hive, etc.). The males (drones), which hatch from unfertilized eggs, appear in the late summer. The entire colony hibernates. The honey-bee is regarded as a domestic animal, though it has never become truly domesticated. It still retains all its natural habits, such as swarming and departure of the swarm from the hive. Provider of honey and wax. Distribution: cosmopolitan.

Order: **Caddis Flies — Trichoptera**

Family: **Rhyacophilidae**

**1.** *Rhyacophila vulgaris* Pict. 7—9 mm, wingspan 24—32 mm. Common species found from late summer until autumn (August to October). Larvae live in fast-flowing streams. They crawl on stones, keeping hold with the claws on their legs. To prevent their being swept away by the current, they also secrete a protective thread. They do not build cases. Only for pupating does the fully grown larva cement together a case of stones in which it transforms in the water. Distribution: most of Europe except the far north. Absent from British Isles.

Family: **Philopotamidae**

**2.** *Philopotamus variegatus* Scop. 7—9 mm, wingspan 21—29 mm. Flies in June to August in foothills and mountains at elevations between 600 and 1,500 metres. Larvae live in tube-like nests, often several together. Full-grown larva is about 20 mm long. Distribution: most of Europe. Absent from British Isles.

Family: **Polycentropidae**

**3.** *Polycentropus flavomaculatus* Pict. 3.5—6 mm, wingspan 13—21 mm. Occurs around streams in July to August. Often rests on tree trunks by the waterside. Larvae inhabit mountain streams, in lowlands only fast-flowing streams. They rest on stones and on vegetation and make about 12-mm-long pouch-shaped cases in which they live. Distribution: Europe, Siberia.

Family: **Hydropsychidae**

**4.** *Hydropsyche angustipennis* Curt. 6—10 mm, wingspan 18—27 mm. Flies in May to August. Very difficult to distinguish from several similar species. Larvae live in flowing streams, spinning funnel-shaped nets to trap food, mostly small insect larvae. Distribution: almost all Europe, Asia Minor.

Family: **Leptoceridae**

**5.** *Athripsodes cinereus* Curt. 7—7.5 mm, wingspan 20—24 mm. Flies from June to mid-October over slow-flowing and stagnant water. Most abundant in lowlands. Larvae likewise live in slow-flowing streams and make slender portable cases. Distribution: the Palearctic and Nearctic.

Family: **Phryganeidae**

**6.** *Phryganea grandis* L. 15—21 mm, wingspan 40—60 mm. Largest of the caddis flies. Found from lowland to mountain elevations but most abundant in lowlands. Adults occur in May to August near stagnant water. They fly in the evening, resting on the bark of trees in the daytime. Larvae live in still water and build cases of plant fragments arranged in spiral form. These may reach 40 mm in length. Larvae occur on aquatic vegetation where they hunt various insect larvae. Distribution: the Palearctic and Nearctic.

Family: **Limnephilidae**

**7.** *Limnephilus griseus* L. 6.5—12 mm, wingspan 19—30 mm. Occurs in May to November, sometimes even until December on still water. Larvae live in ponds and make cases of plant fragments. Distribution: central, northern and eastern Europe, Greenland, Iceland, the Caucasus, Asia Minor, Siberia.

242

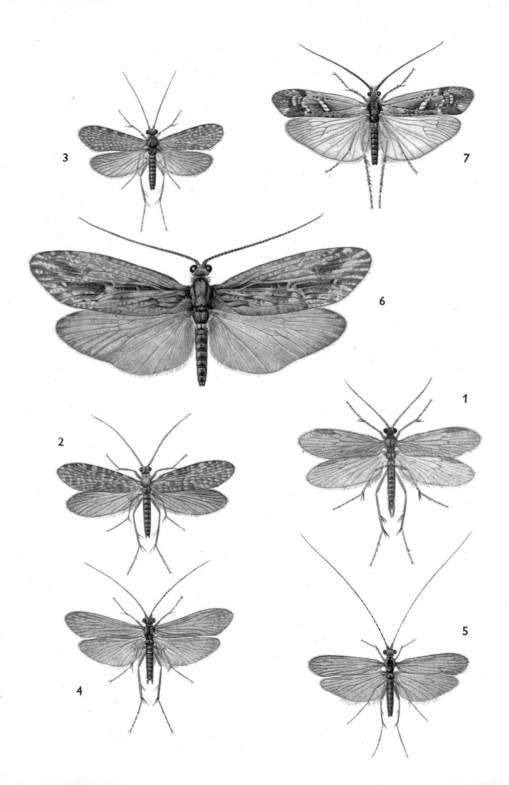

Order: **Butterflies and Moths — Lepidoptera**
(measurements in this section give the length of the fore wing)

Family: **Micropterygidae**

1. *Micropteryx calthella* L. 4—4.5 mm. Common member of this remarkable family related to the caddis flies (Trichoptera). These small insects, which resemble tineid moths, possess mandibles which they use to feed on pollen. Fly in daytime from May to June. Common on buttercups and their relatives (Ranunculaceae). Distribution: Europe, (except the north).

Family: **Swift Moths — Hepialidae**

2. Ghost Swift — *Hepialus humuli* L. 20—35 mm. Found from June to August in damp meadows, forests and in parks. Male and female differ in size and colouring. In the daytime they remain concealed in vegetation; they fly mostly on warm June nights. Female deposits eggs in flight. There are 12 larval stages. Caterpillar burrows in the ground where it feeds on the roots of dandelion, colts-foot, sorrel, hops and other plants. It hibernates (often twice), after which it pupates in the ground. Distribution: much of the Palearctic (north to the Arctic Circle), Middle East.

3. Gold Swift — *Hepialus hectus* L. 10—15 mm. Flies mostly in June to July, sometimes also in early August, in damp meadows, forest edges or on heaths. Caterpillar feeds on the roots of primrose, heather, sorrel and many other grassland and woodland plants. Distribution: north and central Europe, across Asia to Japan.

Family: **Adelidae**

4. *Nemophora degeerella* L. 7—8 mm. Noted for its long antennae, which are unusually long in the males. Flies in spring round plants and in forest undergrowth. Flight is jerky, slow, often compared to the dance of mayflies. Distribution: throughout Europe to Asia Minor.

Family: **Carpenter Moths — Cossidae**

5. Leopard Moth — *Zeuzera pyrina* L. 18—35 mm. Found in June to August at the edges of forests, in fruit orchards, in tree-lined avenues and in parks. Male is smaller (wingspan about 40—50 mm) than the female (60—70 mm); the bottom halves of his antennae are plumose, whereas the female's are filiform. Female lays several hundred eggs in crevices in bark. Caterpillars gradually make their way into the young and older branches as well as trunks of the host plant — apple, pear, ash, birch, elm, maple and other deciduous trees. Caterpillar hibernates once or twice. Distribution: southern and central Europe (including British Isles), temperate regions of Asia (China, Japan), north Africa, North America.

6. Goat Moth — *Cossus cossus* L. 30—41 mm. Found in May to September from lowlands to mountains (1,500 metres). Flies only at night, resting pressed tight against the bark of trees during the day. Female lays several hundred eggs, always in batches of 15—50, in crevices in the bark of diseased and dying trees. Host plants are chiefly deciduous forest and fruit trees. Caterpillars first make their way to the cambium layer, later boring deep into solid wood. They are red, measuring up to 10 cm when fully grown, and are recognized by the characteristic smell they emit. They hibernate twice. Distribution: much of the Palearctic.

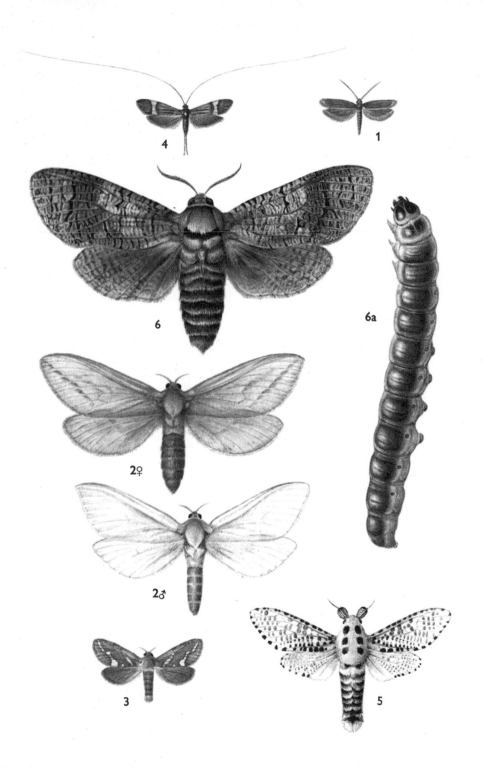

Family: **Burnets and Foresters — Zygaenidae**

1. *Zygaena ephialtes* L. 14—16 mm. Flies in July to August at the edges of forests, in clearings and sunny situations. Exhibits marked variation in colouring and has many colour forms named after the colour and number of spots on the front wings. These include combinations of red and white or yellow and white spots. Caterpillars generally feed on crown vetch *(Coronilla varia)*, clover and thyme. Distribution: from western across central Europe, east to Siberia. Absent from British Isles.

2. Six-spot Burnet — *Zygaena filipendulae* L. 14—18 mm. Occurs abundantly in summer on sunny slopes, in hedgerows, clearings and meadows where it visits flowers. Found from lowland to mountain elevations. The black-spotted caterpillars are found on Papilionaceae. They hibernate, and pupate in June. Distribution: almost all Europe (e. g. Transcaucasia, Canary Islands). Many colour forms and geographic races exist.

3. *Zygaena carniolica* Scop. 12—15 mm. Flies from June to August in sunny situations, favouring areas with limestone substrate. Quite variable in colouring and number of spots on the front wings; there are several colour forms. Caterpillars found from August on birdsfoot-trefoil *(Lotus corniculatus)* and other *Lotus* spp. They hibernate and pupate in cocoons on the ground. Distribution: Europe as far north as Latvia (absent from Great Britain), Transcaucasia (Armenia), Asia Minor, Iran.

4. *Adscita statices* L. 11—14 mm. Occurs abundantly from May to August in damp meadows, forest margins and steppes from lowland to mountain elevations (1,000 metres). Caterpillars feed on sorrel. Distribution: from northern and southern Europe to southern Scandinavia.

Family: **Bagworm Moths — Psychidae**

5. *Apterona crenulella* Brd. ♂ 6—7 mm. A very remarkable species which occurs in two forms. The one has both sexes and is widespread in the south (Italy), the other, so-called *helix,* is parthenogenetic (females only) and is found in most of Europe (not British Isles) and western Asia. Larva feeds on various herbs. It makes a coiled case resembling a snail-shell attached to grasses and tree trunks.

6. *Canephora unicolor* Hufn. 12—14 mm. A common species of forest margins and meadows. Larva makes a fairly large sac 3—4 cm long. Distribution: most of the Palearctic.

Family: **Tineidae**

7. Tapestry Moth — *Trichophaga tapetzella* L. 6—8 mm. A troublesome pest. Larvae feed on woollen fabrics, felt, etc. Distribution: cosmopolitan.

8. Common Clothes Moth — *Tineola biselliella* Humm. 4—8 mm. Most common moth in houses. Flies in spring. Eggs are laid in woollen fabrics, furs, garments, etc. Distribution: cosmopolitan.

Family: **Lyonetiidae**

**1.** *Lyonetia clerkella* L. 4 — 6 mm. Found from lowlands to mountains (in the Alps at c. 2,000 metres). Three generations a year, moths of the third generation hibernating in crevices in bark, moss, etc. Eggs are laid singly in the leaves of plants. Larva hatches after one to two weeks and makes a serpentine mine in the leaf with a central line of excrement. When fully grown it leaves the mine and pupates on the leaf. Pest in some regions. Larvae feed chiefly on fruit trees (apple, pear, cherry, etc.) as well as on rowan, birch, etc. Distribution: much of the Palearctic.

Family: **Gracillariidae**

**2.** *Lithocolletis blancardella* F. 2 — 5 mm. In central and western Europe it has two generations, in the Mediterranean region three or four. Eggs are laid singly on the underside of leaves of various trees (rowan, hawthorn, apple, pear, etc.). Young larva bores into the plant tissue where it makes a blotch mine. Larva of the second generation hibernates in the cooler regions. Distribution: Europe, Siberia, Japan, North America (introduced).

Family: **Clearwings — Sesiidae**

**3.** Hornet Moth — *Sesia apiformis* Cl. 15 — 20 mm. Resembles a wasp in colouring. Flies in full sunlight from May to July, chiefly in avenues of poplars and along streams bordered by poplars on which the larvae feed. The first year they live under the bark, in their second year in the wood of the trunk close to the ground and in the roots. They pupate in a cocoon in the bark. Distribution: from western Europe to Siberia, Asia Minor, North America (introduced).

**4.** Red-belted Clearwing — *Conopia myopaeformis* Borkh. 8 — 9 mm. Flies from May to July in fruit orchards. Larvae live in old diseased trees (apple, rowan, pear, etc.). They pupate under the bark. Distribution: western and central Europe, the Balkans, Asia Minor.

Family: **Yponomeutidae**

**5.** *Yponomeuta padella* L. 9 — 10 mm. Flies in June to July. Female lays the eggs in July in batches in the twigs of hawthorn or plum and covers them with a protective layer. Larvae hatch in the autumn and hibernate communally under a protective plate. In spring they feed on buds, later moving to the leaves round which they spin webs. They live in a communal web where they also pupate. Distribution: the entire Palearctic.

Family: **Case Moths — Coleophoridae**

**6.** *Coleophora laricella* Hbn. 4 — 5 mm. Found from May to June in larch stands. Distribution: central and northern Europe.

Family: **Nebs and Groundlings — Gelechiidae**

**7.** *Scrobipalpa ocellatella* Boyd. 5 — 6 mm. Flies already in April. Larvae feed on wild beet, as well as cultivated forms to which they are injurious. Distribution: much of Europe, Asia Minor, Middle East, north Africa, etc.

Family: **Cochylidae**

**8.** *Eupoecilia ambiguella* Hb. 7 — 8 mm. Larvae feed on a very wide range of plants and are particularly fond of grapevine. Distribution: most of Europe, Asia (China, Japan, etc.).

Family: **Tortricidae**

**1.** *Pandemis heparana* Den. Schiff. 8—11 mm. There are two generations. The first flies in June to July, the second from late August to September, after dusk. Eggs are laid in batches on leaves. Full-grown larva is green, about 2.5 cm long. It lives on deciduous trees and shrubs in forests and gardens. Larva hibernates. Distribution: all Europe, Middle East, Siberia, China, Japan.

**2.** *Archips crataegana* Hb. 8—11 mm. Flies in June to August. Better known than the moth are the clusters of eggs cemented in batches of about 30 in the crevices of various trees. They are covered by a whitish protective layer. Eggs hibernate. Larvae hatch in spring, feeding firstly on buds, later on leaves which they roll into tubes. Distribution: most of Europe, Asia Minor, Siberia, Japan.

**3.** *Epinotia tedella* Cl. 5—6 mm. Flies from May to July in spruce forests. Eggs are laid on the needles on which the larvae feed when they hatch. They live communally in a sort of nest made of needles, in which they also store their excrement. Before the onset of winter they leave the nest, hibernate and then pupate in spring. Distribution: Europe, except the south.

**4.** Codling Moth — *Cydia pomonella* L. 7—9 mm. Usually one or two but sometimes even more generations. Larvae feed on apples and pears. They are about 2 cm long, coloured pink. When fully grown they leave the fruit and hibernate, usually in crevices and other hiding places. They may cause damage in apple-growing regions. Distribution: cosmopolitan.

**5.** Green Oak Tortrix Moth — *Tortrix viridana* L. 9—11 mm. Flies from June to August but lives only one week. Found in tops of oaks. Eggs are laid in twos on slender oak twigs. They hatch in spring. Young larvae enter opening buds, later they feed on the leaves of oaks and other plants such as elder and honeysuckle. Older larvae bend leaves and fasten them together with silken threads. May be a troublesome pest if it occurs in greater numbers. Distribution: much of Europe, Asia Minor.

Family: **Alucitidae**

**6.** *Orneodes desmodactyla* Zell. 5 mm. Easily identified as a member of this small family by having the wings divided into six plumes each. Flies in June to August. Larvae feed on the flowers of *Stachys recta*, *S. silvatica* and others. Distribution: from southern Europe to the southern parts of central Europe.

Family: **Pyralidae**

**7.** Mediterranean Flour Moth — *Ephestia kuehniella* Zell. 10—12 mm. Occurs abundantly in storehouses and households, for the larval stage is passed in flour. Distribution: probably native to India but now cosmopolitan.

**8.** Meal Moth — *Pyralis farinalis* L. 8—12 mm. A pest of flour, in which the larval stage is passed. Plentiful everywhere. Distribution: Eurasia, North America, Australia.

Family: **Grass Moths — Crambidae**

**1.** *Catoptria myella* Hb. 11 — 12 mm. Flies in June to July, primarily at higher elevations. Larvae are found under moss. Distribution: central and northern Europe (Alps, Carpathians). Rare in British Isles (Scotland).

Family: **Plume Moths — Pterophoridae**

**2.** *Oxyptilus pilosellae* Zell. 9 mm. Its relationship to the family is evidenced not only by the fissured wings but chiefly by the extremely long legs. Adults fly from June to August. Larvae occur in May to June on hawkweed *(Hieracium* spp.*)* where they pupate on the stem and leaves. Distribution: much of Europe, north to Finland and Latvia, Transcaucasia.

**3.** *Emmelina monodactyla* L. 12 mm. Very common. Larvae feed on the flowers and leaves of bindweed *(Convolvulus arvensis),* sometimes also on orach, goosefoot, and other plants. Adults hibernate. Distribution: Europe, Asia Minor, North America.

Family: **Skippers — Hesperiidae**

**4.** Silver Spotted Skipper — *Hesperia comma* L. 14 — 17 mm. Sexes differ in colouring. Male has a black patch with silvery streak on the front wing. Adults fly from July to August in widely varied situations. Eggs overwinter. Larvae emerge in spring and are found in April to June on grasses *(Poa, Festuca,* etc. *).* Several forms exist. Distribution: Eurasia, from British Isles to Japan.

**5.** Grizzled Skipper — *Pyrgus malvae* L. 10 — 11 mm. There are two successive generations between April and August. Usually found in forest clearings, forest margins and fields from lowland to mountain elevations. Larvae feed on raspberry, bramble, strawberry, *Potentilla reptans* and other plants. They are concealed in rolled leaves. Distribution: Europe, from the Balkans to southern Scandinavia, Asia.

**6.** Chequered Skipper — *Carterocephalus palaemon* Pall. 13 — 14 mm. Occurs in May to July mostly in damp forest margins, damp meadows and along pathways where there are ample flowers on which it likes to rest. Larvae appear from July till the following May (they hibernate) on various herbs, favouring ribwort plantain, couch grass and brome grass. Distribution: common in certain parts of Europe, elsewhere rarer, especially in British Isles and other parts of north-western Europe; Asia (to the Amur); North America.

**7.** Dingy Skipper — *Erynnis tages* L. 13 — 14 mm. Two generations: the first in April to June, the second in July to August. Abundant on sunny paths, in glades and in gardens. Larvae found on bird's foot trefoil, crown vetch, *Eryngium campestre* and other herbs. They hibernate. Distribution: Europe, northern Asia.

4

6

7

5

3

1

2

Family: **Swallow-tails and Apollos — Papilionidae**

**1.** Swallow-tail — *Papilio machaon* L. 34—45 mm. Two generations occur (April to May, July to August), in the south also a third (September to October). Occurs even in mountains (at elevations of 2,000 metres in the Alps). In hilly country often found on Umbelliferae. Caterpillar feeds primarily on fennel, caraway, wild carrot, etc.; in the Near East also on citrus trees. Distribution: almost all Europe except the northern parts; temperate regions of Asia; North America. Very rare in Great Britain; during the past two decades it has also been disappearing in central Europe in places where it was once plentiful.

**2.** Scarce Swallow-tail — *Iphiclides podalirius* L. 35—45 mm. Flies from May to early July, sometimes a second generation occurs in July—August. Most often found on warm sunny slopes in hilly country with limestone substrate. Caterpillars occur on blackthorn, hawthorn, fruit trees, etc. They pupate before the onset of winter and the pupae hibernate. Distribution: Europe, Transcaucasia, Asia Minor, Iran, western China. Absent from British Isles. The northern limits of its range in Europe are 51°N. It is protected by law in Germany and Czechoslovakia.

**3.** Southern Festoon — *Zerynthia polyxena* Den. Schiff. 22—30 mm. Occurs only locally from late April to May. Flight quite clumsy, close to the ground. Caterpillars feed on various species of birthwort *(Aristolochia rotunda, A. pistolochia, A. clematidis, A. sicula)* from May. Their development lasts about four to five weeks, after which they pupate. Pupa overwinters. A warmth-loving species with a limited range. Distribution: south-eastern and central Europe as far north as Austria and Czechoslovakia; found also in the Balkans, Greece and certain parts of Asia Minor.

**4.** Apollo — *Parnassius apollo* L. 34—50 mm. Flight slow and cumbersome. Found on mountain slopes, meadows and valleys, usually resting on thistles. Flies in June to August. Caterpillar feeds on *Sedum album.* It hibernates and then pupates in spring. Several hundred forms have been described throughout its range. In some places, e. g. Bohemia, it has become extinct. Distribution: from the Pyrenees across the Alps and Carpathians, the Caucasus as far as the Altai. Protected by law in Germany and Czechoslovakia.

**5.** Clouded Apollo — *Parnassius mnemosyne* L. 27—32 mm. Flies in May to July close above the ground. Rests on vegetation bordering mountain streams, in meadows and on forest rides. Found in lowlands and mountains up to c. 1,500 metres. Caterpillars occur on *Corydalis.* Many geographic races exist, e. g. the dark race *Parnassius mnemosyne* ssp. *hartmanni* in the Bavarian Alps. Distribution: from the Pyrenees across central Europe north to Norway; eastward as far as the Caucasus and central Asia. This butterfly is rapidly declining in numbers and is therefore protected by law in some countries (Czechoslovakia, Germany).

Family: **Whites and Yellows — Pieridae**

1. Large White — *Pieris brassicae* L. 29—34 mm. In central Europe two to three generations occur; in the south as many as five. Often found in large numbers. Eggs are laid on the leaves of Cruciferae — cabbage, cauliflower, turnip, etc. Prior to pupation the caterpillars leave the host plant and hide in a sheltered place. Caterpillars in large numbers are injurious. Pupae overwinter. Distribution: almost the entire Palearctic.

2. Small White — *Pieris rapae* L. 20—26 mm. Two to three successive generations occur, so that it may be seen from early spring till autumn. Caterpillars feed mainly on Cruciferae, and in large numbers are injurious. Pupa overwinters. One of the commonest butterflies. Distribution: from western Europe to Japan; north Africa, North America (introduced), Australasia (introduced).

3. Green-veined White — *Pieris napi* L. 20—25 mm. Two generations. Found in fields, gardens, forest margins, etc. Distribution: Europe, temperate regions of Asia, north Africa, North America.

4. Black-veined White — *Aporia crataegi* L. 32—35 mm. Flies in May to July. Formerly a pest of fruit orchards, it is now much rarer. In some places (e. g. Great Britain) it has recently become extinct. Caterpillars found on fruit trees. Distribution: most of Europe across the temperate regions of Asia to Korea and Japan, north Africa.

5. Orange Tip — *Anthocharis cardamines* L. 21—25 mm. Occurs in April to June from lowlands to mountains in forest margins, glades, forest rides, meadows and gardens. Male has a large orange patch on each forewing. Eggs usually laid on flower buds or the underside of leaves of Cruciferae, on which the caterpillars feed — mostly cuckooflower, garlic mustard, *Biscutella*, *Sisymbrium* and *Turittis*. Distribution: Europe, temperate regions of Asia, Japan.

6. Clouded Yellow — *Colias croceus* Fourcr. 22—28 mm. Migrant whose main home is north Africa and the Mediterranean area. Moves north across Europe in April to May, flying mainly in fields with vetch and clover which, besides other papilionaceous plants, are the chief food of the caterpillar. Summer brings up to three more generations. In autumn a large number of butterflies return south. Adults and larvae remaining in northern and central Europe do not survive the winter. Distribution: most of Europe, Asia Minor, Middle East (Iran), north Africa, Canary Islands, Madeira.

7. Brimstone — *Gonepteryx rhamni* L. 27—30 mm. One of the earliest species to appear in spring, when it emerges from its winter shelter. Male is bright yellow, female whitish with a green shade. Caterpillars found on buckthorn *(Rhamnus frangula)* in June to July. Butterflies emerge from the pupae in summer but a few days later they fall into a summer sleep, resuming their flight again in autumn. They hibernate. Distribution: Europe, Asia Minor, Middle East, eastern Siberia, north Africa.

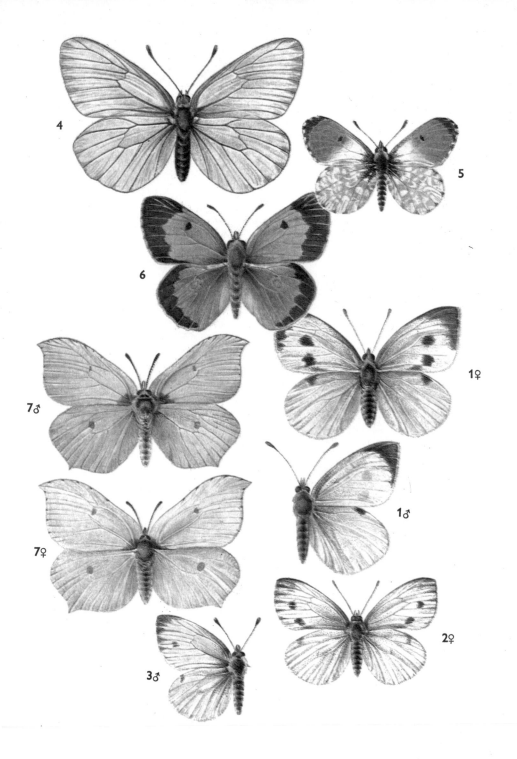

Family: **Blues, Coppers and Hairstreaks — Lycaenidae**

**1. Purple Hairstreak** — *Quercusia quercus* L. 17—18 mm. Flies in July to August in the tops of oaks. Eggs overwinter. Caterpillars hatch in late spring and are most abundant in June on oak leaves. Distribution: in two geographic races from north Africa (Morocco, Algeria) to southern Scandinavia, Asia Minor.

**2. White-letter Hairstreak** — *Strymonidia w-album* Kn. 16—18 mm. Name derived from the white markings on the underside of the hind wings resembling the letter 'W'. Found in June to August chiefly in hilly country and in stony and rocky places, but not in large numbers. Eggs overwinter. Caterpillars emerge in May to June. They feed mainly on elm leaves. Distribution: Europe, from the Pyrenees and Italy to southern Scandinavia, across Asia to Japan.

**3. Green Hairstreak** — *Callophrys rubi* L. 15—17 mm. Wings sombrely coloured above, green on the underside. Found in dry situations — heaths, dry pine forests, etc. — as early as March to April, when the butterflies emerge from the pupae. In warmer regions (north Africa) a second, usually partial generation occurs in July to August. Butterflies found up to elevations of 1,800 metres. Caterpillars, which may be seen from May until late summer, are polyphagous. Distribution: from north Africa to northernmost parts of Scandinavia, Siberia.

**4. Small Copper** — *Lycaena phlaeas* L. 14—16 mm. Occurs in forest margins, fields, gardens and city parks. Found up to elevations of 2,000 metres. Two or more generations a year, depending on the local conditions. Caterpillars found mostly on sorrels *(Rumex acetosella* and *R. acetosa)*, also on marjoram. Distribution: throughout its extensive range (from north Africa to northernmost Europe, North America, and across Asia to Japan), it occurs in several geographical races and colour forms.

**5. Scarce Copper** — *Heodes virgaureae* L. 18—20 mm. Only one generation occurs, from June to August, in flat country and mountains up to 2,400 metres. Favours forest edges and meadows. Eggs overwinter. Caterpillars emerge in April, feed on sorrels *(Rumex acetosa, R. acetosella)*. Distribution: most of Europe (absent from Great Britain and southern Italy), Asia Minor, central Asia, Far East.

**6. Sooty Copper** — *Heodes tityrus* Poda 15—17 mm. Two generations occur; in the south also a partial third generation. Common in meadows and fields, found also in mountains (in the Alps up to 2,000 metres). Caterpillars feed on sorrels and broom. Distribution: most of Europe (absent from Great Britain, southern Spain and Scandinavia), Asia Minor, central Asia.

**7. Purple-shot Copper** — *Heodes alciphron* Rott. 18—20 mm. Occurs in foothills and mountains along streams and on forest rides. A rarer species. Distribution: Europe (absent from British Isles, part of western Europe and Scandinavia), Asia Minor.

1

2

7

3

5a

3a

5♀

5♂

6

4a

4

Family: **Lycaenidae**

**1. Large Blue** — *Maculinea arion* L. 18—23 mm. Flies in June to July on steppe-like meadows as well as those with thickets, and in the sunny margins of forests. Largest member of the family. Larvae feed first on wild thyme, later in anthills. Distribution: from western Europe to Siberia and China. Very rare in British Isles.

**2.** *Lycaeides argyrognomon* Brgstr. 10—16 mm. Two generations occur (May to June, July to August), but it is nowhere abundant and even absent in some regions. Flies at the edges of forests and round thickets where crown vetch, the caterpillar's foodplant, grows. Eggs laid by summer generation overwinter and larvae emerge in early spring. Distribution: France and Scandinavia and across central Europe and Asia to Japan. Absent from British Isles.

**3. Brown Argus** — *Aricia agestis* Schiff. 13—14 mm. In central Europe two and in southern Europe three generations. Found in dry situations. Distribution: western and southern Europe, except Iberian peninsula, across the whole of central Europe to Siberia.

**4. Mazarine Blue** — *Cyaniris semiargus* Rott. 16—18 mm. Common on forest rides and dry slopes, mostly in foothills. Occurs also in mountains (in the Alps c. 2,500 metres). One or two generations a year. Caterpillars usually found on *Trifolium, Melilotus, Anthyllis, Genista* and other papilionaceous plants. They hibernate and pupate in spring. Distribution: from north Africa (Morocco) to southern parts of northern Europe, temperate parts of Asia, Mongolia. Extinct in Britain.

**5.** *Agrodiaetus damon* Schiff. 17—19 mm. Flies in July to August, favouring situations in foothills with a limestone substrate. Caterpillars feed on *Onobrychis sativa* from September onward. They hibernate and pupate in late spring. Distribution: sporadic from Spain and France through central Europe to central Asia.

**6. Chalkhill Blue** — *Lysandra coridon* Poda 17—20 mm. Marked difference in the colouring of the male and female. Favours steppe-like terrain and downland, especially with limestone substrate. Also found on railway embankments and field paths; locally abundant. Occurs up to elevations of about 2,000 metres. Only a single generation — in July to August. Young caterpillars hibernate. Their chief foodplants are horseshoe vetch, crown vetch and other vetches. Distribution: from the Pyrenees and southern part of Great Britain across western and central Europe to Italy and the Balkans (rare). Absent from Scandinavia.

**7. Common Blue** — *Polyommatus icarus* Rott. 14—18 mm. Very abundant European blue. Female has brown wings with coloured spots on the edges. One to three generations a year, depending on the geographical location. Found from lowland to mountain elevations (in central Europe even above 2,000 metres). Caterpillars hibernate; they feed on clover *(Trifolium)*, rest-harrow *(Ononis)* and *Genista*. Distribution: all Europe, north Africa, temperate Asia.

Family: **Nymphalidae**

1. Purple Emperor — *Apatura iris* L. 35—40 mm. Found in June to August in damp deciduous forests. Females fly round the tree tops; males often settle in groups on forest rides to drink from puddles. They also visit horse and cattle dung. Caterpillars found on various species of willow, occasionally also on aspen. They hibernate. Distribution: from western Europe across the temperate parts of Asia to Japan. Absent in southern Europe and Scandinavia. Occasional visitor to Finland.

2. Southern White Admiral — *Limenitis reducta* Stgr. 26—31 mm. Fond of sunny slopes because it is a southern species. In the south there are three generations a year; northward the number of generations declines. In central Europe, which marks the northern limits of its range, only one generation occurs. Caterpillars feed on honeysuckle from July on and, after hibernating, in April and May. Distribution: chiefly southern Europe, Transcaucasia (Armenia), Middle East (Iran) and elsewhere.

3. Pearl-bordered Fritillary — *Clossiana euphrosyne* L. 21—25 mm. Widespread in lowlands and mountains. One to two generations a year, depending on the climate of the region. Found in forest rides, clearings and margins, also on hillsides covered with thickets. Caterpillars feed on various violets. They hibernate. Distribution: most of Europe (absent from the Mediterranean islands) and right across Asia to the Sea of Japan.

4. High Brown Fritillary — *Fabriciana adippe* L. 29—34 mm. Often visits flowering thistles, together with other related fritillaries, in forest rides and clearings. General colouring like that of other fritillaries. Recognized by the pattern on the underside of the wings— two rows of pearly spots and in between round brownish spots with pearly centre; there are also pearly spots at the wing base. Flies from June to August. Young caterpillars, or those that are already developed but still enclosed in the eggshell, hibernate. They feed on various violets on which they may be found from early spring till July. Distribution: all Europe, except the far north, and across the temperate parts of Asia to Japan.

5. Silver-washed Fritillary — *Argynnis paphia* L. 33—38 mm. Fairly common in forests — mostly in clearings, round rides, along edges, etc. On the wing most abundantly in July to August when it visits the flowers of various thistles and blackberry. Caterpillars feed on the leaves of various violets. Eggs are sometimes laid on violets, but much more frequently in a spiral arrangement on tree trunks. Distribution: almost all Europe far to the north (southern Norway, Finland, Sweden), temperate parts of Asia, as far as Japan, north Africa (Algeria).

Family: **Nymphalidae**

**1.** Painted Lady — *Vanessa cardui* L. 27 — 31 mm. Flies a zig-zag course on dry fields and meadows. A migrant. Arrives in central and northern Europe from the south as early as April to May. Progeny of this generation usually return south again in autumn. Caterpillar favours nettle, thistle and the leaves of colts-foot. Distribution: almost worldwide.

**2.** Red Admiral — *Vanessa atalanta* L. 27 — 30 mm. Arrives in northern and central Europe from the south in spring; produces a generation that is on the wing in summer and early autumn in meadows, gardens, forest margins, rides and clearings. Settles on stumps and injured trunks to suck the oozing sap. Also sucks over-ripe fruit. North of the Alps the butterflies seek out sheltered places in which to hibernate, but most of them die. Caterpillars feed on leaves of nettles. Distribution: all Europe, Asia Minor, Iran, north Africa, North America, New Zealand (probably introduced).

**3.** Camberwell Beauty — *Nymphalis antiopa* L. 35 — 45 mm. Emerges from its winter shelters in early spring. Most abundant round water, in sunny forest margins and broad forest rides as well as clearings from lowlands to mountains. Caterpillars occur in June to July on birch, aspen, poplar, willow, etc. Butterflies emerge from the pupae and are on the wing in midsummer and autumn. They hibernate. Distribution: most of Europe (a rare visitor to the British Isles), temperate parts of Asia, North America (where it is called the mourning cloak).

**4.** Large Tortoiseshell — *Nymphalis polychloros* L. 29 — 33 mm. Formerly regarded as a pest of gardens, but nowadays rare in many regions. Hibernated butterflies appear in spring and the new generation flies from July until hibernation. South of the Alps there are usually two generations each year. Caterpillars feed on various deciduous trees (poplar, willow, elm, fruit trees — chiefly pear, cherry and apple). Distribution: most of Europe, north Africa, parts of Asia.

**5.** Small Tortoiseshell — *Aglais urticae* L. 23 — 28 mm. Emerges from its winter shelter in March. Found in clearings, by forest edges, in meadows and in fields as well as gardens from lowland to mountain elevations (3,000 metres). Caterpillars found on nettles in May. A new generation of butterflies appears in July, and a further crop of caterpillars feeds on the nettles in late July and August. The butterflies from these caterpillars fly in late summer and then hibernate. There is only one brood in northern areas. Distribution: from western Europe to Japan.

**6.** Peacock Butterfly — *Inachis io* L. 27 — 35 mm. Visits flowers in the first days of spring. Individuals that hibernated fly until May; their offspring fly from July onward. Caterpillars feed on the leaves of nettle. Butterflies found in widely varied localities from lowland to mountain elevations. Distribution: Europe, temperate parts of Asia to Japan.

**7.** Comma Butterfly — *Polygonia C-album* 22 — 25 mm. Scientific name derived from the white pattern on the underside of the hindwings resembling the letter 'C'. Butterflies hibernate and lay eggs in spring. Caterpillars occur in May to June on nettles, black and red currant, hops and the like. Adults of this generation fly from June to July and a second generation flies in August to September before hibernating. Distribution: Eurasia, north Africa.

264

Family: **Browns** — Satyridae

1. Marbled White — *Melanargia galathea* L. 23—28 mm. Comparatively variable in the shape of the wing spots and general colouring, which may be whitish to deep yellow. Occurs abundantly from June to August on shrub-covered hillsides, in forest rides, forest margins and on railway embankments. Ascends to about 1,700 metres in mountains, and even higher in Africa. Caterpillar feeds on various grasses such as cocksfoot, brome, timothy, Yorkshire fog, etc. Caterpillar hibernates. Distribution: most of Europe (absent from Scandinavia), Transcaucasia, Iran, north Africa.

2. Woodland Ringlet — *Erebia medusa* Den. Schiff. 23—24 mm. Occurs from lowlands to mountains. Flies mainly in May to June, in mountains also in July. Most frequently found in forest clearings. Caterpillars feed on various grasses. They hibernate. Distribution: central and eastern Europe, from central France eastwards. Absent from Scandinavia and most of Italy.

3. Mountain Ringlet — *Erebia epiphron* Kn. 17—19 mm. Relic of the Ice Age. Found in European mountains from June to August at elevations up to 3,000 metres. Flies slowly and settles on plants. Caterpillars feed on various grasses, hibernate, and pupate in June. Forms several geographical races throughout its range. Distribution: most of Europe's mountains including Scotland and northern England. Not in Scandinavia.

4. Meadow Brown — *Maniola jurtina* L. 22—28 mm. Flies from June to August almost everywhere from lowlands to mountains. Caterpillars feed on grasses. Distribution: from north Africa to southern part of northern Europe, to the Urals, to Asia Minor and Iran.

5. Small Heath — *Coenonympha pamphilus* L. 14—16 mm. Two to three generations so that in the south it may be seen as early as April; farther north from May until autumn. Found everywhere, even in the neighbourhood of cities, from lowlands to mountains (1,800 metres). Flight is slow and fluttering as it moves from one flower to another. Caterpillars feed on various grasses. Distribution: all Europe far to the north, Asia Minor, Middle East (Iraq, Iran), north Africa.

6. Speckled Wood — *Pararge aegeria* L. 22—25 mm. At lower elevations two generations occur; at high elevations only one. Flies jerkily for short distances at the edges of forests, in small glades, clearings and forest rides. Caterpillars found on various grasses. Hibernates in caterpillar or chrysalis state. Distribution: Europe, Asia Minor, Middle East, central Asia, north Africa.

7. Large Wall Brown — *Lasiommata maera* L. 20—29 mm. In more northerly regions flies in June to July; in the south two generations occur that fly May to June and August to September in forest glades and clearings. Usually abundant, occurs even at mountain elevations (2,000 metres). Caterpillars feed on various forest grasses; hibernate. Distribution: Europe (far to the north; absent from Great Britain, Corsica, Sardinia, Crete), Asia Minor, Middle East, central Asia, the Himalayas, north Africa.

## Family: Lasiocampidae

**1. Lackey Moth** — *Malacosoma neustria* L. 13—20 mm. Found from late June to mid-August in deciduous forests, orchards, and tree-lined roads. Caterpillars feed primarily on the foliage of fruit trees and oaks. Eggs are laid in dense rings round slender twigs. They overwinter. Caterpillars appear in May to June and live most of their life in a communal tent of silk. They pupate singly in a cocoon on or between leaves. Sometimes regarded as a pest. Distribution: the Palearctic (except the northern part).

**2. Small Eggar Moth** — *Eriogaster lanestris* L. 15—22 mm. Flies in March to April on sunny hillsides and in glades with young birch trees. Female is stouter than the male and has a tuft of grey hairs on the abdomen. Caterpillars generally found in birch thickets, on hawthorn, blackthorn, willow bushes, etc. They live communally in a large nest which they spin. They pupate in a sturdy cocoon in or on the ground. Pupa overwinters, often remaining in the cocoon for several years. Distribution: central and northern Europe, northern part of southern Europe, Siberia.

**3. Oak Eggar** — *Lasiocampa quercus* L. 26—37 mm. There are several forms differing in general coloration as well as life habits. The sexes also differ in size and colouring. Flies mainly in July to August in oak or mixed woodlands.and on heaths. Caterpillar feeds on the leaves of oak, willow, blueberry, etc. Young caterpillar hibernates as a rule, but may feed up in the autumn to produce an overwintering pupa. Distribution: western, central, and southern Europe, Asia Minor, Transcaucasia, Siberia.

**4. Fox Moth** — *Macrothylacia rubi* L. 24—33 mm. Flies from May to July in meadows, fens and heaths. Caterpillar feeds on small plants, often on the foliage of blackberry or raspberry. It is fully grown by winter and hibernates. In spring it pupates on the ground in a grey cocoon. Distribution: most of Europe, Asia Minor.

**5. Lappet Moth** — *Gastropacha quercifolia* L. 27—43 mm. Greatly varied in colouring. In July and early August it flies in the evening in orchards and ornamental gardens, in groves and on heaths. In the daytime it rests with the fore wings folded roof-like over the abdomen and the hind wings extended far out beyond. Caterpillar feeds on fruit trees, hazel, willow and others. It hibernates and in spring pupates inside a grey-black cocoon in bark crevices or in the forks of branches. Formerly it was regarded as a pest but today it has become extinct in many places. Distribution: Europe, Asia Minor, China, Japan.

**6. Pine Lappet Moth** — *Dendrolimus pini* L. 25—36 mm. Colouring ranges from dark to light. Flies from June to August in dry pine forests and mixed woods with stands of pine, the needles of which are the chief food of the caterpillar. Caterpillar hibernates once or twice and pupates in a cocoon in the forks of branches or on tree trunks. Distribution: much of Europe, China, Japan. Not in British Isles.

Family: **Lemoniidae**

**1.** *Lemonia dumi* L. 25 — 29 mm. A moth of late summer and autumn (August to November). Female is a paler colour than the male because she has thinner layers of scales on the wings. Found from lowlands to hilly country, usually at the edges of forests, in meadows, etc. Eggs are whitish and darkly speckled; caterpillars dark brown. Caterpillars are found in May to June on various Compositae, chiefly dandelion and various species of hawkweed. Pupates either under fallen leaves or in the ground. Distribution: from the Balkans to southern Sweden and Finland, Urals.

Family: **Saturniidae**

**2.** Great Peacock Moth — *Saturnia pyri* Den. Schiff. 60 — 72 mm. Largest European moth. Male differs from female by the pectinate antennae. On the wing at night in May, generally in vineyards, orchards and parks. In daytime it rests concealed on stones, fences, and in grass. Caterpillar found chiefly on pear, apple, apricot and other fruit trees as well as on ash. In late summer it is about 12 cm long and pale-green with a great many bluish-tipped warts. When danger threatens it emits audible sounds. It pupates inside a sturdy cocoon on trees, in the forks of branches, sometimes simply on the ground. Pupa sometimes passes through two winters. Distribution: chiefly southern Europe, Asia Minor, Middle East (Iran). Northern limit of its range passes through central Europe; absent from British Isles.

**3.** Emperor Moth — *Saturnia pavonia* L. 28 — 40 mm. Male differs from female in having pectinate antennae and differently coloured wings — rich orange-brown (especially the hind wings), whereas the female's are greyish. Flies as early as April, chiefly at the edges of forests and in clearings. Males sometimes fly swiftly even on sunny days; females, however, usually rest on branches. Found from lowland to mountain elevations (2,000 metres). Young caterpillars are black and live gregariously. Later they turn green and scatter over the foodplants — blackthorn, rose, heather, blueberry, raspberry, willow and others. They pupate inside a brown cocoon. This species sometimes crossbreeds with the preceding and other related species. Distribution: much of the Palearctic.

Family: **Syssphingidae**

**4.** Tau Emperor Moth — *Aglia tau* L. 27 — 42 mm. Classed until recently in the family Saturniidae. The specific name is derived from the white markings in the dark spots on the wings which resemble the Greek letter 'tau'. Male is smaller and a deeper yellow-brown than the female. On the wing in beechwoods and other deciduous woods from late March to May. Caterpillar feeds on the leaves of beech, birch, lime, alder, oak and other trees. Pupa hibernates. Distribution: central Europe; absent from British Isles.

Family: **Endromididae**

1. Kentish Glory — *Endromis versicolora* Ll. 25 — 39 mm. Occurs very early in spring, even in mid-February and March, depending on the location. Flies in open woodlands with birch and other deciduous trees (lime, hazel, alder, etc.) on which the caterpillars feed. Female rests on branches in the treetops; male flies about in circles on sunny days. Caterpillar pupates in a black cocoon on the ground. Pupa overwinters. Distribution: Europe (except the south), Siberia.

Family: **Drepanidae**

2. Pebble Hooktip — *Drepana falcataria* L. 16 — 18 mm. One to two generations occur; under extremely favourable conditions a partial third. Lives from April to August in deciduous groves, along streams, in heaths and clearings. Caterpillar feeds on the leaves of birch and alder. Pupa overwinters. Distribution: much of Europe.

Family: **Thyatiridae**

3. Peach Blossom — *Thyatira batis* L. 18 — 19 mm. Flies after sundown in glades, forest clearings and margins, gardens and parks. Occurs from May to early July, sometimes also as a partial second generation. Larva feeds on raspberry and blackberry. Pupa overwinters. Distribution: much of Europe, Transcaucasia, Siberia, Japan, northern India.

Family: **Geometridae**

4. Orange Underwing — *Archiearis parthenias* L. 18 — 19 mm. Flies in daytime from early March in birch woods, clearings, along pathways etc. Caterpillars feed mostly on birch. Pupa overwinters. Distribution: central and northern Europe (including British Isles), Siberia.

5. Large Emerald — *Geometra papilionaria* L. 21 — 29 mm. Found from June to August at the edgess of birch or mixed hardwood forests. Caterpillar feeds on the leaves of birch, hazel, lime, beech, alder, etc. Larva overwinters. Distribution: central and northern Europe, Asia Minor, Siberia, Japan.

6. Blood-vein — *Calothysanis amataria* L. 14 — 17 mm. Usually two generations on the wing from May to October in riverine woods, waterside thickets and forest margins. Visits parks, gardens and even enters houses. Caterpillar feeds on the leaves of various docks, sorrels, and knotgrass. It hibernates. Distribution: the Palearctic. In Europe absent only in the north.

7. Lace Border — *Scopula ornata* Scop. 11 — 12 mm. Occurs abundantly in two generations from May to September in dry localities. Foodplants of the caterpillar are thyme, marjoram, speedwell, yarrow, sorrel and others. Larva hibernates. Distribution: Europe (except the north), Asia Minor, central Asia, Amur region, north Africa.

8. Riband Wave — *Idaea aversata* L. 14 — 15 mm. Very variable. More frequently seen than the typical form, which has a dark band on the wings, is f. *spoliata* shown in the illustration. Two generations on the wing from May to September in open woodlands, glades etc. Larva hibernates. Distribution: much of Europe (absent in the north and in certain parts of Spain), Transcaucasia, Asia Minor, Middle East.

Family: **Geometridae**

1. *Aplocera plagiata* L. 18—23 mm. A large and common species. Occurs in two generations (May to October) mostly on dry and warm hillsides, at the edges of forests, in steppes, etc. Caterpillar feeds on St John's wort *(Hypericum perforatum)*. Autumn caterpillars hibernate. Distribution: much of the Palearctic; absent from the north of Europe.

2. Winter Moth — *Operophtera brumata* L. 16—18 mm. Marked differences between the sexes. Male has normal wings; female only wing stumps, which makes flight impossible. Males fly from mid-October to December in the late afternoon. Found not only on forest margins but also abundantly in orchards and parks. Caterpillar feeds chiefly on fruit trees and other deciduous trees. Eggs hatch in April. Distribution: central and northern Europe (absent from the south), Transcaucasia, Amur region.

3. Scallop Shell — *Rheumaptera undulata* L. 17—18 mm. Striking pattern on all four wings. Flies from June to August in thickets at the edges of woods, in riverine groves, glades, parks and gardens. Caterpillars feed mostly on the leaves of elm, alder, blueberry, aspen, etc. Pupa overwinters. Distribution: central and northern Europe, temperate regions of Asia, North America.

4. Purple Bar — *Cosmorhoe ocellata* L. 13—14 mm. Two generations (May to June, July to August) on the wing in meadows, heaths, forest margins and gardens. Caterpillars feed on bedstraw *(Galium)*. Fully grown by autumn, they spin a case in which they hibernate and then pupate the following spring. Distribution: most of Europe, Asia Minor.

5. *Spargania luctuata* Schiff. 14—15 mm. Two generations (May to June, July to August). Found most often at the edges of forests, in waterside thickets, glades, etc. Caterpillar feeds on the leaves of willow-herb *(Epilobium)*. It hibernates. Distribution: central and north-eastern Europe (absent from north-German lowlands), Siberia, central Asia, North America.

6. Magpie Moth — *Abraxas grossulariata* L. 17—21 mm. Exceedingly variable in the patterning on the wings. Found in gardens, parks and forest margins. Flies from June to August. Caterpillar feeds on the leaves of gooseberry, currant, bird-cherry, blackthorn, as well as willow, hazel, etc. It hibernates and then pupates in June of the following year. This moth was formerly regarded as a pest, but now it is no longer plentiful and in many places has even become extinct. Distribution: most of Europe, western Asia and elsewhere.

7. Clouded Border — *Lomaspilis marginata* L. 12—14 mm. Very variable in pattern. One, sometimes also a partial second, generation occurs from April to August. Found in waterside alder thickets, by forest margins, in valley meadows, heaths, parks and gardens. Caterpillar feeds on sallow, willows, aspen, hazel, birch etc. Pupa overwinters. Distribution: most of Europe, central Asia, south-eastern Siberia.

1

2

6

3

5

6

4

7

Family: **Geometridae**

**1.** September Thorn — *Ennomos erosaria* Schiff. 16—21 mm. Found from June to September in deciduous woods (mainly oak stands) and in gardens. Caterpillar feeds on the leaves of oak, beech, birch and lime. Eggs overwinter. Distribution: central, south-western and eastern Europe, Transcaucasia.

**2.** Swallowtailed Moth — *Ourapteryx sambucaria* L. 27—30 mm. Occurs sporadically in June to July at the edges of forests, in parks and gardens, and by the waterside. Caterpillar feeds on the foliage of common elder *(Sambucus nigra),* ivy, alder, blackthorn and other plants. It hibernates and then pupates the following June. Distribution: central and southern Europe, Transcaucasia, Japan.

**3.** Brimstone Moth — *Opisthograptis luteolata* L. 19—22 mm. Usually one generation, on the wing in May to June. In favourable years there is a second generation (f. *aestiva*), smaller and a deeper yellow. Found in open woodlands, glades, parks and gardens. Caterpillar feeds chiefly on leaves of hawthorn, fruit trees, willow, hazel, etc. Pupa overwinters. Distribution: Europe, western and central Asia, north Africa.

**4.** Mottled Umber Moth — *Erannis defoliaria* Clerck 22—26 mm. Found in forests and gardens where the caterpillars were formerly serious pests. Male on the wing from late September to early December; female crawls on trees at the same time. Larva feeds on the leaves of various trees. Eggs overwinter. Distribution: from northern Italy to southern Scandinavia, Transcaucasia.

**5.** Peppered Moth — *Biston betularia* L. 21—32 mm. Occurs in several forms, best known being the dark-winged f. *carbonaria.* Flies in May to June at night, resting on tree trunks in the daytime. Caterpillar feeds primarily on the leaves of various trees (oak, poplar, elm, blackthorn, pear, rose, etc.). Distribution: Europe, Transcaucasia, Siberia, Japan.

**6.** Mottled Beauty — *Alcis repandata* L. 21—25 mm. Flies from May to August, mainly in forests, bushy steppes and gardens. Caterpillar feeds on deciduous and coniferous trees and many species of herbaceous plants. Hibernates. Distribution: Europe, central Asia.

**7.** Common Heath — *Ematurga atomaria* L. 14—17 mm. At higher elevations only one generation occurs, at lower elevations there is also a partial second generation. Flies on heaths, in groves and woodland meadows, sometimes in fair numbers. Larva feeds on heather, vetch, wormwood and other plants. Distribution: Europe, Asia Minor, Middle East, central Asia, Siberia.

**8.** Bordered White Moth — *Bupalus piniarius* L. 19—22 mm. Usually abundant in pine and mixed coniferous forests, where it is found from late April to late July. Caterpillar feeds on the pine needles and may thus be destructive in places. Pupa overwinters. Distribution: central and northern Europe, Transcaucasia, Siberia.

**9.** Latticed Heath — *Semiothisa clathrata* L. 11—15 mm. The typical form has yellowish white wings. These may also be a deep yellow or else white. Flies in meadows, at the edges of forests and along paths. Caterpillar feeds on clover. Pupa overwinters. Distribution: Europe, western and central Asia, Siberia, Japan.

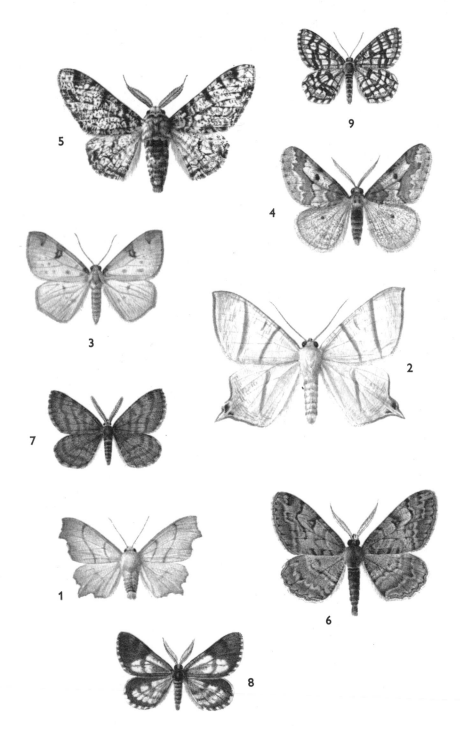

Family: **Hawk Moths — Sphingidae**

**1.** Eyed Hawk — *Smerinthus ocellatus* L. 33—44 mm. Flies from May to July late at night until dawn. Found in riverine groves, parks, gardens and alongside rivers from lowland to mountain elevations (2,000 metres in the Alps). Rests on tree trunks and branches. When disturbed, discloses the brightly coloured hind wings with large spots. In northern and central Europe usually only one generation (in the south also a second), which is on the wing until October. Caterpillar feeds mainly on various species of willow, poplar, lime, bird-cherry, blackthorn and certain fruit trees. It is full grown by autumn and pupates underground where it remains all winter. Distribution: Europe, Transcaucasia, Asia Minor.

**2.** Oak Hawk — *Marumba quercus* Den. Schiff. 45—55 mm. A southern species, its numbers decrease northward towards central Europe. On the wing in oakwoods from May, in more northerly regions from June. In the daytime it rests in the tops of low trees or in thickets. Female lays a little over 100 greenish eggs singly on oak leaves. Caterpillars hatch within two weeks. They feed on the leaves of oak *(Quercus)* and holly *(Ilex)*. Their growth is slow and they remain on the foodplant about seven weeks. When fully grown the caterpillar changes colour and hides under leaves or burrows to a shallow depth in the soil to pupate. Pupa overwinters. Distribution: southern and western Europe (not British Isles), in central Europe, Austria and Czechoslovakia (northern limit of its range); visits Germany; Transcaucasia, Asia Minor, Middle East.

**3.** Lime Hawk — *Mimas tiliae* L. 30—40 mm. A common hawk moth. Extremely variable in size and colouring. In northern and central Europe there is usually only one generation (April to July), but in the south there is another in August to October. Flies at dusk in lime-tree avenues, parks and forest margins. Found also in mountains. Female lays a great number of greenish eggs singly on the underside of leaves in the tops of the foodplants, generally lime or elm — sometimes also alder, birch, maple, ash, horse chestnut, walnut and others. Caterpillars emerge after one or two weeks and remain in the higher branches. Only when fully grown do they descend to the ground and pupate in an earthen cell. Pupa overwinters. Distribution: much of the Palearctic.

**4.** Death's Head Hawk — *Acherontia atropos* L. 45—60 mm. Well known for the startling pattern on the thorax which resembles a human skull. A warmth-loving migrant species which arrives in Europe from tropical Africa in early summer. Eggs are usually laid on leaves of the potato and related plants such as deadly nightshade. In the autumn, when full-grown, the larva burrows in the ground where it pupates in a large earthen cell. If the pupae survive the winter the adult moths emerge in spring, but the species does not normally survive the European winter. Distribution: African and Madagascar region; casual migrant to Europe, Transcaucasia, Iran, etc.

Family: **Sphingidae**

**1. Pine Hawk** — *Hyloicus pinastri* L. 33—45 mm. Found mostly in pine forests. In the daytime it rests on tree trunks, its colour blending with the bark so that it is practically invisible. Its colouring is not striking, but extremely variable. In some individuals there are distinct dark spots on the wings; in others, the wings are dark and the pattern indistinguishable. These dark, so-called melanic forms are often found in the neighbourhood of large cities. Eggs are laid singly or in batches on pine needles, on which the caterpillars feed. When fully grown the caterpillars pupate close to the tree trunk. Distribution: almost all the temperate regions of Eurasia, but absent from Scotland and Ireland and much of northern Europe.

**2. Bedstraw Hawk** — *Celerio gallii* Rott. 32—35 mm. In the evening visits flowering campion, bindweed, willow-herb and other plants in forest clearings. Caterpillars are not particular as to food but are often found on bedstraw which they consume entirely. Newly hatched caterpillars are black; later they turn green or blackish-grey. The yellow oval spots on each side of the body make them resemble the caterpillars of the spurge hawk *(Celerio euphorbiae)*, but the latter have the spots doubled and the tip of the abdominal spine black. Attempts at crossing the two species have been successful. The hybrid of a male *C. gallii* and female *C. euphorbiae* is named hybr. *galliphorbiae;* and that of a male *C. euphorbiae* and female *C. gallii* hybr. *kindervateri*. Distribution: temperate parts of Eurasia; only an occasional visitor to British Isles.

**3.** *Chaerocampa alecto* L. 37—43 mm. A moth of the tropics and subtropics where it has several generations a year. In Europe it occurs only in the south. Caterpillars are large and coloured green with striking oval spots on the sides. They feed on the leaves of grapevines. Distribution: tropics and subtropics.

**4. Striped Hawk** — *Celerio lineata* ssp. *livornica* Esp. 37—41 mm. A warmth-loving southern species. Caterpillars feed chiefly on the leaves of grapevine, also willow-herb, bedstraw, sometimes also sorrel, etc. Distribution: the typical form *(Celerio lineata)* occurs in North America, ssp. *livornica* inhabits southern Europe and southern Asia. An occasional but rare visitor to the British Isles and northern Europe.

**5. Oleander Hawk** — *Daphnis nerii* L. 47—56 mm. One of the loveliest moths of the family. The robust caterpillars are easily recognized by the two large spots on the front third of the body. The foodplant is oleander *(Nerium oleander)*. Distribution: native to the tropics of Africa and Asia and the subtropical regions of southern and south-eastern Europe, whence it travels long distances, not only to central Europe but even far north to Finland and Sweden. It also visits the British Isles occasionally.

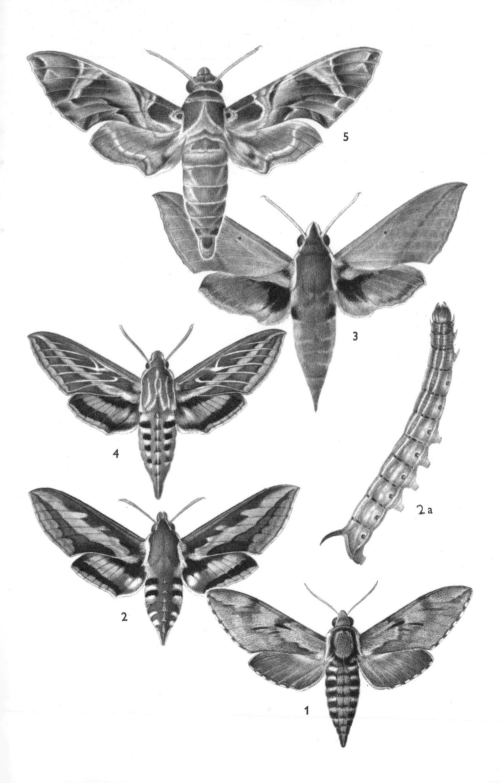

5

3

2a

4

2

1

Family: **Sphingidae**

**1.** Privet Hawk — *Sphinx ligustri* L. 44—50 mm. On the wing at dusk from May to July. In daytime it rests tightly pressed against the bark of trees, on walls, etc, with wings folded roof-like over the body. May still be seen frequently in large city parks, mainly round privet and lilac bushes. The pale-green eggs are laid singly, mainly on the leaves of privet, lilac and ash. Caterpillars emerge after about ten days and remain on the underside of the leaves. Caterpillar rests with the front part of the body raised, thus resembling a sphinx (hence its generic name *Sphinx*). Before the onset of winter it burrows in the ground where it pupates. Pupa overwinters. Distribution: almost all Europe (absent from Ireland), much of the temperate part of Asia.

**2.** Elephant Hawk — *Deilephila elpenor* L. 25—32 mm. On the wing from sundown till late at night from May to August. Visits flowering lilac, honeysuckle, petunia, bugloss, soapwort and other plants from which it sucks nectar on the wing. Eggs are laid singly on the underside of leaves of the foodplants — willow-herb, honeysuckle, grapevine, loosestrife, balsam, etc. Caterpillars have warning marks on the front part of the body. They pupate in the ground. Distribution: much of the Palearctic.

**3.** *Proserpinus proserpina* Pall. 19—24 mm. A rare species that has disappeared entirely in many places in recent years. After sundown in May to June it visits flowering willow-herb, evening primrose, bugloss and other plants to suck nectar. Eggs are quite small and glossy green. Caterpillars hatch after about ten days and feed chiefly on willow-herb, evening primrose and loosestrife. They pupate in the ground at a shallow depth. Pupa overwinters. Distribution: central and southern Europe, Transcaspian region.

**4.** Hummingbird Hawk — *Macroglossum stellatarum* L. 21—24 mm. A migrant; appears in northern and central Europe in May. A day-flying moth on the wing in sunny as well as cloudy weather. Excellent flier. Occasionally found even in city parks and gardens. Caterpillar usually found on bedstraw, bird-cherry and woodruff. Distribution: the Palearctic (except the far north), North America.

**5.** Narrow-bordered Bee Hawk — *Hemaris tityus* L. 19—21 mm. Differs from most other large hawk moths in that the wings are transparent. Flies by day, chiefly around noon. Found in meadows, hedgerows and clearings on various flowers from which it sucks nectar while continually fluttering its wings. One or two generations a year. The pale-green eggs are laid singly. Caterpillars generally feed on field scabious and devil's bit scabious. Distribution: most of Palearctic.

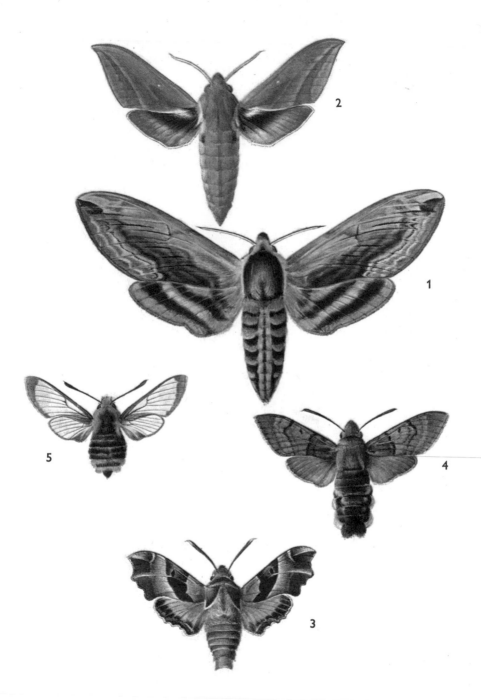

Family: **Prominents — Notodontidae**

**1.** Puss Moth — *Cerura vinula* L. 28—36 mm. On the wing from late April to early July in meadows, along streams, in abandoned quarries and in parks. Caterpillar is very striking both in shape and colouring. It feeds on the leaves of willow, poplar and aspen. Pupates in a sturdy cocoon cemented of wood shavings. Pupa overwinters. Distribution: Europe, Asia Minor, central Asia, Siberia, Japan, north Africa.

**2.** Plumed Prominent — *Ptilophora plumigera* Esp. 18—20 mm. A late autumn species. On the wing from October to late November, mostly in deciduous forests and parks. Eggs overwinter. Caterpillars hatch in May and feed on the leaves of field maple and sycamore, less frequently on the foliage of beech, etc. Distribution: Europe (from northern Italy to southern Scandinavia, rare in British Isles), northern Asia, Japan.

**3.** Buff-tip Moth — *Phalera bucephala* L. 24—32 mm. Easily recognized by the striking coloration. In central Europe there is another similarly coloured species, *P. bucephaloides*, with a larger and paler yellow spot at the apex of the fore wings and another roundish yellow spot in the front section. Flies from May to July near streams, in riverine woods and in parks. In the south there is a second generation. Caterpillars occur in July to August on willow, poplar, birch, alder, oak and other hardwood trees. Pupates in the ground. Pupa overwinters. Distribution: most of Europe (absent in the far north), Asia Minor, Siberia, north-east Africa.

**4.** *Peridea anceps* Goeze 25—35 mm. Flies in oak woods on sunny slopes from late April to late May. Caterpillar feeds on oak leaves. Pupa overwinters. Distribution: Europe (from central Italy to Scandinavia), Transcaucasia, Amur region.

Family: **Thaumetopoeidae**

**5.** European Processionary Moth — *Thaumetopoea processionea* L. 13—18 mm. Found in oak woods. On the wing chiefly in July to August. Female lays the eggs in large batches which she covers with hairs as protection against cold and enemies. Eggs overwinter and hatch in May. Caterpillars live in nests on branches. At night they leave the nest and crawl in dense rows over the trunks and branches to feed on the leaves of oak. They pupate in loose cocoons inside the nest which contains also cast-off larval skins and excrement. Caterpillars may occasionally be destructive. Distribution: central and southern Europe (entirely absent in some places), Asia Minor.

**6.** *Thaumetopoea pinivora* Treitsch. 17—19 mm. Found in dry pine forests, where it flies in July to August. Eggs are laid on pine needles on which the caterpillars feed. They spin a nest for themselves in the branches and pupate underground. Pupa overwinters, sometimes remaining in this stage for one or two years. Occasional pest. Distribution: northern and central Europe, locally abundant. Absent from British Isles.

Family: **Tussock Moths** — **Lymantriidae**

**1.** Pale Tussock Moth — *Dasychira pudibunda* L. 21—29 mm. Flies at night from April to June in hardwood forests and in parks. Female lays several tens of eggs at one time on tree trunks. Caterpillars generally feed on beech, hornbeam, oak, birch; sometimes also on rose, pear, willow, elm and other trees. In autumn they pupate in loose cocoons amidst dry leaves. Pupa overwinters. Distribution: Europe (chiefly central and western, less abundant towards the south), Transcaucasia, central Asia, western Siberia.

**2.** Vapourer Moth — *Orgyia antiqua* L. 11—15 mm. Marked sexual dimorphism: female is stout and has vestigial wings, male is winged. On the wing from June to October. Eggs overwinter. Caterpillar feeds on the leaves of various deciduous trees and shrubs such as oak, beech, willow, fruit trees, etc. Pupates in a loose cocoon. Distribution: Europe (western, central and northern), Transcaucasia, Siberia, northern China, Japan, North America.

**3.** Brown-tail Moth — *Euproctis chrysorrhoea* L. 17—22 mm. Usually white-winged. Some individuals, however, have black dots on the fore wings. On the wing from June to September in orchards, tree avenues and deciduous forests. Female lays eggs on branches and leaves and covers them with a layer of goldish hairs. Caterpillars feed on fruit trees as well as many other deciduous trees, such as oak. At first they live communally in nests woven of silk fibres, where they also hibernate. Distribution: much of Europe, the Caucasus, Transcaucasia, Asia Minor, north Africa.

**4.** White Satin Moth — *Leucoma salicis* L. 22—26 mm. Most abundant in July in poplar stands bordering streams, along highways and in parks. Caterpillar feeds on the foliage of poplar and willow. It hibernates. Distribution: Europe (from Italy to Scandinavia), Asia Minor, central Asia, Siberia, north Africa.

**5.** Black Arches Moth — *Lymantria monacha* L. 19—27 mm. Extremely variable in colouring. Adult moths occur from June to September. Females rest on tree trunks; males fly. Found chiefly in coniferous forests. Female lays 100—400 eggs successively in batches under bark scales. Eggs hatch in April. Caterpillars have caused catastrophic damage in places, chiefly in spruce monocultures. Nowadays, however, such calamities are rare. Distribution: Europe (from western across central to eastern Europe), Transcaucasia, Siberia, Japan.

**6.** Gipsy Moth — *Lymantria dispar* L. 18—36 mm. As in all related species, the sexes differ. On the wing from July to August in deciduous forests and gardens. Female lays the eggs all at once and covers them with a layer of hairs, the whole slightly resembling a tree fungus. Larvae are polyphagous and feed on the leaves of various deciduous trees. Sometimes destructive. Distribution: most of Europe (now extinct in British Isles), Transcaucasia, Asia Minor, Middle East, central Asia, Siberia, China, Japan, north Africa, North America (introduced, and now a pest).

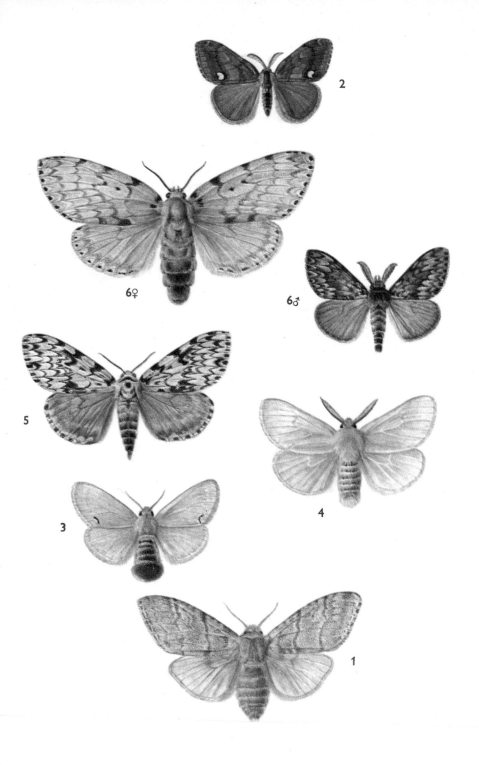

## Family: Tiger Moths — Arctiidae

**1. Speckled Footman** — *Coscinia cribraria* L. 15—21 mm. On the wing from June to August in heaths or pinewood clearings. Caterpillars hatch in the autumn and feed on plantain, dandelion, heather and various other plants. They hibernate and pupate in the ground. Distribution: Europe, northern Asia (to the Amur River).

**2.** *Rhyparia purpurata* L. 20—26 mm. Found in June to July in damp meadows where the larvae feed on various herbs and woody plants, e. g. bedstraw, heather, broom, blackthorn, birch, etc. Caterpillar hibernates and in spring pupates on the ground. Distribution: much of Europe (less on the west and absent from British Isles), northern Asia, Japan.

**3. Garden Tiger** — *Arctia caja* L. 26—37 mm. Best-known member of the family. Like the other species it, too, is extremely variable in wing markings. In daytime it rests on tree trunks, plants, walls, etc., with the bold pattern on the fore wings breaking up its outline. Flies in July to August. In the south a partial second generation occurs. The stout caterpillar with long russet and black hairs feeds on widely varied plants such as raspberry, blueberry, blackthorn, heather, deadnettle, docks, etc. It hibernates and pupates the following year in a loose cocoon on the ground. Distribution: Europe, Asia Minor, Middle East, Siberia, Japan.

**4. Cream-spot Tiger** — *Arctia villica* L. 28—32 mm. Found on steppe-like slopes, in forest-steppes and in city gardens. Flies in June to July. Caterpillar feeds on deadnettle, dandelion, yarrow, etc. It hibernates. Pupates on the ground. Distribution: Europe (now disappearing in some places), Middle East.

**5. Scarlet Tiger** — *Callimorpha dominula* L. 21—27 mm. On the wing from May to July in daytime in woodland meadows and by running water. Occurs also high up in mountains (Alps, High Tatras). Caterpillars feed on deadnettle, nettle, buttercup, forget-me-not and many other plants. They hibernate and pupate on the ground. Distribution: Europe (absent from Holland, Ireland, Scotland), some parts of Asia.

**6. Jersey Tiger** — *Euplagia quadripunctaria* Poda 26—30 mm. On the wing in greatest numbers in August. Favours quarries, rocky valleys with limestone substrate, and waterside places where marjoram grows. Caterpillars emerge in September, feeding first on a wide variety of low-growing plants such as deadnettle, nettle, dandelion and plantain. After hibernation they may also feed on hazel, raspberry and other shrubs. Distribution: much of Europe (except the north), Asia Minor, Middle East (Iran), western Asia.

**7. Cinnabar Moth** — *Thyria jacobaeae* L. 18—21 mm. Found from May to June in damp valleys, quarries and forest margins. Caterpillars feed from July to September on ragwort *(Senecio jacobaea),* in mountains on the leaves of butterbur and coltsfoot along streams. They pupate before the onset of winter. Pupa overwinters in a loose cocoon on the ground. Distribution: Europe, western Asia (to the Altai).

Family: **Noctuidae**

**1.** Turnip Moth — *Agrotis segetum* Den. Schiffm. 16—21 mm. One of the commonest moths. The female has setaceous, the male pectinate antennae. Flies mostly in fields and gardens. Usually one generation each year, but two occur in warmer areas. First generation is on the wing in May to June, second in August to October or even November. Visits flowers at night and rests during the day. Female lays several hundred eggs on goosefoot, orache, plantain and other plants. Caterpillars feed on about 50 kinds of plants. Older caterpillars burrow in the ground, where they eat plant roots during the day; at night they crawl up the plants and eat the leaves. Because they sometimes also feed on the leaves of cultivated plants (e. g. sugar-beet, maize, sunflowers, vegetables, etc.) they may be destructive. Larva hibernates. Distribution: Europe (including the north), Asia (absent from Siberia), Africa, North America.

**2.** Hearth and Dart Moth — *Agrotis exclamationis* L. 17—19 mm. Tends to produce black (melanic) forms. The patch on the wing resembles an exclamation mark. There are one or two generations, as in the preceding species. Distribution: Europe, Siberia to China, north Africa.

**3.** Setaceous Hebrew Character — *Xestia C-nigrum* — 19—21 mm. Name is derived from the black marking on the front wing which resembles the letter 'C'. In northern Europe there is one generation a year, but there are two in central Europe and three in the south. Caterpillars are not particular as to food: of the economically important plants they eat maize, clover, various vegetables, etc. Fully grown caterpillars burrow in the ground where they pupate. Distribution: Europe, Iran, Siberia, Japan, India, North America.

**4.** Great Brocade — *Eurois occulta* L. 24—30 mm. A rarer species. On the wing from June to August in peat moors and pine forests where blueberries and cranberries, foodplants of the caterpillars, grow. Caterpillar hibernates. Distribution: central and northern Europe, northern part of southern Europe, Siberia to Korea, North America.

**5.** Large Yellow Underwing — *Noctua pronuba* L. 26—29 mm. In colder regions one, in warmer regions two to three, generations a year occur; adult moths emerge in June. They fly at night and rest during the day. Fond of parks and gardens. Caterpillar feeds on the leaves of numerous grasses (including grain and weeds) and other low-growing plants. Hibernates. Distribution: the Palearctic (except the northernmost part).

**6.** Cabbage Moth — *Mamestra brassicae* L. 19—23 mm. Flies at night in various localities, often in vegetable fields and gardens. Caterpillars are polyphagous, found often on vegetables — cabbage, beet, lettuce, peas, sunflowers, etc. Pupa overwinters. Distribution: Eurasia.

**7.** Brown-line Bright-eye — *Mythimna conigera* Schiff. 17—18 mm. Visits flowers from June to August. Caterpillar feeds on grasses and small plants. Distribution: Europe, Transcaucasia, Siberia, Japan, India.

**8.** *Cucullia argentea* Hfn. 16—18 mm. On the wing in May to July in sandy situations. Larva feeds on wormwood *(Artemisia)*. Distribution: chiefly southern Europe, east to the Altai and Amur River.

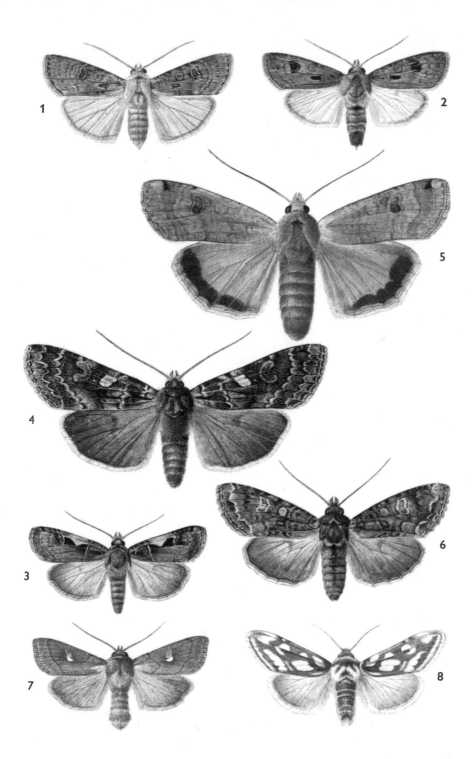

Family: **Noctuidae**

1. *Xanthia togata* Esp. 16—17 mm. Found from July to October at the edges of forests, in abandoned quarries, beside water and in gardens. Eggs hatch in March and caterpillars feed on the catkins of sallow at first; later they feed on small plants. Distribution: Europe (from central Italy to southern Scandinavia), Ural and Altai regions, Japan, North America.

2. Grey Dagger Moth — *Acronicta psi* L. 16—21 mm. One or two generations occur practically everywhere. Caterpillars feed chiefly on willow, poplar, lime, birch, elm, hazel, cherry, pear and other trees. Pupa overwinters. Distribution: Europe (except the north), Transcaucasia, Asia Minor, Middle East, eastern Asia.

3. Old Lady — *Mormo maura* L. 33—35 mm. Not plentiful. On the wing from July to August in grassy valleys, favouring the vicinity of water. Caterpillars feed on dandelion, sorrels, deadnettle and the foliage of various shrubs. They hibernate. Distribution: Europe (not far north), Middle East.

4. *Apamea monoglypha* Hfn. 22—26 mm. Found from June to September in forest clearings, heaths, in the neighbourhood of water and often also in houses. Caterpillar feeds on the roots of various grasses. It hibernates. Distribution: Europe (except the far north and south), Middle East, Siberia.

5. *Staurophora celsia* L. 20—22 mm. On the wing from late August to early October in open pine forests and at the edges of heaths. Caterpillars feed on the roots of various grasses. Eggs overwinter. Distribution: central and northern Europe (not British Isles), eastern Siberia, Amur region.

6. Pine Beauty — *Panolis flammea* Den. Schiff. 16—17 mm. Adult moth emerges from pupa in April. On the wing in stands of pine and spruce in the small sapling stage. Eggs are laid in rows on the previous year's needles and hatch in one week — later at lower temperatures. Caterpillars feed on the needles from the tip down. When fully grown they descend to the ground, either down a thread they have spun or down the tree, and pupate under the forest litter. They are pests in some regions. Distribution: Europe (from central Italy to northern Scandinavia), Asia to Japan.

7. Cream-bordered Green Pea — *Earias chlorana* L. 9—11 mm. On the wing during May and June in meadows and willow thickets by water, in gardens and parks. Sometimes a second generation in autumn. Eggs are laid at the tips of willow branches. Caterpillars weave the terminal leaves together as a shelter. Fully grown caterpillars leave their shelters and pupate on branches or leaves. Pupa overwinters. Distribution: Europe (from the northern part of southern Europe to southern Scandinavia), Siberia.

8. Nut-tree Tussock — *Colocasia coryli* L. 17—19 mm. Usually a single generation is formed in April to May, sometimes also a second one in July to August. Common in hardwood forests, parks and gardens. Caterpillars feed on the leaves of oak, beech, lime, birch, hazel and other trees. Pupa overwinters. Distribution: Europe (from northern Italy to Scandinavia), Transcaucasia, eastern Asia.

Family: **Noctuidae**

**1.** Silver Y Moth — *Autographa gamma* L. 17—20 mm. Name derived from the markings on the fore wings which resemble the Greek letter 'gamma'. Occurs abundantly from April to November chiefly in fields, meadows and gardens. In spring and summer its numbers are augmented by many new arrivals from the south and south-east, whose offspring (one, sometimes two, generations) return south in summer and early autumn. Caterpillars feed on about 100 kinds of plants (e. g. clover, deadnettle, cabbage, peas, vetch, sunflowers). Usually the caterpillar hibernates but it does not survive in cooler regions. Destructive when it overmultiplies. Distribution: the Palearctic, Ethiopian and Oriental regions.

**2.** Burnet Companion — *Euclidia glyphica* L. 13—14 mm. Usually two successive generations occur, on the wing from late April to late August. Moths are extremely variable in colouring. Abundant in meadows, clearings and forest margins. Caterpillar feeds preferably on the leaves of clover. Pupa overwinters. Distribution: Europe (except the northern polar regions), Asia Minor, central Asia, Amur region, Japan.

**3.** Clifden Nonpareil — *Catocala fraxini* L. 40—48 mm. One of the largest European moths. On the wing from late July to mid-October in wooded valleys, edges of hardwood forests, by water, etc. Caterpillars feed mostly on leaves of poplar. Eggs overwinter. Distribution: Europe (from northern part of southern Europe to southern Scandinavia), Transcaucasia, Amur region, North America.

**4.** Dark Crimson Underwing — *Catocala sponsa* L. 30—33 mm. Hind wings red with dark bands. Flies from July to mid-September chiefly in oak woods; visits also parks and gardens. Caterpillar feeds on oak leaves. Eggs overwinter. Distribution: all Europe.

**5.** *Ephesia fulminea* Scop. 23—25 mm. Continually declining in numbers in recent years. Found from June to August on sunny hillsides and in forest margins, also visits gardens. Caterpillars feed on the leaves of blackthorn, bird-cherry, plum, and other trees. Eggs overwinter. Distribution: Europe (absent from Great Britain and the south), Ural region, Ussuri region, Japan.

**6.** Herald Moth — *Scoliopteryx libatrix* L. 19—24 mm. Occurs in the neighbourhood of fens, around water, at the edges of forests as well as in parks and gardens. On the wing August to October, after which it hibernates and then lives until the following June. Moths hibernate in cellars, caves and hollow trees. Larva feeds on the leaves of willow and poplar from June to August. Distribution: Europe (except the south and north), Asia Minor, Siberia to Korea and Japan, North America.

**7.** Snout Moth — *Hypena proboscidalis* L. 18—20 mm. One or two generations occur and are on the wing in forest margins, clearings, near water, fens, in gardens and near human habitations from May to September. Caterpillars found on nettles, woundwort, hops etc; they hibernate. Distribution: most of Europe, Asia Minor, central Asia, eastern Siberia.

## Order: Scorpion Flies — Mecoptera

### Family: Panorpidae

**1.** *Panorpa communis* L. 20 mm, wingspan 25 — 30 mm. Common from spring to autumn in forests, waterside thickets and hedgerows. Male easily distinguished from female by the glossy brown clasping organs held scorpion-like over the abdomen. Adults and larvae eat small insects and also take dead plant and animal matter. Distribution: most of Europe.

### Family: Bittacidae

**2.** *Bittacus italicus* Müll. Wingspan 35 — 40 mm. Its membership of this family is evidenced by the shape of the head prolonged into a deflexed, brown-coloured 'beak'. Otherwise the long legs and general appearance are slightly reminiscent of the crane-flies. In daytime remains concealed in vegetation, where it catches other insects with its long back legs. At the onset of evening it flies along streams and on hillsides. Distribution: Mediterranean region.

## Order: Two-winged Flies — Diptera

### Sub-order: Nematocera

### Family: Crane-flies — Tipulidae

**3.** *Tipula oleracea* L. 15 — 23 mm. On the wing from May to August. Female lays 700 — 1,000 eggs in soil, favouring fields with papilionaceous plants. Larva feeds on roots; pupates in the ground after winter hibernation. Distribution: Europe (more plentiful in the west than in the east, extends northward to central Sweden, Norway and Finland), north Africa.

### Family: Mosquitoes — Culicidae

**4.** *Culex pipiens* L. 3.4 — 5 mm. Three or four generations. Females hibernate in cellars and emerge in early spring. They suck the blood of birds, but do not molest man. Larvae live in water near man's dwellings. Pupa is also aquatic. Distribution: almost worldwide.

### Family: Midges — Chironomidae

**5.** *Chironomus plumosus* L. 10 — 12 mm. Resembles a mosquito but does not suck blood. Flies in large numbers near stagnant water, where the larval and pupal stages are passed. Larvae are up to 25 mm long and coloured blood-red. Important as fish food. Distribution: western, central and northern Europe.

### Family: Black-flies — Simuliidae

**6.** *Simulium equinum* L. 2.2 — 3.5 mm. Flies in large numbers from March to September near streams. Females plague man and animals and suck their blood, particularly on warm days before a storm. Males swarm at dusk above water. Distribution: Europe, north Africa.

### Family: March-flies — Bibionidae

**7.** St Mark's Fly — *Bibio marci* L. 10 — 13 mm. Commonest and best known of the family. On the wing in March and April; flight cumbersome. Larvae live in the ground and feed on roots; common in gardens. Distribution: Europe.

### Family: Gall-midges — Cecidomyidae

**8.** *Mikiola fagi* Hart. 4 — 5 mm. Best known for the galls produced by the larvae and located on the upper side of beech leaves, often in large numbers. They are 4 — 12 mm long and shaped like small skittles. Adults emerge in late March. Distribution: Europe.

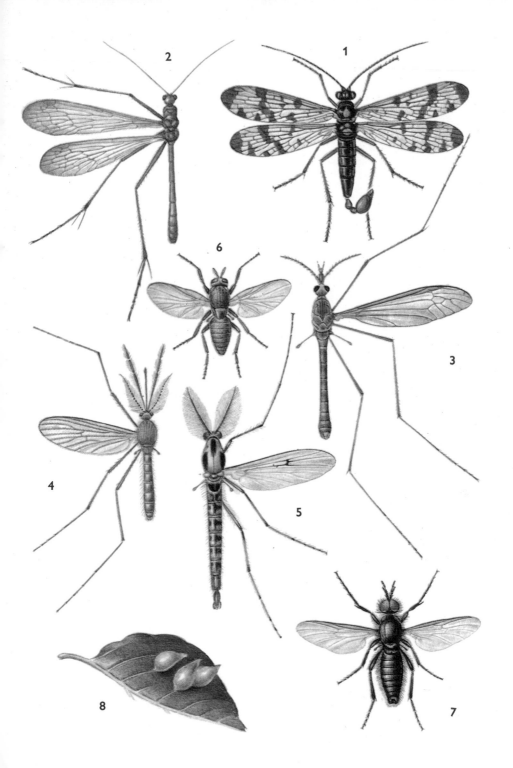

Sub-order: **Brachycera**

Family: **Soldier-flies — Stratiomyidae**

**1.** *Stratiomys chamaeleon* L. 14—15.5 mm. Found on flowering Umbelliferae and other plants in damp meadows and along pathways in foothills and mountains (c. 2,000 metres). Eggs are laid on the underside of leaves of aquatic plants. Larvae are aquatic and predacious. Distribution: central and southern Europe, Transcaucasia, Siberia.

**2.** *Chloromyia formosa* Scop. 6.5—9 mm. Very common from May to July on flowers and thickets. Favours damp situations. Larvae are saprophagous, feeding on decaying matter — often found in compost heaps. Distribution: Europe, north Africa.

Family: **Horse-flies — Tabanidae**

**3.** *Tabanus bovinus* L. 19—24 mm. Very common from spring till autumn in forests and meadows from lowlands to mountain elevations (2,000 metres in the Alps). Females, which feed on the blood of mammals, often attack grazing horses and cattle in large numbers. Males feed on nectar. Rarely attacks man. The commonest horse-fly which bites man is *Tabanus bromius*. Distribution: all Europe, Siberia, north Africa.

**4.** *Haematopota pluvialis* L. 8—12 mm. In summer a common and very troublesome pest of warm-blooded animals and man. Often occurs in large numbers from May until late autumn, mainly in forests and on pathways. It is particularly annoying before a storm. Found up to mountain elevations (over 2,000 metres in the Alps). Distribution: the entire Palearctic.

**5.** *Chrysops caecutiens* L. 7.5—11 mm. Abundant in summer, chiefly in damp situations. Female sucks the blood of cattle, horses and man. Distribution: all Europe, Siberia.

Family: **Snipe-flies — Rhagionidae**

**6.** *Rhagio scolopacea* L. 13—18 mm. Common from May to August on tree trunks and felled logs in forests. Rests in characteristic position with legs outspread and front part of body raised. Greatly resembles female scorpion-flies. Larva is predacious, feeds on various insects. Lives in wood and in the ground. Distribution: much of Europe, including British Isles.

Family: **Stiletto-flies — Therevidae**

**7.** *Thereva plebeia* L. 8—12 mm. Found from May to September in forest clearings and in gardens. Occurs even in the mountains up to 2,500 metres. Larva is long, white and predacious, feeding on the larvae of various insects; found in litter. Distribution: Europe, Siberia, north Africa.

Family: **Window-flies — Scenopinidae**

**8.** *Scenopinus fenestralis* L. 3—6 mm. Very abundant in June to July on window-panes, especially indoors. Larva is saprophagous, feeding on decaying matter. Distribution: Europe, north Africa, North America, eastern India.

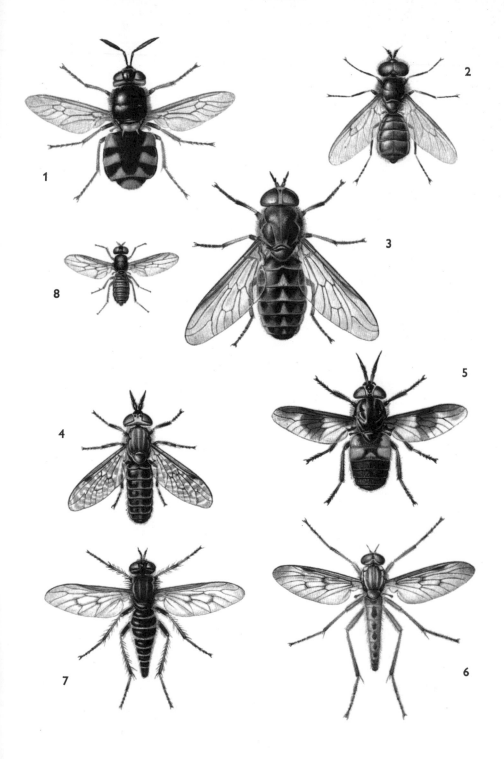

Family: **Robber-flies — Asilidae**

**1.** *Asilus crabroniformis* L. 16—30 mm. Predacious, as are other members of the family. Found from June to September on heathlands, in pine forest clearings and in dry fields. Fond of waiting for prey on logs. Feeds on various flies, locusts and Hymenoptera, including wasps. It pierces the victim with the proboscis and sucks its juices. One of the largest European flies. Distribution: Europe, Asia, north Africa.

**2.** *Laphria flava* L. 16—25 mm. One of the best-known members of the family. Occurs from spring till autumn but is most plentiful in June to July. It rests on logs in forests, along with other related species. Also favours willowherb, where it waits for the arrival of prey. Feeds on beetles, Hymenoptera, Diptera, bugs and other insects. Found up to 2,000 metres or more in the mountains. Distribution: all Europe.

**3.** *Neoitamus cyanurus* Loew 11—17 mm. On the wing from May to August in pine and birch woods, also in pastureland. Hunts all kinds of insects, often large species of Lepidoptera, dragonflies, Diptera, beetles, etc. Distribution: all Europe.

Family: **Bee-flies — Bombyliidae**

**4.** *Bombylius major* L. 8—12 mm. An expert flier. In general somewhat resembles a small male bumblebee. In spring it is found on flowers, into which it plunges its long proboscis to suck nectar. Larvae are parasites in the nests of certain solitary bees *(Andrena, Colletes)*. Distribution: Europe, Japan, north Africa, North America.

**5.** *Villa hottentotus* L. 12—16 mm. Locally abundant on flowers in July and August. Favours sunny situations. Larvae are parasitic on caterpillars of the cabbage moth and other noctuid moths. Distribution: Europe (not British Isles), north Africa.

Family: **Dance-flies — Empididae**

**6.** *Empis livida* L. 8—9 mm. A small nick on the inner margin of the eye is a characteristic feature of the family. The long proboscis points straight downward. Adults often congregate in large dancing swarms. Before mating the male brings the female a gift, usually a fly, which she sucks dry. Larvae are predacious and live in the ground. Distribution: most of Europe.

Family: **Long-legged Flies — Dolichopodidae**

**7.** *Dolichopus ungulatus* L. 4.8—7 mm. Found in both dry and damp situations. Occurs abundantly from June to August. Distribution: Europe, from Italy to northern Scandinavia.

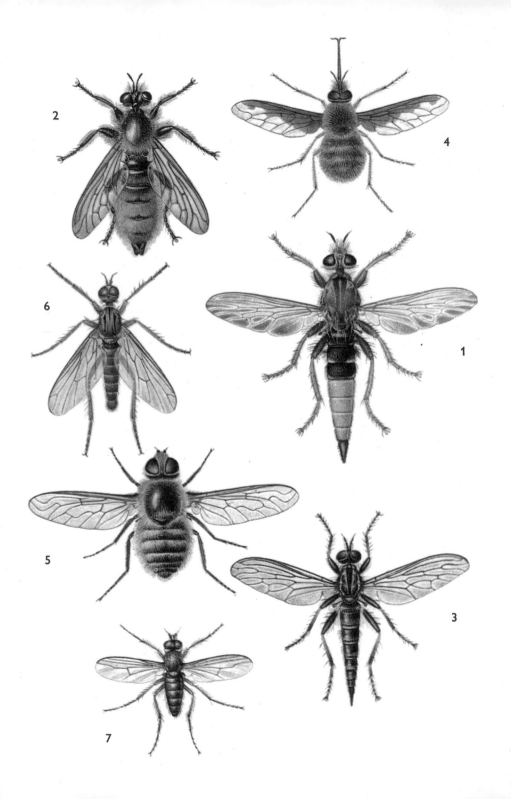

Family: **Hover-flies — Syrphidae**

**1.** Drone-fly — *Eristalis tenax* L. 15—19 mm. Commonest member of the family. Slightly resembles a bee. On the wing from April to October; settles on flowers. Larvae live in dung heaps and foul water and are regular inhabitants of country privies, etc. Larva is grey, cylindrical, with a 2—3-cm-long breathing tube at the hind end, hence the name 'rat-tailed maggot'. Distribution: cosmopolitan.

**2.** *Myiatropa florea* L. 12—16 mm. Occurs abundantly from spring till autumn on various flowers. The markings on the thorax somewhat resemble the 'skull' on the thorax of the death's head hawk moth. Distribution: much of the Palearctic.

**3.** *Volucella pellucens* L. 15—16 mm. Scutellum is bordered with dark hairs. Adults visit flowers from April onwards, sometimes even into October. Development takes place in the nests of the common wasp *(Paravespula vulgaris)* and German wasp *(P. germanica)*. The female flies into the underground nest and lays her eggs on a paper envelope. The larva makes its way into a cell and lives as an ectoparasite on the wasp larva. Later it bores a hole in the cell wall and leaves it to feed on dead wasps at the bottom of the nest. It hibernates in the ground and then pupates in spring. Distribution: Europe, Siberia to Japan.

**4.** *Pipiza quadrimaculata* Panz. 6—8 mm. A small species common on flowers from April to July. Distribution: Europe (not British Isles), North America.

**5.** *Cheilosia illustrata* Harris. 9 mm. Found on Umbelliferae. Distribution: all Europe.

**6.** *Scaeva pyrastri* L. 14—19 mm. On the wing from May to October. Settles on flowering Umbelliferae. Found high up in the mountains. Distribution: Europe, northern and western Asia, north Africa, North America.

**7.** *Episyrphus balteatus* Deg. 11—12 mm. A very common European species often occurring in large swarms in coastal areas — possibly migrating. Flies on forest rides, in parks and in gardens. 'Hovers' in the air, then suddenly flies off, only to return again to the same place. Distribution: Europe, Asia, north Africa, Australia.

**8.** *Baccha elongata* F. 7—11 mm. Has an extremely slender abdomen broadened to form a club at the hind end. Adults visit flowers from April to October. Larvae hunt aphids. Distribution: all Europe.

**9.** *Sericomyia silentis* Harris. 16—18 mm. Occurs from May to August. Fond of thyme. Larvae found in damp meadows. Distribution: much of Europe, Japan, North America.

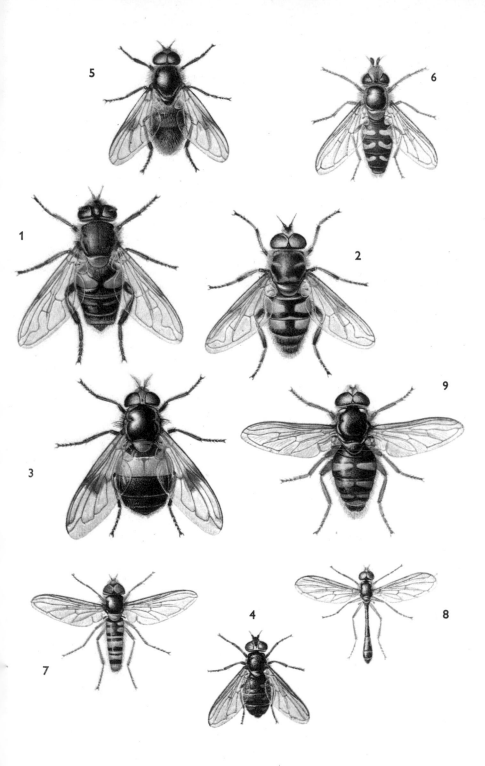

Family: **Thick-headed Flies — Conopidae**

**1.** *Sicus ferrugineus* F. 9—13 mm. A moderately large insect. Very plentiful everywhere. Larvae develop in the nests of various bumblebees, such as *Bombus terrestris* and *B. lapidarius*. Distribution: the Palearctic.

Family: **Psilidae**

**2.** Carrot-fly — *Psila rosae* F. 4.5—6 mm. Two generations a year — in the second half of May (adults emerge from overwintered pupae) and in August. Eggs are laid in the ground near the roots of carrot, parsley and celery. Larvae infest the roots and bore tunnels in the direction of the root tip. Young plants often die; roots of older plants decay and turn bitter. Distribution: Europe, Middle East (Syria), north Africa (Algeria), North America.

Family: **Tephritidae**

**3.** Mediterranean Fruit-fly — *Ceratitis capitata* Wiedm. 4.5—6.5 mm. Serious pest in orchards, with up to seven or even more generations a year. Eggs are laid inside fruit (oranges, peaches, apricots, pears, and also tomatoes, peppers, etc.). The long white larvae eat the pulp and cause the fruit to decay. Infested fruit falls prematurely. Distribution: introduced with fruit cultures to practically all parts of the world, chiefly the tropics and subtropics. A serious pest in the Mediterranean area; its range extends to Austria, Hungary, Switzerland and Great Britain (rare, probably only immigrants).

**4.** *Rhagoletis cerasi* L. 3.5—4 mm. Occurs most abundantly in May and June. Female pierces the skin of cherries with her short ovipositor and lays her eggs in the pulp. The larvae gradually tunnel their way to the pip. The fully grown larva, about 6 mm long, leaves the fruit and burrows in the ground close to the surface. Pupa overwinters. Distribution: most of Europe (absent from Great Britain), the Caucasus.

Family: **Piophilidae**

**5.** Cheese-skipper — *Piophila casei* L. 2.5—4 mm. Pest of stored goods. Larva infests cheese, meat, and is found also in excrement. It can leap more than 20 cm, forward as well as upward. Distribution: almost worldwide.

Family: **Lonchaeidae**

**6.** *Lonchaea chorea* F. 3—5 mm. The living insect has striped eyes. On the wing from spring till autumn. Larvae live in excrement and under rotting bark. Distribution: Europe.

Family: **Braulidae**

**7.** Bee-louse — *Braula coeca* Nitsch. 1—1.5 mm. Wingless, resembles a louse. Parasite of honey bees, favouring queens. Consumes the food of bees, does not suck blood. Often large numbers of these insects are found on a single bee. Development takes place in the hive. Distribution: cosmopolitan, wherever bees are kept.

Family: **Fruit-flies — Drosophilidae**

**8.** Vinegar-fly — *Drosophila melanogaster* Meig. 2 mm. Found in households, fields and gardens, chiefly round fruit and fruit juices. Distribution: cosmopolitan.

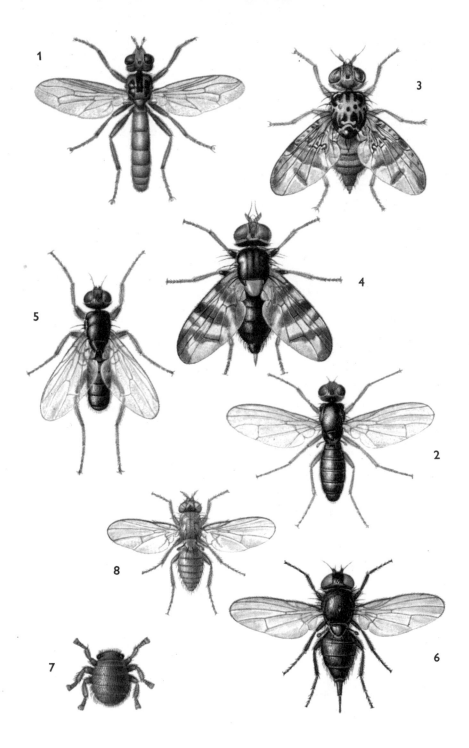

Family: **Chloropidae**

**1.** *Chlorops pumilionis* Bjerk. 2.5—3.5 mm. Collects nectar and honeydew on plants. Flight is cumbersome and brief. Two generations. Eggs are laid on the leaves of couchgrass and cereal crops (wheat and barley). Larvae cause deformation of the upper parts of the stems and even burrow into the ears, particularly in barley. Larvae of the spring generation may cause damage to cereal crops; larvae of the autumn generation are economically of no importance. Distribution: all Europe, Siberia, North America.

**2.** Frit-fly — *Oscinella frit* L. 1.5—2 mm. Notorious and widespread pest of cereal crops of all kinds, chiefly barley and oats. Flies appear in fields in May. Several generations a year. Adults of the second and later generations are smaller and a lighter colour. Distribution: Europe, Siberia, North America.

Family: **Anthomyiidae**

**3.** Cabbage-root Maggot — *Delia brassicae* Bouché 5.5—7.5 mm. Pupae overwinter. Adult flies are on the wing in April and May. Eggs are laid in batches on the ground or on various wild and cultivated cruciferous plants (cauliflower, cabbage, turnip, etc.). Larvae burrow in the ground and feed on the roots. They pupate inside the host plant. Destructive. Two or three generations a year. Distribution: Europe, North America.

Family: **Dung-Flies — Scatophagidae**

**4.** Yellow Dung-fly — *Scatophaga stercoraria* L. 9—11 mm. Widespread up to mountain elevations (3,000 metres in the Alps). Flies around excrement, dung heaps and refuse from early spring, hunting small insects found there. Distribution: the Palearctic and Nearctic.

**5.** *Nanna flavipes* Fall. 4—5 mm. On the wing in spring. Eggs are laid on the topmost leaves of timothy grass. Larvae burrow into the developing spikes and feed on the individual spikelets. Full-grown larvae are lemon yellow and about 8 mm long. They pupate in soil. Pupa overwinters. Distribution: central and northern Europe.

Family: **Muscidae**

**6.** Common House-fly — *Musca domestica* L. 7—8 mm. A synanthropic fly found in the vicinity of man. Emerges from its winter shelter in March. Does not bite or sting. Female lays about 150 eggs on foul-smelling animal and vegetable matter (excrement, rotting meat, etc.). Before pupating the larvae usually burrow in the ground. A troublesome species that has as many as five generations a year in Europe. Distribution: cosmopolitan.

**7.** Stable-fly — *Stomoxys calcitrans* L. 5.5—7 mm. Several generations occur in a year; in the south one follows immediately after another. Occurs primarily in the country, less common in cities. Feeds on the blood of various mammals, including man. It bites severely. Eggs are laid in excrement. Distribution: cosmopolitan.

**8.** Lesser House-fly — *Fannia cannicularis* L. 5—7 mm. Very common. Occurs from spring till autumn and is also plentiful in man's dwellings. Flies around lamps. Distribution: cosmopolitan.

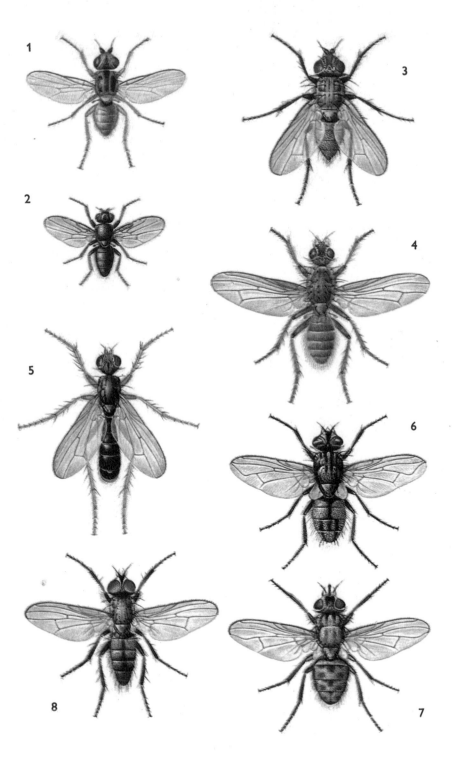

Family: **Bot-flies — Gasterophilidae**

**1.** Common Bot-fly — *Gasterophilus intestinalis* Deg. 12—15 mm. Well-known parasite of horses and donkeys. Female lays several hundred eggs on the host's body, usually on the front part. Larva remains inside the egg-shell for a long time. Not till it is licked up by the host does it emerge, remaining on the tongue for several days and then continuing its growth in the stomach. It passes out of the body with the faeces and either pupates in the excrement or in the ground. Distribution: cosmopolitan.

Family: **Louse-flies — Hippoboscidae**

**2.** Forest-fly — *Hippobosca equina* L. 7—8 mm. Body is depressed from above. Usually found on cattle; sometimes also on horses and dogs. Feeds on blood and settles in a spot where the infested animal cannot get at it. Distribution: cosmopolitan.

**3.** Deer-fly — *Lipoptena cervi* L. 5.2—5.8 mm. Found chiefly in autumn on red deer, roe deer, badgers, wild boar; frequently attacks man. When it first emerges it has two wings, but these are shed as soon as it finds a host. Feeds on blood. Distribution: the Palearctic.

**4.** Sheep Ked — *Melophagus ovinus* L. 5—6.2 mm. Does not have wings or even halteres. A troublesome pest of sheep. Distribution: cosmopolitan.

Family: **Bat-ticks — Nycteribiidae**

**5.** *Phthiridium biarticulatum* Herm. 2.8 mm. Wingless. Fairly abundant parasite of various species of bats. Distribution: Europe, Asia Minor, north Africa.

Family: **Blow-flies — Calliphoridae**

**6.** *Calliphora vicina* Rob. Desv. 6—13 mm. Very common. Synanthropic to a great degree. Found on decaying animal matter. Female lays an average of about 600 eggs on dead organisms. Larvae hatch shortly after and burrow inside the dead body. Distribution: most zoogeographic regions.

**7.** *Lucilia caesar* L. 6—11 mm. Has a bright metallic colouring. There are several more similarly coloured species in Europe. Like other members of this family, it is a common species and locally very abundant around man's dwellings. Found often in large numbers on excrement, carrion and decaying material. Eggs are laid in decaying animal material. Distribution: much of the Palearctic.

Family: **Sarcophagidae**

**8.** Flesh-fly — *Sarcophaga carnaria* L. 13—15 mm. Occurs commonly and abundantly in the vicinity of man. Frequents both flowers and excrement. Females avidly seek meat, in which they lay their eggs; these are also laid in all sorts of food remnants. An extremely unpleasant species, particularly in the south. Distribution: Europe, Africa.

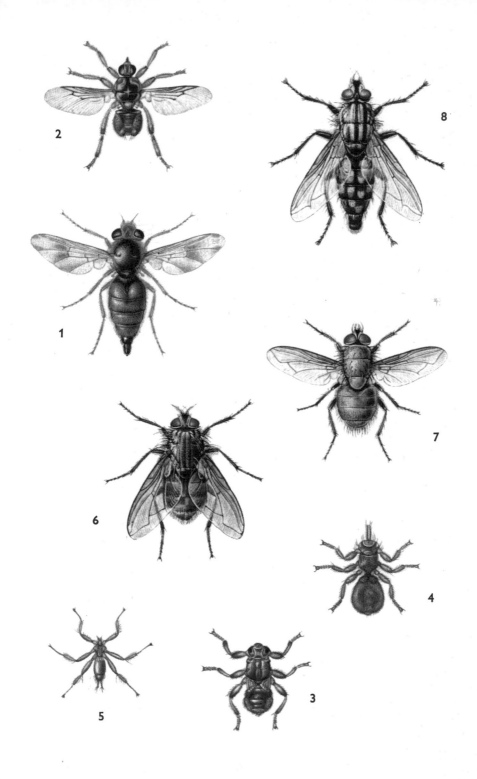

Family: **Tachinidae**

1. *Phryxe vulgaris* Fall. 5—8 mm. One of the many species of the family which helps greatly in the control of various forest and agricultural pests. Adult insects are found from early May to late September on flowering Umbelliferae in meadows, often also on common elder. Larvae are internal parasites of numerous butterflies and moths (some 70 host species have been recorded to date). Distribution: all Europe.

2. *Tachina grossa* L. 15—20 mm. Largest of the tachinids. Found throughout its range in August, but singly, as a rule. Larvae are internal parasites of the caterpillars of various large moths such as the pine hawk, oak eggar, and fox moth. Distribution: Eurasia. There are several similarly coloured species in Europe.

3. *Tachina fera* L. 11—14 mm. Has a brightly coloured abdomen. Common in summer on thyme. Larvae are internal parasites of the caterpillars of the black arches moth, gipsy moth and pine beauty. Distribution: Europe, Asia Minor, Turkestan, north Africa.

Family: **Oestridae**

4. Sheep Nostril-fly — *Oestrus ovis* L. 10—12 mm. Found wherever sheep are kept. Female deposits already hatched larvae in the nostrils of sheep. The larvae first crawl into the nasal cavity and later into the sinuses. They irritate the mucous membrane, causing the sheep to sneeze and lose weight. They feed on mucus. When fully grown (22—28 mm long — fig. 4a), they are ejected through the nostrils when the sheep sneezes. Pupation takes place below ground. Distribution: cosmopolitan.

Family: **Hypodermatidae**

5. Ox Warble-fly — *Hypoderma bovis* L. 13—15 mm. Terror of cattle, which take to their heels when the female insects fly about them. Eggs are laid on the hide, usually on the hind part of the body or legs of cattle. Larvae bore in through the skin and make their way through the body to the back where they produce the swellings known as 'warbles' just under the skin. Observations have revealed that there are many times more larvae in bulls than in cows. Larva is oval, 30 mm long. Distribution: the Palearctic, North America.

Order: **Fleas — Siphonaptera**

Family: **Pulicidae**

6. Human Flea — *Pulex irritans* L. 2—3.5 mm. Most numerous in late summer. Attacks domestic and wild animals (cats, dogs, wolves, badgers, etc.) as well as man. Feeds on blood. The laterally compressed body facilitates movement through the fur of the host. It is also a good jumper. It is believed that this troublesome parasite found its way to man via the dog. Female lays about 400 eggs in dust-laden spots and in the holes of mammals. Larvae feed on debris. Development takes a very short time. Distribution: cosmopolitan.

Family: **Hystrichopsyllidae**

7. Mole Flea — *Hystrichopsylla talpae* Curtis 3.5—6 mm. Largest of the European fleas. Found on various mammals (moles, shrews, mice, voles, etc.), and in their burrows. Not abundant, restricted to lower elevations (chiefly where trees and bushes grow). Occurs in nests throughout the year. Distribution: Eurasia (from Great Britain to Siberia) and the Caucasus.

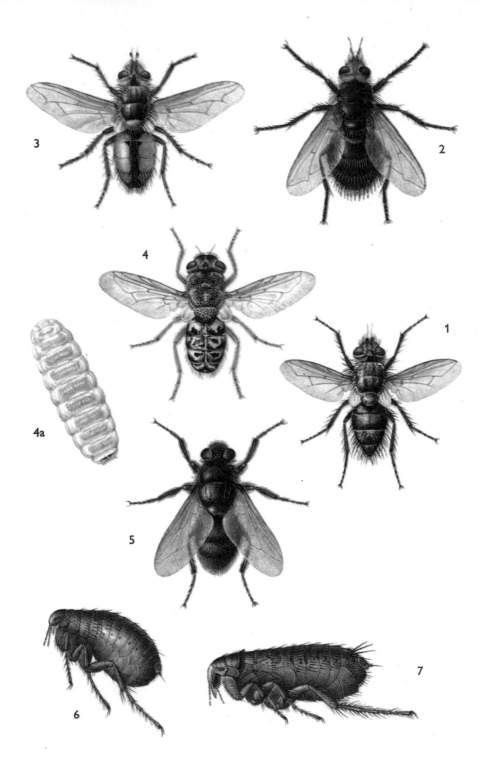

# Bibliography

Alford, D.: Bumblebees. London 1975

Andrewes, C.: The Lives of Wasps and Bees. London 1969

Balfour-Browne, F.: British Water Beetles, 1—2. London 1940—58

Borror, D. J. and M. D. Delong: An Introduction to the Study of Insects. London 1971

Chinery, M.: A Field Guide to the Insects of Britain and Northern Europe. London 1973

Chvála, M., L. Lyneborg and J. Moucha: The Horse Flies of Europe. Kopenhagen 1972

Colyer, C. N. and C. O. Hammond: Flies of the British Isles. London 1968

Corbett, P. S.: A Biology of Dragonflies. London 1962

Crowson, R. A.: The Natural Classification of the Families of British Coleoptera (reprint 1967, E. W. Classey).

Forster, W. and T. A. Wohlfahrt: Die Schmetterlinge Mitteleuropas, 1—5. Stuttgart 1954 —1976

Freude, H., K. W. Harde and G. Lohse: Die Käfer Mitteleuropas. Krefeld, from 1964

Goddard, J.: Trout Fly Recognition. London 1966

Handbooks for the Identification of the British Insects. London (appears continually)

Harz, K.: The Orthoptera of Europe I. Den Haag 1960

Higgins, L. G. and N. D. Riley: A Field Guide to the Butterflies of Britain and Europe. London 1970

Imms, A. D.: Insect Natural History, London 1971

Larson, P. P. and M. W. Larson: Lives of social Insects. N. York 1968

Leftwich, A. W.: A Dictionary of Entomology. London—N. York 1976

Linssen, E. F.: Beetles of the British Isles I—II. London—N. York 1959

Möhres, F. P.: Käfer. Form und Farbe, Fülle und Pracht. Stuttgart 1963

Oldroyd, H.: Collecting, Preserving and Studying Insects. London 1958

Ragge D. R.: Grasshoppers, Crickets, and Cockroaches of the British Isles. London 1965

Reitter, E.: Fauna Germanica. Die Käfer des Deutschen Reiches, 1—5. Stuttgart 1908 —1916

Sandhall, A.: Insekten und Weichtiere. BLV München, Bern, Wien

South, R.: The Moths of the British Isles, 1—2. London 1961

Southwood, T. R. E. and D. Leston: Land and Water Bugs of the British Isles. London—N. York 1959

Spradbery, J. P.: Wasps. An Account of the Biology and Natural History of Solitary and Social Wasps. London 1973

Stokoe, W. J.: The Caterpillars of British Butterflies. London 1944

Stokoe, W. J.: The Caterpillars of British Moths, 1—2. London 1948

Tweedie, M. W. F.: Pleasure from Insects. London 1968

Van Emden, F.: A Key to the Genera of the larval Carabidae. Trans. Ent. Soc. London vol. 92, 1—100, London 1942

Zahradník, J.: Les Coléoptères. Marabout Service, Verviers 1977

# Index of Common Names

# Index of Latin Names